crown street cooks

food from the heart of surry hills

光貿易有限公司

Spelling
home
dome
name
shame
wrong
belong

PHOTO: SHAO

SCOTTISH SHORTBREAD

contents

- 9 brunch
- 25 lunch
- 41 dinner
- 73 soups, salads, sides
- 87 dessert
- 103 cake stall
- 127 celebration
- 149 crown street eats

- 181 directory
- 184 thank-yous
- 187 measurements
- 188 index

HEALTH FOOD

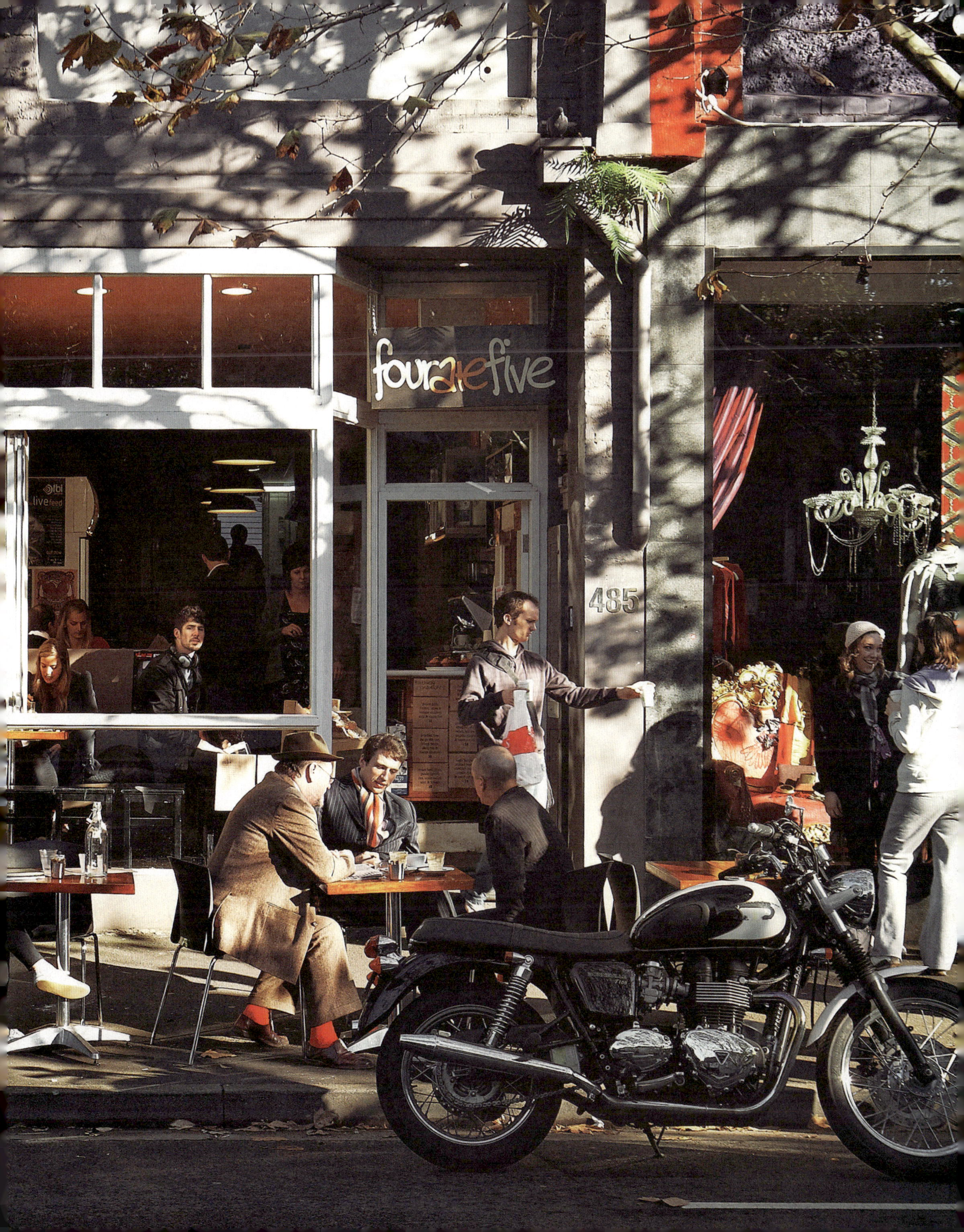

fouratefive
485

Kawa cafe
346-350 Crown Street, Surry Hills, NSW 2010 |
T 02 9331 6811 | E kawaoncrown@gmail.com

Pull up a pew at Kawa and enjoy yummy feel-good food, made from fresh, organic ingredients. A comfortable meeting place just a hop and a skip from Crown Street School.

Photo: Michael Wee

brunch

piping hot chocolate

Serves 2 | Prep 2 mins | Cooking 5 mins

75g dark chocolate, in pieces (I use Lindt 70%)
2 tsp sugar
1 vanilla pod, split
250ml milk
150ml pouring cream
Chocolate flakes
Whipped cream (optional) to serve

Place all ingredients other than chocolate flakes into a saucepan and heat gently. Using a whisk, stir briskly until the chocolate has melted and the mixture is nice and hot. Divide equally between two cups and dust with chocolate flakes.

Notes: For added joy, add a dollop of whipped cream to the hot chocolate before serving.

— Fiona Macneall

CHEF'S RECIPE

breakfast couscous

Serves 4 | Prep soak overnight + 15 mins | Cooking 21 mins

DRIED-FRUIT COMPOTE
250g dried apricots, peaches, prunes, figs, pears
½ cup honey
1 cinnamon stick
2 peppercorns
2 whole cloves
1 bay leaf
1 star anise
2 cardamom pods
COUSCOUS
1 cup dry couscous
Generous knob of butter
1 tbsp dark brown sugar
1 level tsp ground cinnamon (or cassia)
½ tsp ground nutmeg
Pinch ground cloves
Pinch ground allspice
Pinch ground cardamom
2 tsp orange flower water
2 tbsp dried currants or barberries (try Herbie's Spices)
TO SERVE
Yoghurt, honey, crushed pistachios &/or almonds (roasted for 10 mins at 150°C)
A little warm milk

For the compote, soak dried fruit overnight in enough water to cover, + 2cm. Once soaked, place a colander over a saucepan and drain fruit into it. Set fruit aside. Add honey, cinnamon stick, peppercorns, cloves, bay leaves, star anise and cardamom pods to liquid and simmer for about 20 mins. Strain liquid, pour back over fruit and leave to cool. Refrigerate until needed.

For the couscous, place dry couscous in a large bowl with a generous knob of butter. Add boiling water to cover couscous by 1cm-2cm. Cover and stand for 5 mins. Fluff up with a fork. In a small bowl, mix brown sugar, ground spices, orange flower water and currants/barberries into a runny paste. Adjust to taste. Mix paste through warm couscous. Refrigerate until needed.

To serve, heat bowl of couscous in microwave for 1 min until hot. Divide into 4 individual bowls. Top with compote, a dollop of yoghurt, a drizzle of honey and crushed nuts. Serve with warmed milk to moisten.

— Hugh, Cafe Mint

mint tea

Serves 4 | Prep 5 mins | Brewing 3 mins

4 cups water
10 sprigs fresh mint, plus extra to garnish
3 tsp green tea
3 tbsp sugar (or more to taste)

Boil water and pour a small amount into a teapot, swishing it around to warm the pot. Place mint, green tea and sugar in teapot, then fill with rest of hot water. Let tea brew for 3 mins.

Fill 1 glass with tea, then pour back into pot. Repeat. This helps to dissolve and distribute the sugar. Now pour the tea. You want a nice foam on the tea, so always pour with the teapot a fair height above the glasses. If you do not have at least a little foam on the top of the first glass, pour tea back into pot and try again until the tea starts to foam up nicely.

Garnish with remaining sprigs of mint. — *Louise Bickle*

PHOTO: MICHAEL WEE

winner bacon & egg pies

Serves 4-6 | Prep 20 mins | Cooking 25 mins

3 sheets frozen puff pastry, thawed, each cut into 4 square pieces
1 cup grated tasty cheese
1 cup chopped bacon, cooked until crispy
¼ cup pine nuts
1 cup shredded baby spinach
2 tbsp chopped flat-leaf parsley
Salt & cracked black pepper
6 eggs
2 cups cream

Preheat oven to 200°C. Grab 2 x 6-hole Texas muffin tins (non-stick are best). Place a square of pastry over each muffin hole and press down carefully so that corners poke up. Sprinkle a little grated cheese into base of each pastry case – this will "waterproof" the bases.

In a bowl, mix together bacon, pine nuts, spinach and parsley. Season to taste. Divide mixture evenly among the 12 cases. In a separate bowl, beat eggs and cream together well, then pour evenly among cases. Sprinkle rest of cheese over the top of each.

Bake until eggs are set and pastry is golden and crisp (about 25 mins). Check pastries after 15 mins to make sure they are browning evenly and not burning. Turn tins or change to different oven shelves if necessary. When cooked, remove from oven. Gently ease pies out of muffin tins as soon as you can handle the heat. Serve.

– Louise Bickle

"This is a great alternative to bacon and eggs when cooking for a big group. One weekend away I managed to make them in an antique Metters Early Kooka gas oven with no temperature gauge. They were a huge hit."

chocolate & banana muffins

Makes 12-16 | Prep 15 mins | Cooking 20 mins

60g butter, softened
½ cup caster sugar
2 ripe bananas, mashed
1 egg, beaten
½ tsp vanilla essence
½ cup dark choc chips
1 cup self-raising flour

Preheat oven to 180°C. In a large bowl, mix butter, sugar, bananas, egg, vanilla and choc chips with a wooden spoon, then sift in flour. Mix well. Place 12 pattycases in a cupcake or muffin tray. Using a spoon, divide mixture evenly among pattycases. Bake for about 20 mins.

– Henrie Stride

baked beans with chorizo & eggs

Serves 4 | Prep 10 mins | Cooking 25 mins | Baking 10-15 mins

8cm piece spicy chorizo sausage, diced
3 spring onions, finely sliced
4 cloves garlic, finely chopped
4 sprigs oregano, leaves torn
1 bay leaf
2 x 400g cans cannellini beans, drained, rinsed (or use 2 cups dried cannellini beans, soaked overnight & drained)
4 tbsp red wine vinegar
4 tbsp tomato paste
400g can crushed tomatoes
2-3 tbsp water
Sea salt & cracked black pepper
4 free-range eggs
50ml extra virgin olive oil
Toasted sourdough fingers, to serve

Preheat oven to 170°C. Fry chorizo in a lightly greased heavy-based saucepan over medium heat for 3-5 mins. Add spring onions, garlic, oregano and bay leaf and cook, stirring occasionally, for 2-3 mins. Add beans and vinegar and stir well.
Add tomato paste, tomatoes and water and simmer for about 15 mins or until thick. Season to taste.
   Transfer mixture to a medium (1.5-litre capacity) ovenproof dish. Use the back of a spoon to make 4 holes in bean mixture. Crack an egg into each hole, drizzle with oil and bake for 10-15 mins or until eggs are cooked. Serve with toasted sourdough fingers.

— Fran Nicholson

Notes: Crumble cheese (manchego) on top before baking.

CHEF'S RECIPE

blueberry griddle cakes

Makes 8 | Prep 10 mins | Resting 15 mins | Cooking 20 mins

6 tbsp sugar
2 eggs
1 tbsp melted butter
1 cup milk
2 cups plain flour
½ tsp salt
4 tsp baking powder
Vegetable oil
1 cup blueberries
Maple syrup & icing sugar (optional), to serve

Whisk sugar and eggs well in a mixing bowl. Add melted butter and half the milk. Sift in flour, salt and baking powder. Mix, gradually adding remaining milk, until you have a smooth batter. Do not overmix! Rest batter for 15 mins before cooking.
   Heat a little oil in a frypan pan. Spoon mixture into pan (⅓ to ½ cup of batter per griddle cake; you could use a measuring cup for this) to form a circle. Sprinkle blueberries on top of mixture. Turn when underside is golden. Brown other side. Serve in a stack, drizzled with maple syrup and dusted with icing sugar, if desired.

— Pauline, Pieno

crown street cooks

PHOTO: TOBY BURROWS

homemade yoghurt

Makes 2L | Cooking 15 mins | Cool & set 6-12 hrs

2L milk (initially we used full cream, but low-fat milk works just as well)
5 heaped tbsp skim-milk powder
1 cup natural yoghurt

You will need a milk thermometer. Pour milk into a deep saucepan and whisk in skim-milk powder. Bring milk to just below boiling point – about 90°C. Remove from heat and cool until it drops to 50°C.

Whisk in natural yoghurt. Pour into containers and wrap in a towel/blanket. Leave on benchtop for at least 6 hrs or overnight, then refrigerate.

Notes: You can use the last cup of your homemade yoghurt to make your next batch, but after doing this for 4 or 5 times you will need to start again with a fresh tub of bought yoghurt.

You can add pureed fruit or honey or simply eat with your muesli (see recipe below). — *Schofield family*

crunchy granola

Serves 10 | Prep 10 mins | Cooking 30-40 mins

⅓ cup brown sugar
75ml honey
1 tbsp oil (such as canola oil)
2½ cups rolled oats
¾ cup desiccated coconut
¾ cup chopped almonds
¼ cup sunflower seeds
¼ cup pumpkin seeds

Preheat oven to 120°C. In a small saucepan, bring brown sugar, honey and oil to boil.

Place dry ingredients in a large bowl and mix well. Pour hot sugar mix over dry ingredients and stir well until everything is coated. Make sure you stir it thoroughly – for the granola to be really crunchy you need to make sure that every single oat is coated with some honey mix.

Spread over an oven tray (or 2) and bake for 40 mins or until golden (it normally takes our oven about 30 mins). Store in an airtight container.

— *Downing family*

mandazi (east african doughnuts)

Makes about 16 | Prep 10 mins + 4-5 hrs resting time
Cooking approx 5 mins

2 cups plain flour, plus extra for rolling
5 tbsp sugar
1 tsp coarsely ground cardamom
1 sachet dried yeast
1 cup coconut milk
Vegetable oil, for frying

In a large bowl, mix dry ingredients with coconut milk and bind into a dough. Leave bowl of dough in a warm place for 4-5 hrs to rise. Sprinkle a work surface with plain flour and knead dough well. Roll out to approx 13mm thick.

Cut into triangles or whatever shape you like (using a scone cutter would be ideal) and leave for a further 15 mins.

Deep-fry *mandazi* in small batches in hot oil over a medium heat, turning until both sides are a deep golden colour. Remove with a slotted spoon and drain on kitchen paper to remove excess oil.

Notes: These yummy doughnuts are best eaten warm or on the day they are made. In Tanzania they are typically served with tea with milk and sugar.

— *Raaijmakers family*

best banana bread ever

Serves 8 | Prep 30 mins | Cooking 50-60 mins

65g butter, plus a little extra for the cake tin
¾ cup sugar
2 eggs
3 really ripe bananas (the riper the better)
1½ cups self-raising flour (you can use white or wholemeal), plus a little extra for the cake tin
Pinch salt
2 tbsp milk
1 level tsp bicarb soda

Preheat oven to 180°C. Grease and flour a 30cm loaf tin. In a mixing bowl, beat butter and sugar until pale and fluffy. Beat eggs, then mash bananas and combine both with butter mixture. Sift flour and salt and fold into mixture.

Mix milk and bicarb soda together, then fold into mixture (always add the milk and bicarb soda last). Bake for 50-60 mins, until a skewer inserted into middle comes out clean. Cool on a wire rack.

— *Charley family*

"This is a 100-year-old Red Cross recipe that was passed down to us."

crown
street
cooks
17

tattie scones (scottish potato scones)

Serves 4-6 | Prep 5 mins | Cooking 8 mins

225g mashed potato (use leftover mash from the night before, or cook & mash a couple of potatoes)
65g self-raising flour
Pinch salt
Milk – a splash (if you are using leftover mash made with milk &/or cream there is probably no need for extra milk)
Butter, to serve

In a bowl, mix all ingredients with a fork to create a dough that is not too soft or wet. It should have an almost-dry feeling.

Turn out onto a floured work surface and knead and turn lightly with your hands. Roll out with a floured rolling pin to a flat thin round (like a pizza base). Cut round into 6 segments and prick with a fork (see picture, above left).

Cook dough segments on a hot griddle, BBQ hotplate or in a heavy-based frying pan. You want to dry-fry them, so don't add butter or oil when cooking. Watch during cooking – they can burn. When underside has browned, flip to cook other side.

Serve immediately with lots of butter.

– Louise Bickle

zopf (swiss bread)

Makes 2 loaves | Prep 25 mins | Resting 1 hr Cooking 40 mins

1kg plain flour
50g fresh yeast or 15g dried yeast (2 sachets)
500ml milk
½ tsp sugar
1 egg, separated
3-4 tsp salt
200g butter

Sieve flour into bowl. Make a hollow in the centre. Dissolve yeast in cold milk, then add sugar. Add eggwhite to milk mixture and beat gently. Add salt and beat gently.

Melt butter in pan over low heat. Add butter and milk/yeast mixture to flour and mix into a soft dough. Knead dough on a lightly floured flat surface for about 10 mins (or 4-5 mins in mixer fitted with dough hook) until texture is smooth and silky. Place dough in a lightly oiled bowl. Cover with tea towel and rest for 1 hr in a warm place or until dough doubles.

Preheat oven to 200°C. Divide dough into 4 equal parts. Form into long strands (about 60cm) that taper at each end. Each *zopf* is made up of 2 strands braided together as follows:
• Lay 1 strand horizontally on work surface. Place other stand vertically across middle to form a cross.
• Take right end of horizontal strand and lay it leftwards across vertical one. Take left end and lay it rightwards. Next take the 2 ends of the vertical strand and repeat, bringing upper end downwards and lower end upwards.
• Continue, alternating, until braid is complete. Press ends together and tuck under.

Mix egg yolk with a little water and brush each *zopf*. Place on flat baking tray in lower part of oven and bake for approx 40 mins. Increase heat a little towards the end to brown the loaves.

Notes: We love it served warm with butter and jam but it goes well with eggs and anything brunchy.

— Raaijmakers family

mediterranean eggs

Serves 2 | Prep 10 mins | Cooking 15 mins

1 tbsp olive oil
1 brown onion, peeled, diced into small cubes
1 ripe tomato, diced into small cubes
2 tbsp water
1 tsp tomato paste
2 eggs
Salt
Pinch five-spice powder
Crusty bread, to serve

Heat olive oil in a frypan; add onion and fry until browned. Add diced tomato and reduce heat. Simmer until tomato has softened (about 2 mins). Add water and tomato paste and mix through.

Add eggs and mix until they start to solidify a little. Add salt to taste and five-spice powder. Stir and serve in a bowl with crusty bread for dipping.

— Abby Hamdan

bircher muesli

Serves 4-6 | Prep 10 mins | Soaking 3 hrs or overnight

3 cups rolled oats (traditional or instant)
½ cup sultanas or dried cranberries ("craisins")
3 cups fruit juice (orange, apple or any juice you like)
2 Granny Smith apples
2 tsp ground cinnamon
1 tsp ground nutmeg
500g vanilla yoghurt
2 tbsp honey (or to taste)
3 tbsp crushed hazelnuts
3 tbsp crushed pecan nuts

Soak oats and sultanas/craisins in juice overnight (or at least 3 hours), covered with plastic wrap in fridge. Peel and roughly grate apples and stir through soaked oats and sultana mixture.

Mix in cinnamon, nutmeg and yoghurt until well combined. Sweeten with honey to taste. Top with crushed hazelnuts and pecans and serve.

Notes: For a creamier, more decadent bircher muesli, freshly whipped cream can be added with the yoghurt.

— Eizenberg family

molly's flapjacks

Makes 12 slices | Prep 20 mins | Cooking 20 mins

115g butter
115g soft brown sugar
1 tbsp golden syrup
200g rolled oats
60g chopped nuts
½ tsp salt

Preheat oven to 160°C. Line a flat, well-greased cake tin (approx 25cm) with baking paper. Melt butter, brown sugar and golden syrup in saucepan and mix in oats, nuts and salt. Push mixture evenly into tin – you should get a depth of about 3 cm.

Bake for about 20 mins (or until done). Cut into squares and remove from tin before the slices harden.

– Kirwan family

corn fritters

Makes about 10 | Prep 20 mins | Cooking 15 mins

1¼ cups plain flour
1½ tsp baking powder
130g corn kernels (fresh or canned), drained
130g can creamed corn
½ cup milk
2 eggs, lightly beaten
Herbs such as freshly chopped parsley or basil
Salt & pepper
½ cup oil

Sift flour and baking powder into a medium bowl. Make a well in centre and add corn kernels, creamed corn, milk, eggs, herbs and salt and pepper all at once. Stir until combined and lumps are gone.

Heat 1 tbsp of the oil in a frying pan. Drop 2 heaped tbsp of mixture into pan (forms 1 fritter) and flatten slightly. Leave some space between them so they don't run together. Cook over medium heat until golden. Turn fritters over and cook other side. Remove from pan and drain on paper towel. Repeat with remaining oil and mixture.

Notes: I like to serve them with crispy bacon, some green leaves and our favourite tomato chutney.

– Lynn Mathot

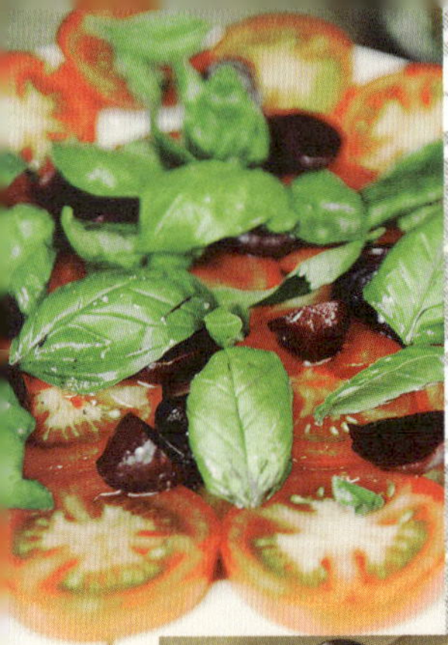
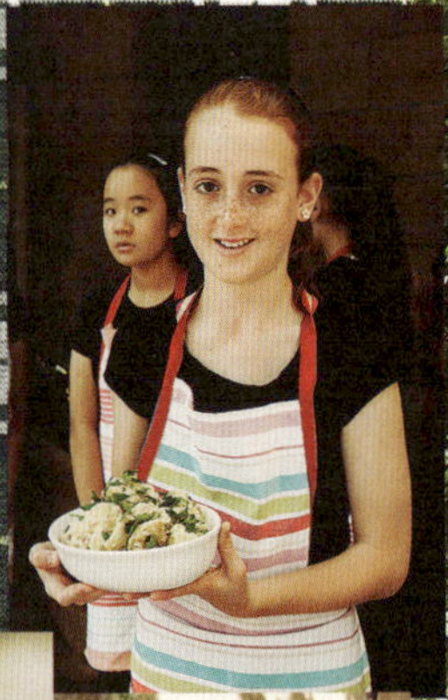
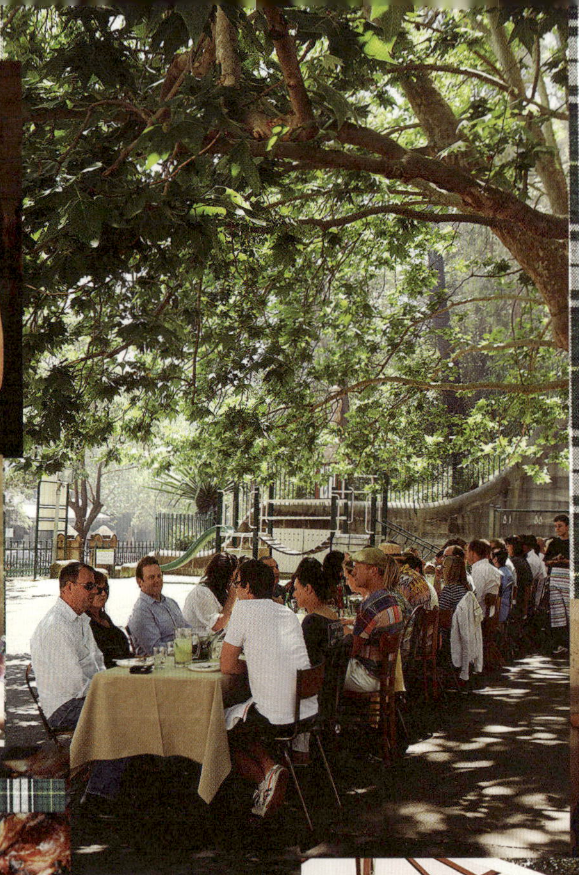
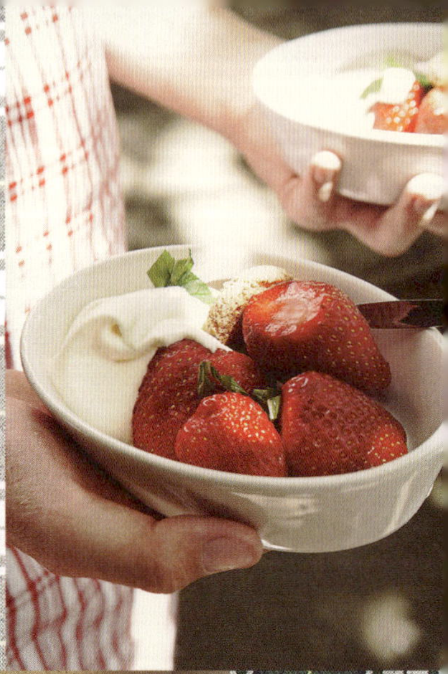
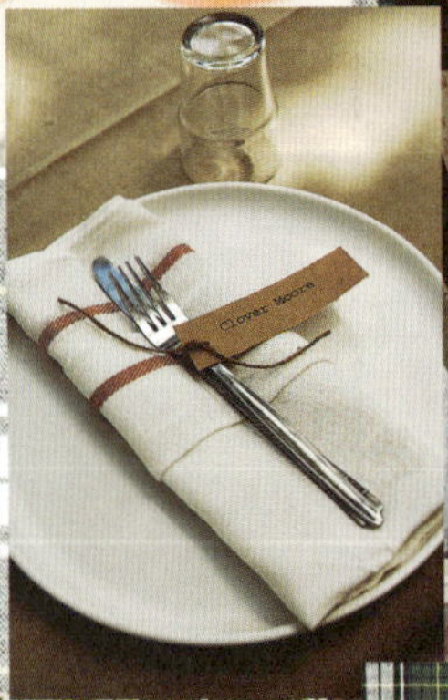
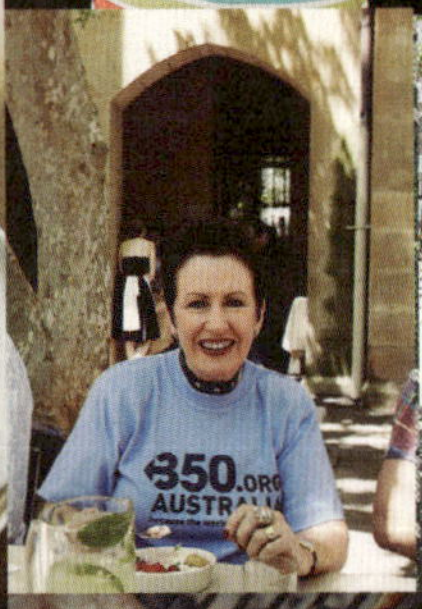
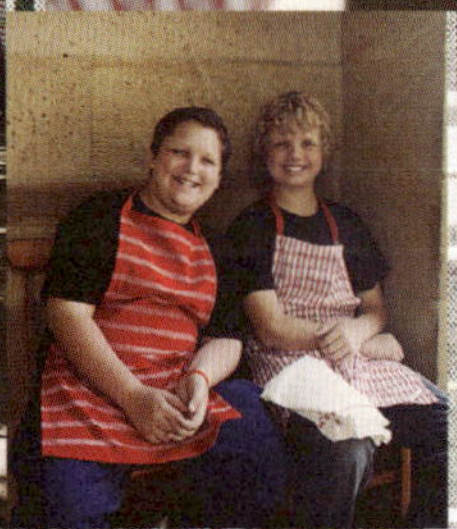
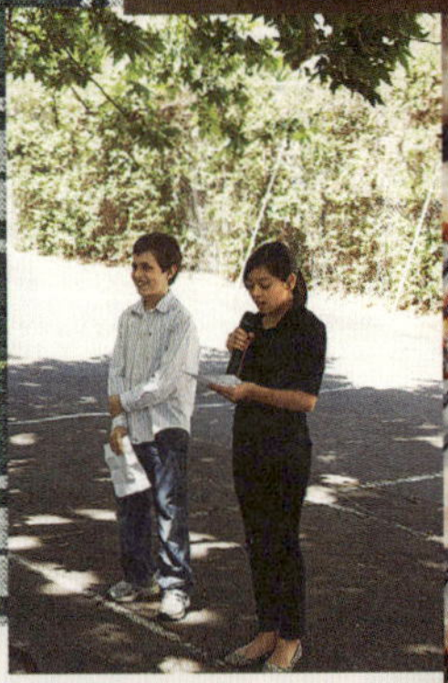
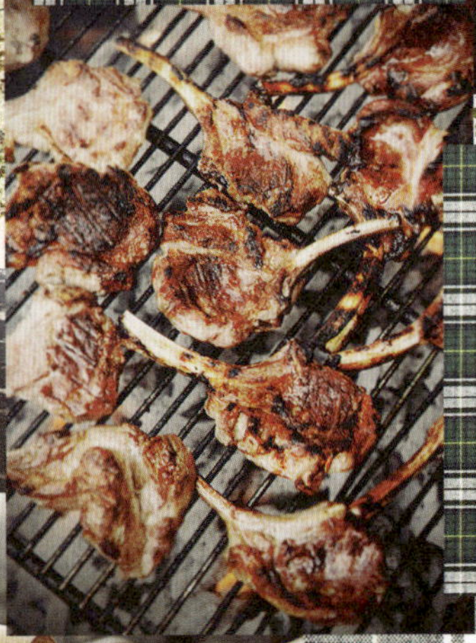
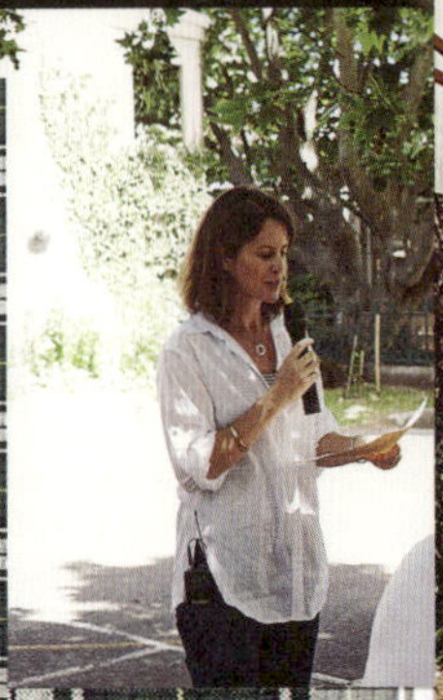
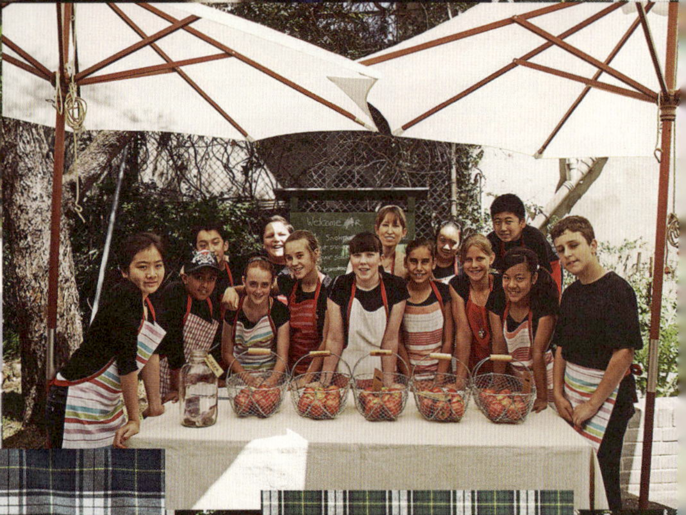
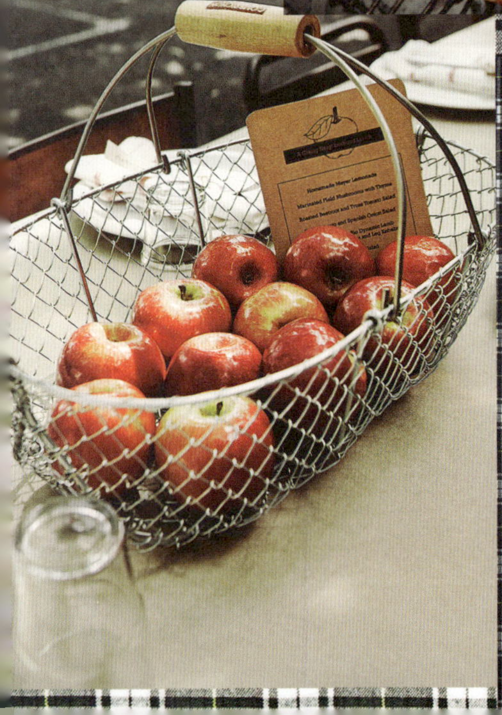
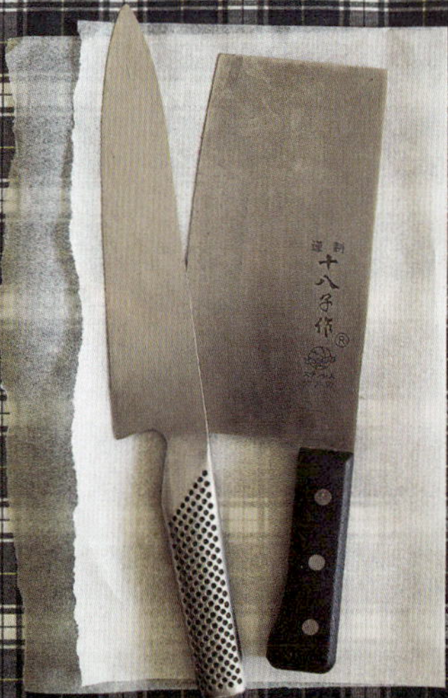
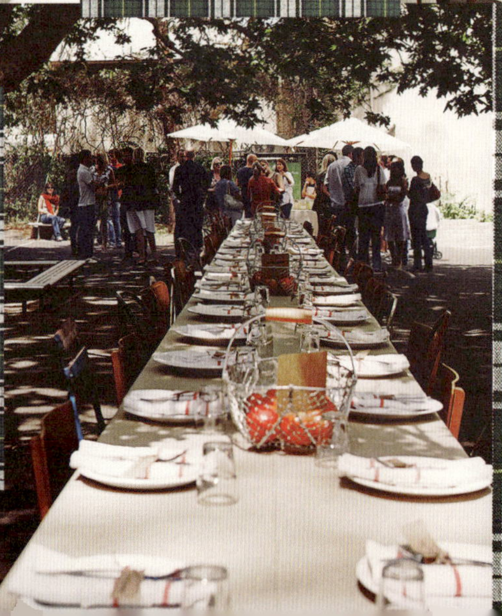

PHOTO: MICHAEL WEE

O Organic Produce

487 Crown Street,
Surry Hills, NSW 2010
| T 02 9319 4009
www.organicproduce.com.au |
Mon to Sat, 7.30am-4.30pm

Everything's organic, in season and delicious at this popular local cafe, which also does catering and sells grocery items. A great place for a healthy snack with the kids.

crown street eats

PHOTO: TIM ROBINSON

lunch

spring pasta

Serves 4 | Prep 15 mins | Cooking 20 mins

Dollop of good-quality olive oil
6 small eschalots (French shallots), finely chopped
2 cloves garlic, finely chopped
8-10 slices prosciutto, finely sliced
300g Swiss brown or portobello mushrooms, sliced
1 medium tub semi-dried tomatoes, roughly chopped
450g linguine, spaghetti or spaghettini (fresh is best)
½ bunch fresh basil, roughly shredded
Fresh red chilli (optional), finely sliced
1 generous handful of rocket
Salt & fresh cracked pepper
1 cup good-quality parmesan cheese, grated

Heat a frypan or large shallow-based pan and add a good dollop of olive oil so the base is generously covered. Add shallots and garlic and cook over medium heat until golden brown and translucent (about 5 mins). Add prosciutto and cook for another 5 mins.

Add mushrooms and stir until cooked through – keep stirring ingredients to prevent them sticking to base of pan. Turn heat to low and stir semi-dried tomatoes through mixture – just long enough for flavours to combine and tomatoes to heat through.

Cook pasta – fresh pasta usually only takes 2-3 mins so can be done immediately the tomatoes go into the pan. If using dried pasta you will need to start cooking earlier, although it is fine to let the sauce cook on a low heat while you wait.

When pasta is nearly al dente, stir basil through mixture (and add fresh chilli, to taste). Drain cooked pasta and toss a little olive oil through to separate it – you can use chilli olive oil if you want more of a kick.

Toss rocket through mixture just before serving and season to taste. NB: You may not need too much salt due to the prosciutto.

Serve pasta in bowls, place mixture on top of pasta and sprinkle generously with parmesan and cracked pepper.

– Analisa Kirby

steamed fish with ginger & spring onion

Serves 4 | Prep 20 mins | Cooking 10-15 mins

400g-500g whole fish, fillets or fish portions (flounder, silver bream or barramundi, gutted & scaled, are all good options)
1 knob fresh ginger, cut into 4 broad slices
SAUCE
1 tbsp peanut oil + a few drops sesame oil
15-20 pieces finely sliced or grated ginger
1 spring onion, finely chopped
100ml soy sauce (we use Lee Kum Kee Seasoned Soy Sauce For Seafood)
Steamed Asian greens, to serve

To make steamed fish, place fish pieces in steamer and lay big slices of ginger on top. Bring water to boil and steam fish for approx 10 mins or until flesh is white and opaque. Remove ginger and place steamed fish portions skin-side up on warm plates.

To make sauce, heat oil in saucepan and add sliced or grated ginger. Fry until golden brown. Add spring onion and fry briefly until just softened. Remove pan from heat and add soy sauce – just to warm through, don't fry!

To serve, pour sauce over fish and serve with steamed Asian greens.

– Sutandya family

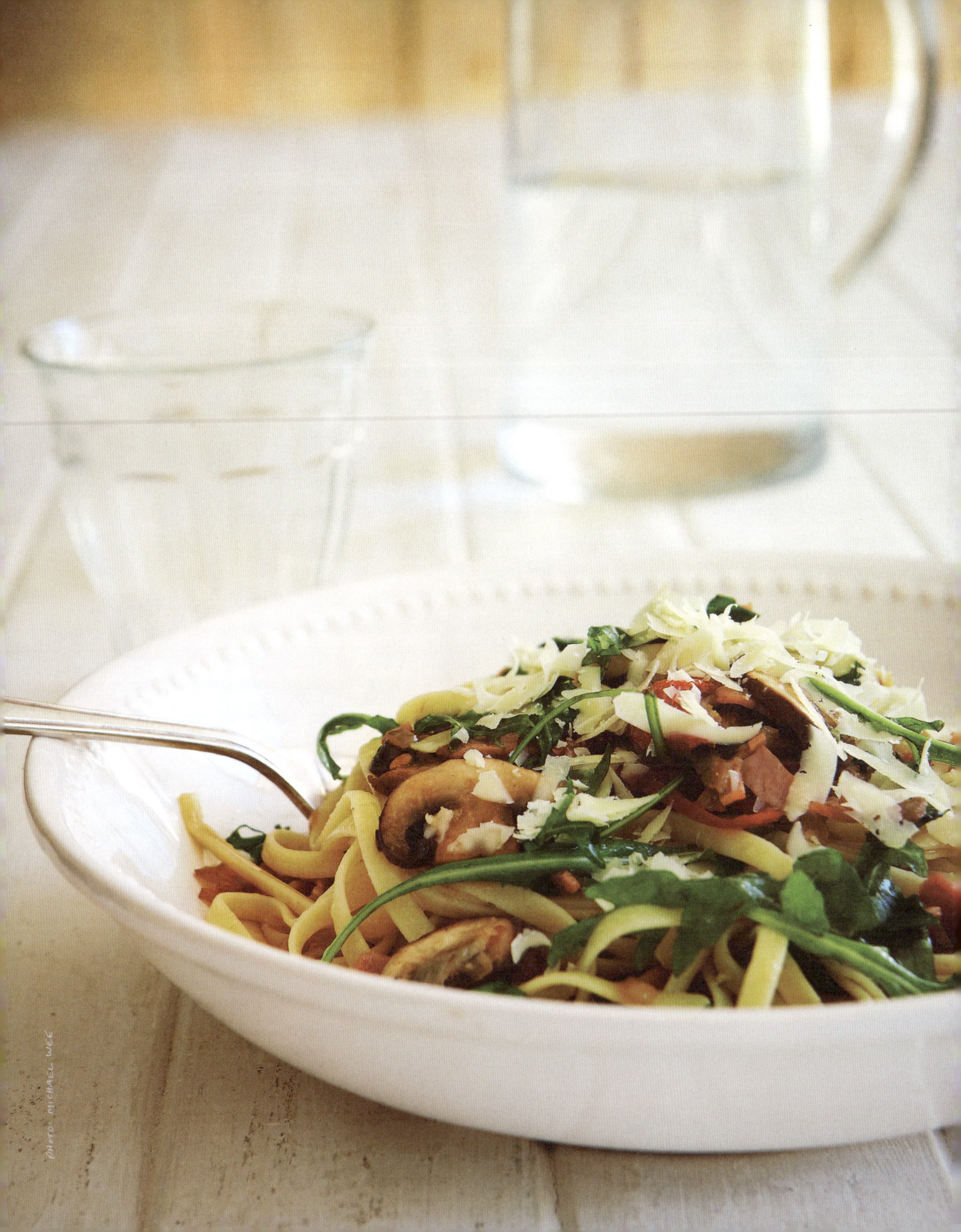

PHOTO: MICHAEL WEE

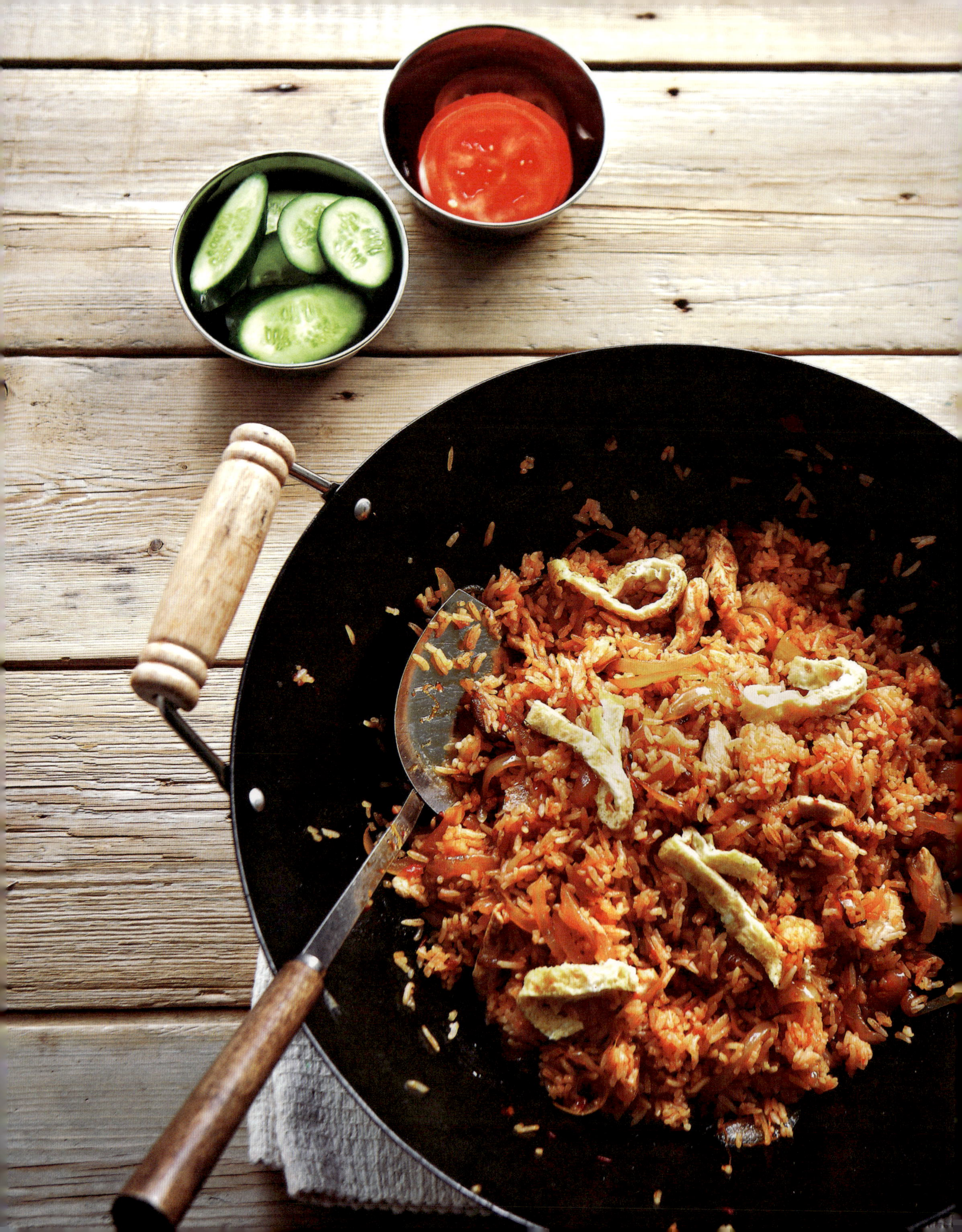

nasi goreng (indonesian fried rice)

Serves 4-6 | Prep 15 mins | Cooking 30 mins including rice

- 2 cups white rice (to make 6 cups cooked)
- 2 eggs (to make omelette to slice for garnish)
- Salt & pepper, to taste
- 3 tbsp peanut oil
- 2 medium brown onions, finely sliced
- 2 cloves of fresh garlic, minced
- ½ tsp *belachan* (dried shrimp paste)
- 3 tbsp mild chilli paste or red capsicum paste
- 200g chicken fillets or other meat, cut into strips
- 1 tbsp soy sauce
- 1 tbsp butter
- 1 cucumber, sliced (to serve)
- 1 tomato, sliced (to serve)

Cook rice and set aside. Meanwhile, whisk eggs and season with salt and pepper. Pour egg into a lightly oiled non-stick pan and make omelette. Set aside.

Bring a separate pan or wok to medium heat and add peanut oil. Fry onions and garlic until light yellow in colour. Add shrimp paste, some salt and chilli/capsicum paste. Fry until red chilli oil appears.

Add chicken and keep stirring until it changes colour. Add cooked rice and stir to combine with onion mixture, then add soy sauce and butter. Stir well until rice is hot and evenly coated. Season to taste.

Serve immediately, with sliced omelette as garnish and cucumber and tomato on the side.

— Latifah Alwiny, Crown Street After School Care

salt & pepper tofu with chilli lime dressing

Serves 4 | Prep 30 mins | Cooking 20 mins

- 2 x 300g packets fresh firm tofu
- 2 tsp coarsely ground black pepper
- 2 tbsp sea salt flakes
- ½ tsp five-spice powder
- ⅓ cup plain flour
- Peanut oil, for deep-frying
- Lime wedges, to serve

VEGETABLES
- 150g (1 small) red capsicum, finely sliced
- 150g (1 small) yellow capsicum, finely sliced
- 100g snow peas, finely sliced
- 70g (1 small) carrot, finely sliced
- 1 cup bean sprouts
- ½ cup loosely packed coriander leaves

CHILLI LIME DRESSING
- 2 tbsp peanut oil
- ¼ cup lime juice
- 2 tbsp sweet chilli sauce

Unwrap tofu blocks and pat dry with absorbent paper. Cut both pieces in half horizontally, then cut each half into quarters (you'll have 16 pieces). Place tofu pieces, in a single layer, on absorbent paper. Cover with more absorbent paper; stand 15 mins.

In a large bowl, combine capsicums, snow peas, carrot, sprouts and coriander.

To make chilli lime dressing, whisk together all ingredients in a small bowl.

In a medium bowl, combine pepper, salt, five-spice and flour. Coat tofu in mixture, shake away excess. Heat oil in wok; deep-fry tofu, in batches, until browned lightly. Drain on absorbent paper.

To serve, divide vegetables among plates, top with tofu and drizzle over the chilli lime dressing. Serve with extra lime wedges, if desired.

— Lynn Mathot

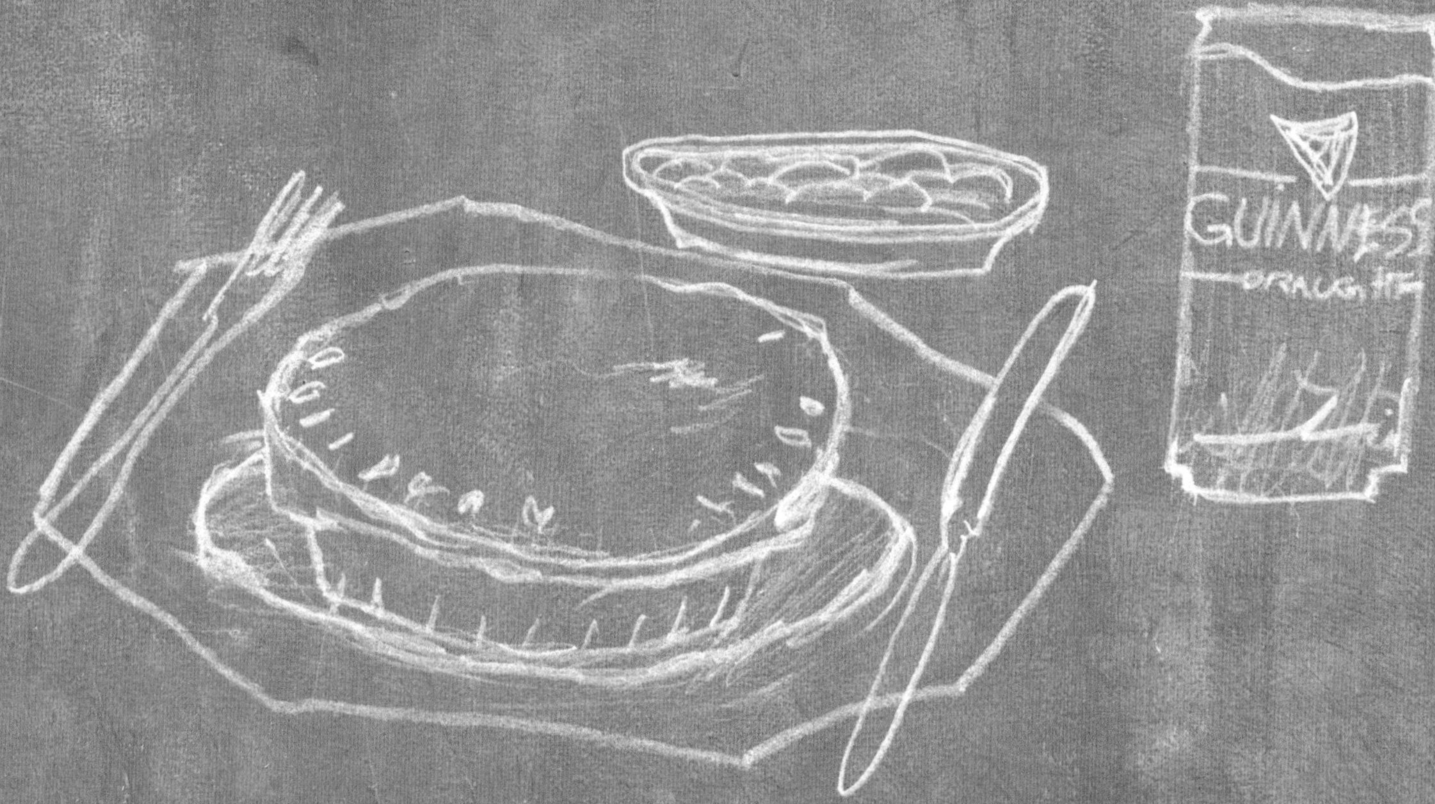
GUINNESS
DRAUGHT

beef, stilton & guinness pie with tomato chutney

Serves 4 | Prep 40 mins + 2-3 hrs marinating | Cooking 20 mins

1kg stewing steak (blade, braising beef, chuck, flank or brisket all work well), trimmed of excess fat, cut into large chunks
2 cloves garlic, chopped
1 tsp thyme
1 tbsp black peppercorns
2 x 440ml cans Guinness (enough to marinate meat in)
6 tbsp flour, seasoned with salt & pepper
Olive oil, for frying
8 eschalots (French shallots), peeled, halved
Salt & pepper
2 tbsp tomato paste
1 tbsp brown sugar
½ tsp salt
500g puff pastry sheets, fresh or frozen (defrosted)
100g Stilton cheese, crumbled
1 egg, beaten, to glaze

SIMPLE TOMATO CHUTNEY
3 tbsp olive oil
2 tsp mustard seeds
4 cloves garlic, sliced
800g fresh tomatoes, chopped
3 tbsp brown sugar
2 tbsp balsamic vinager
Salt & freshly ground black pepper, to taste

Place beef, garlic, thyme, peppercorns and Guinness into a bowl. Marinate, covered in fridge, for 2-3 hrs or overnight.

Take out beef and pat dry (strain marinade and keep reserve liquid). Toss beef through flour.

Heat oil in a large casserole and brown beef all over in batches. Remove beef, then brown shallots in casserole. Return beef to casserole along with marinade, tomato paste and brown sugar. Season to taste. Cover and simmer for about 1 hr, then continue cooking uncovered for 30 mins until beef is tender (or cook in oven on 160°C). Cool slightly.

Heat oven to 200°C. Sprinkle Stilton between 2 sheets of puff pastry then roll them out together until approx 0.5cm thick.

To make pastry lids, turn pie dish/es upside down on pastry and cut around the edge. Turn dish/es back over and spoon in the filling. Brush a little egg around the rims and top pie dish/es with pastry lid. Trim edges, then brush more egg over top. Cook for 20-25 mins until pastry is crisp and golden.

To make simple tomato chutney, heat olive oil in small saucepan over medium heat. Add mustard seeds and garlic. Gently cook until garlic is slightly golden. Add tomatoes, brown sugar, vinegar, salt and pepper. Bring to boil and reduce to a simmer. Cook for about 20 mins, stirring occasionally, until liquid is reduced. Cool before serving.

— Fiona Macneall

salmon with soba noodles

Serves 4-6 | Prep 15 mins | Cooking 10 mins

325g organic soba (buckwheat) noodles
3-4 Atlantic salmon fillets
Handful baby spinach leaves, or as much as desired
2-3 spring onions, finely chopped or sliced thinly on angle in desired lengths

DRESSING
1 tbsp finely grated fresh ginger
10ml sesame oil
25ml rice wine
25ml mirin
50ml salt-reduced soy

Preheat oven to 180°C. Combine dressing ingredients and set aside. Place salmon skin-side down on tray lined with baking paper. Bake for 4-5 mins until just firm but raw in middle. Meanwhile, cook soba noodles for 4 mins (or to packet instructions). Rinse noodles under cold running water. Divide into noodle bowls.

To serve, break salmon into large chunks and divide among bowls. Steam baby spinach leaves until they wilt, then divide among bowls. Drizzle sesame dressing over and toss. Scatter spring onions over the top.

— Lesley Holden

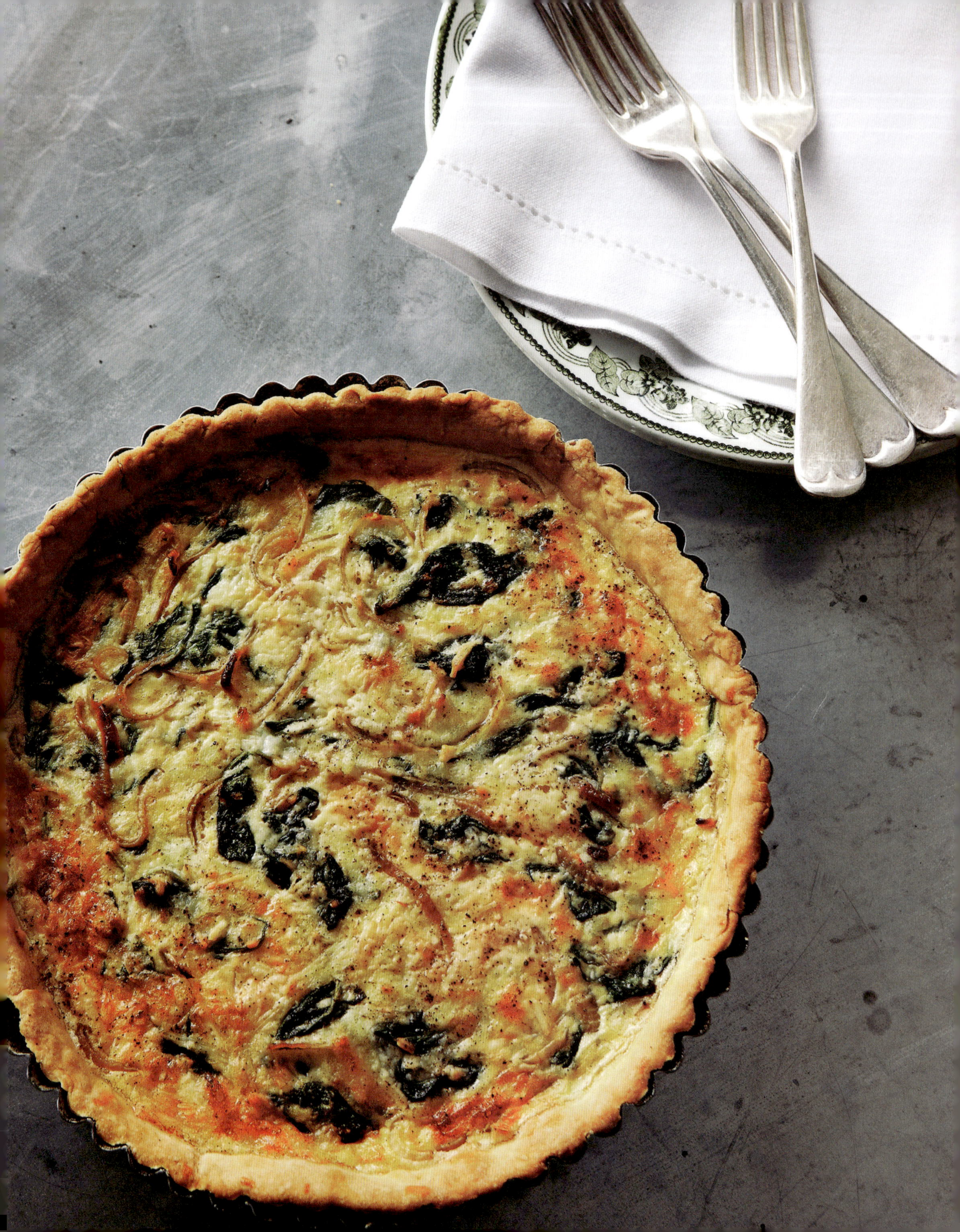

nanna patz's savoury tart

Serves 12 | Prep 30 mins – includes pastry | Cooking 25 mins

3 tsp olive oil
6 anchovy fillets, chopped
1 brown onion, finely sliced
1 clove garlic, crushed
225g spinach
500g shortcrust pastry (good-quality frozen sheets are ok)
50g parmesan cheese, grated
100g gruyère cheese, grated
1 egg yolk
2 eggs
100ml double cream
¼ cup milk
Salad greens, to serve

Preheat oven to 200°C. Heat oil in a frypan and add anchovies, onion and garlic and cook for 5 mins until onion is tender. Cook spinach until tender and drain off excess moisture. Set aside. Roll out pastry and press into lightly greased 24cm quiche tin.

Prick base with a fork and line with foil and baking weights (or rice/dried beans). Bake for 10 mins, then remove foil and bake for a further 5 mins until pale golden. Spread onion mixture over base, then layer spinach, parmesan and gruyère cheese into tart case. Whisk together egg, egg yolk and cream. Season well. Pour into tart case. Reduce oven to 180°C and bake for 20 mins or until filling is set.

To serve, scatter with parmesan (try toasted pine nuts on top too – you'll think you've died and gone to heaven). Serve with extra spinach leaves drizzled with oil and lemon juice.

– Milla & Ava's Nanna Patz

bánh xèo (vietnamese pancakes)

Makes 6 x 13cm crepes | Prep 30 mins | Cooking 20 mins

CHEF'S RECIPE

RICE BATTER
1 cup rice flour
¼ tsp ground turmeric
½ tsp salt
¾ cup canned coconut milk
NUOC CHAM (DIPPING SAUCE)
2 limes, peeled, quartered
¼ cup water
¼ cup fish sauce
1 small carrot, grated
3 heaped tsp brown sugar
1 long red chilli, sliced
1 clove garlic, finely diced
FILLINGS
1 cup lard or vegetable oil
¼ tsp salt
200g pork shoulder, thinly sliced
200g small tiger prawns, peeled, deveined, sliced in half lengthways
½ cup brown onion slices, each about 3mm thick
1 cup sliced mushrooms
3 spring onions, thinly sliced on angle, 6mm thick
2 cups bean sprouts (preferably trimmed)
Iceberg lettuce leaves, to serve

To make rice batter, in a large bowl whisk together rice flour, ground turmeric and salt. Add 1½ cups water and coconut milk. Whisk until mixture is smooth. Strain through sieve. Rest batter for 30 mins.

To make dipping sauce, blitz peeled limes, water, fish sauce and carrot in a food processor. Add sugar, chilli and garlic to taste.

Heat a 25cm non-stick frypan or skillet over high heat. Add 1 tbsp lard/oil and salt, and then add 1 portion of pork, prawns, onions, mushrooms and spring onions. Stir-fry until pork and shrimp are half cooked then ladle ½ cup of batter into pan. Swirl pan to coat bottom evenly. Cover right-hand side of crepe with bean sprouts. Drizzle another 1 tbsp of lard/oil around outer edge of crepe and lower heat to medium.

Cover pan and cook for 1 min. Remove cover and continue to cook until edges begin to brown. Use soft silicone spatula to loosen crepe from bottom of pan (a hard spatula will tear the crepe). When bottom is light brown and crispy, fold crepe to encase bean sprouts.

Place pieces of cooked *bánh xèo* inside a lettuce leaf, dip in *nuoc cham* and eat immediately.

– Ngoc Tuan Nguyen, Chu Bay

Notes: *Bánh xèo* ("bahn SAY-oh") means "sound crepe" – it indicates the sizzling sound the batter makes when it hits the hot skillet.

pesto & cherry tomato prawn pasta

Serves 6 | Prep 30 mins – includes pesto | Cooking 20 mins

Chef's Recipe

500g linguine or pasta of choice
6-8 fresh or frozen tiger prawns per person (peeled, deveined, with tails left intact)
Small bunch fresh rocket
Pesto sauce (see below)
Burst cherry tomato sauce (see below)

PESTO
1 bunch basil
Juice of ½ lemon
2 cups finely grated parmesan cheese
2 tbsp crushed fresh garlic
200g pine nuts
Salt & pepper, to taste
150ml olive oil

BURST CHERRY TOMATOES
1 punnet cherry tomatoes
2 sprigs oregano
100ml olive oil
2 tbsp fresh crushed garlic
Salt & pepper, to taste

To make the pesto, add all pesto ingredients to a food processor, except olive oil. Turn on processor, mix for about 1 min then gradually add olive oil. Process until smooth. Set aside.

To make the burst cherry tomatoes, in a large frypan, heat olive oil then add cherry tomatoes, oregano, garlic, salt and pepper and fry gently over medium heat until tomatoes pop. Remove from heat. Set aside.

Cook pasta according to packet instructions. While pasta is cooking, add prawns to the burst cherry tomatoes in frypan and cook until prawns turn pink. Once pasta is al dente, drain and add to frypan with prawns and tomatoes. Stir through the pesto sauce and fresh rocket.

To serve, divide between bowls and sprinkle extra parmesan over top, if desired.

— Room 9

Photo: Toby Burrows

tofu & snow pea fried rice

Serves 4 | Prep 10 mins | Cooking 15 mins

1 tbsp oil (eg, rice bran oil)
2 squares silken tofu
1 egg
1 tbsp sweet chilli sauce
2 tsp soy sauce
2 cloves garlic, chopped
1 cup cooked rice
12 snow peas
4 spring onions, chopped

Heat a heavy-based frypan or wok, add a splash of oil and the tofu, allowing it to sear for 1 min. Next, add egg in the same manner as a fried egg, but use a spoon to pierce the yolk and swirl it through the white.

Pour sweet chilli and 1 tsp soy sauce onto egg and swirl. Allow to cook for about 1 min until egg is set. Use a spatula to chop egg in pan. Add garlic and stir for about 30 secs. Add rice and continue to stir until rice is hot. Add snow peas, spring onions and remaining 1 tsp soy sauce. Stir for another 30 secs and serve.

— Si Chen

crown street cooks

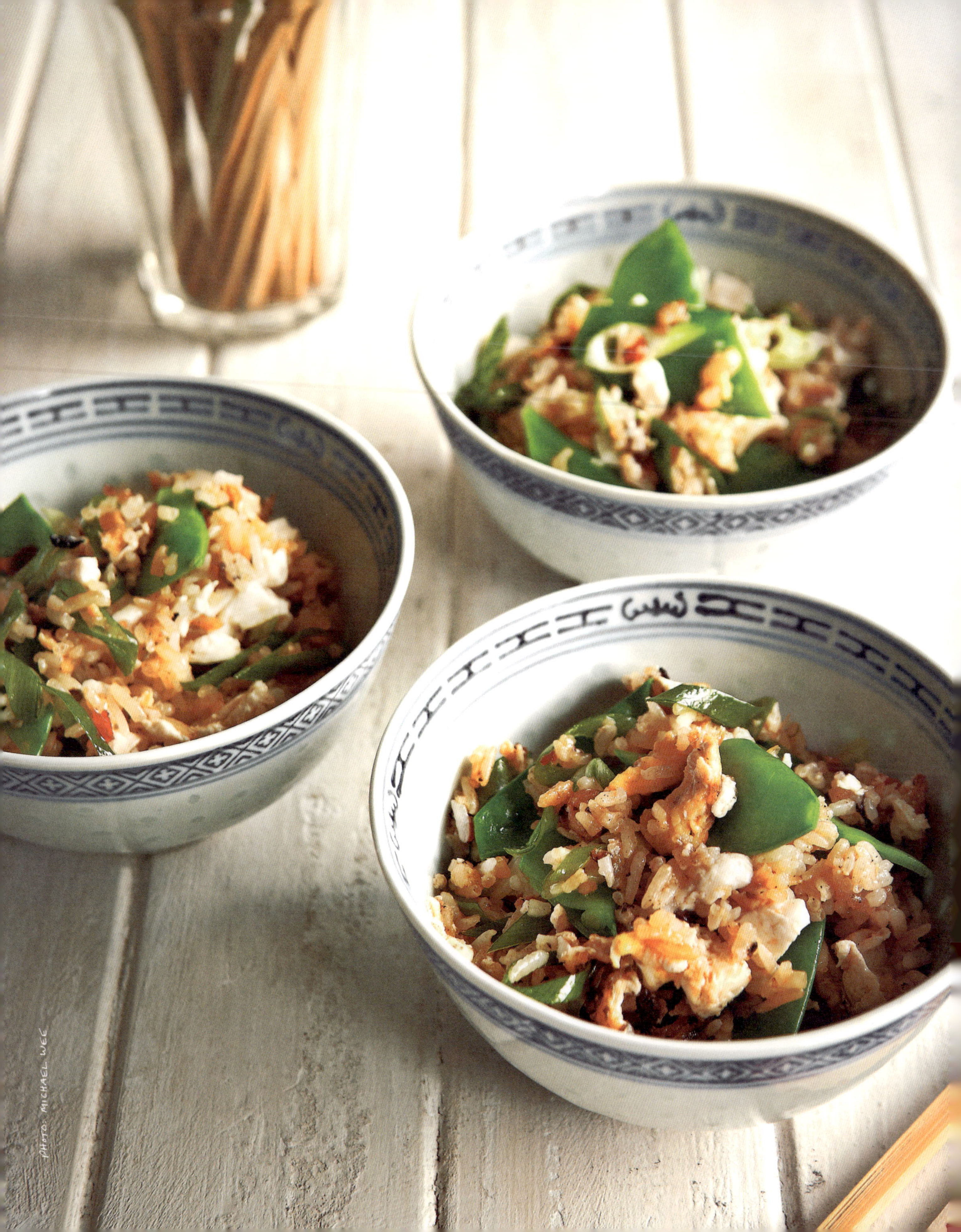
PHOTO: MICHAEL WEE

crown street public school's garden club bruschetta

Serves 4 | Prep 20 mins | Cooking 8 mins

4 slices day-old sourdough bread
1 clove garlic peeled, cut in half
Olive oil, for drizzling
TOMATO TOPPING
2 tbsp olive oil
4 ripe tomatoes, diced
½ cup shredded fresh basil leaves
BROAD BEAN & PEA TOPPING
200g broad beans
100g podded peas
4 tbsp olive oil
Juice of 1 lemon
½ cup shredded fresh mint leaves
140g shaved pecorino cheese

To prepare bread, grill both sides of sourdough until toasted. While hot, rub one side of each piece of toast with cut garlic.

For tomato topping, spoon tomatoes onto bread. Sprinkle with basil and drizzle with olive oil. Season with salt and pepper and serve immediately.

To prepare broad bean topping, cook broad beans in boiling water for 2 mins. Drain and refresh under cold water; drain again. Pop beans from skins.

Cook peas in boiling water for 2 mins. Drain, refresh under cold water and add to a bowl with broad beans, olive oil and lemon juice. Use a potato masher to roughly crush to a chunky paste. Stir in mint and season with salt and pepper.

Spoon broad bean and pea mixture on top of prepared garlic bread. Drizzle with olive oil, scatter pecorino shavings on top and serve immediately.

> "Our garden club meets once a week to weed, plant and harvest our organic vegetable garden. We then use the fresh produce picked from the garden to make something for lunch."

Photo: Michael Wee

We can all do our bit to make Sydney greener and more sustainable. The City of Sydney wants to make it easier for you to live green. For free sustainable living workshops, free cycling courses, information on community gardens and tips on how re-use and recycle go to **www.cityofsydney.nsw.gov.au**

2030 Sustainable Sydney

CITY OF SYDNEY
city of villages

PHOTO: MICHAEL WEE

crown street eats

The Winery by Gazebo
285A Crown Street, Surry Hills, NSW 2010
| T 02 9331 0833 | E info@thewinerybygazebo.com.au
www.thegazebos.com.au | Mon to Thu from 3pm; Fri-Sun from noon

While away an afternoon or dine Gazebo-style at night... With every creature comfort at hand, this unique indoor-outdoor venue is a fave with Surry Hills hipsters. Sublime wine, fabulous food and a frolickingly good atmosphere ensure Thou Shalt Have Fun.

Photo: Tim Robinson

dinner

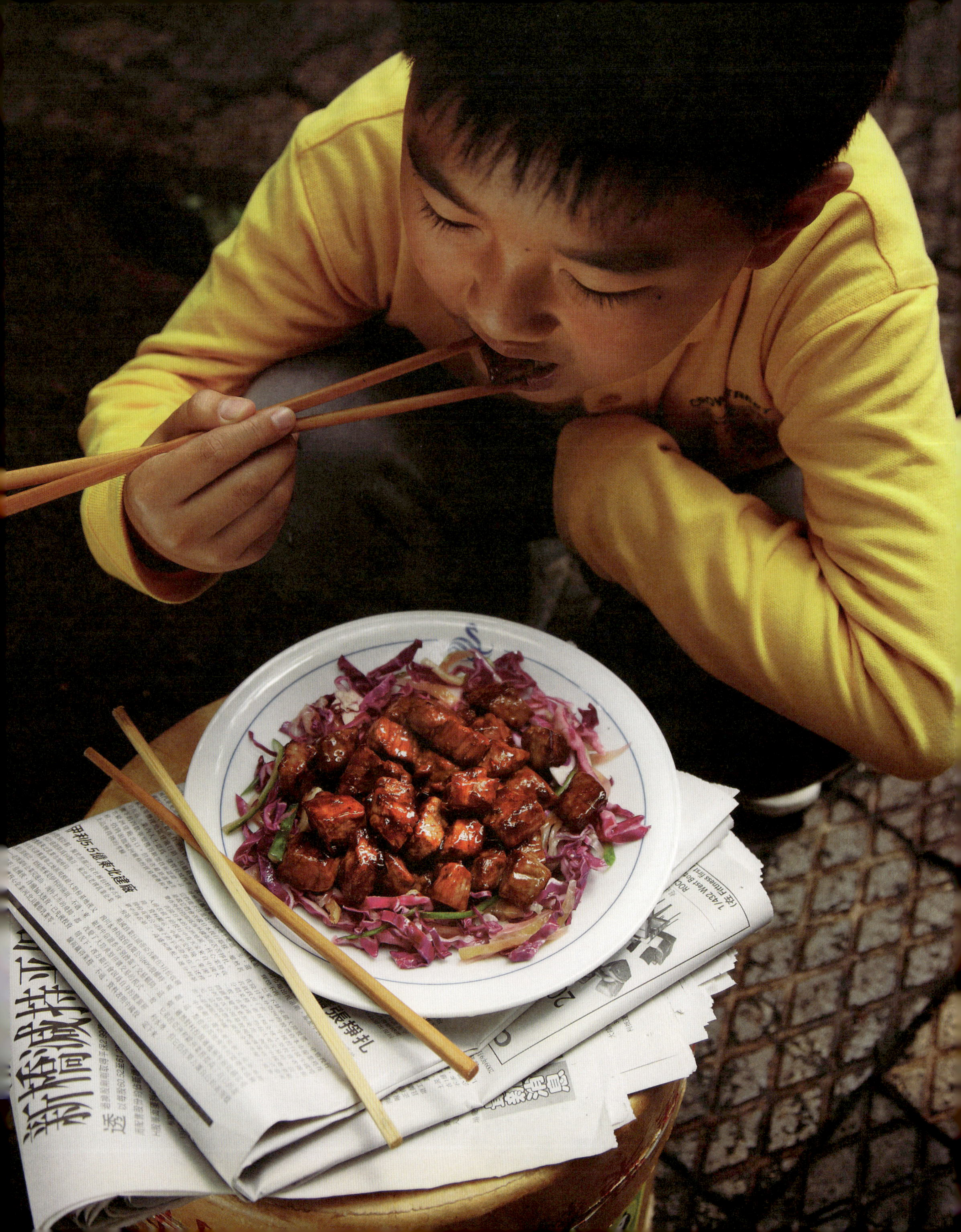

CHEF'S RECIPE

mongolian beef

Serves 2 | Prep 30 mins | Cooking 6 mins

200g T-bone steak
50g onion, cut into thin slivers
50g spring onions, cut into thin slivers
25g large red banana chilli, cut into thin slivers
1½ tsp ground black pepper
1½ tsp steak seasoning
1 tsp honey
1 tsp olive oil
Sweet chilli sauce (a splash, or to taste)
Soy sauce (a splash)

RED CABBAGE SALAD
Wedge of red cabbage
Small handful pickled mustard greens
   (from Asian grocery stores)
1 tsp sugar, or to taste
1 small cucumber
A little mayonnaise

Cut meat away from T-bone and chop into small cubes approx 1.5cm square.

Mix onion, spring onions, chilli, pepper, steak seasoning and honey with steak pieces and leave for 10 mins to marinate.

Heat oil in wok and fry beef for 1 min. Add soy and sweet chilli sauces. Continue to fry until meat is nearly dry.

For the red cabbage salad, slice cabbage into thin slivers. Wash pickled greens, drain, then add sugar to take sour taste away. Cut cucumber into thin sticks approx 10cm long. Mix together and dress with mayonnaise. Arrange cabbage salad on a serving plate and pile beef into centre.

— *Sean Zhang, East Ocean*

> **"I make large quantities and freeze them in meal portions so that when I'm working my son Vincent (pictured) can cook it himself."**

spaghetti & meatballs

Serves 4 | Prep 20 mins | Cooking 20 mins

1 onion
2 cloves garlic
1 stick celery
1 carrot
500g mince (we use half pork, half veal)
½ cup breadcrumbs
1 egg
1 cup grated parmesan, plus extra to serve
Salt & pepper, to taste
1 cup chopped fresh oregano &/or basil,
   or dried herbs to taste
400g jar tomato puree or passata
400g tin chopped tomatoes
Olive oil
Spaghetti

Preheat oven to 180°C. Place onion, garlic, celery and carrot in bowl of food processor and process until finely chopped.

To make the meatballs, place half of the vegetable mixture into a bowl with mince, breadcrumbs, egg, parmesan, salt and pepper, and herbs. Mix together well with clean hands – you need to get stuck in! Roll into small meatballs. Place meatballs onto a lightly oiled baking tray and bake for 10 mins or until just browned, so they don't fall apart when added to sauce.

To make the sauce, put some olive oil in a frying pan and sauté other half of onion, garlic, celery and carrot mixture. Add puree/passata and chopped tomatoes and cook on a medium heat for 10 mins. Transfer meatballs to sauce and cook for 20 mins on a low to medium heat. Keep stirring to make sure the sauce doesn't catch on the bottom of the pan.

Meanwhile, cook spaghetti in lightly salted water according to packet instructions. Top spaghetti with meatballs and sauce. Sprinkle with parmesan cheese.

– Schofield family

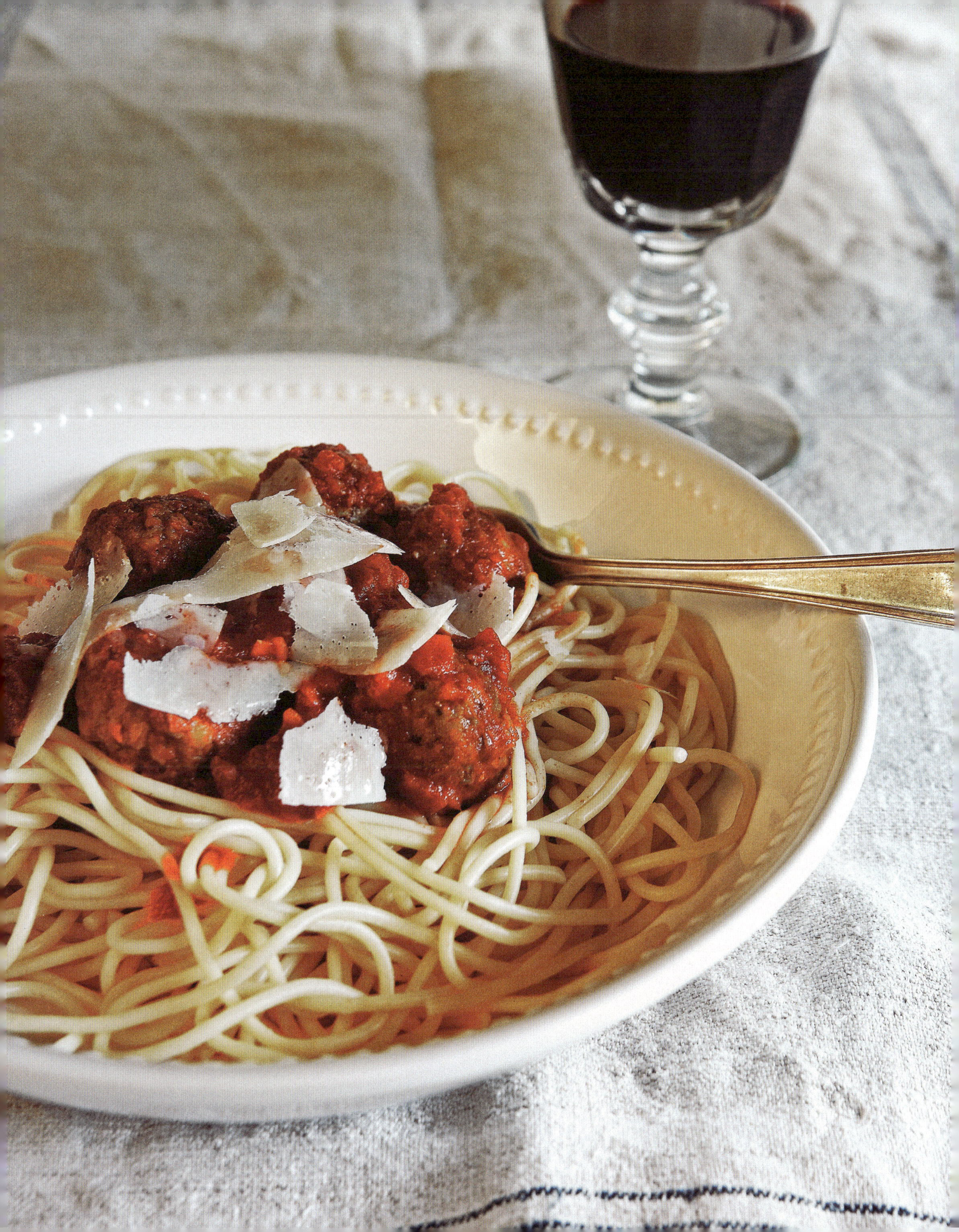

psari plaki (greek baked fish)

Serves 6 | Prep 30 mins | Cooking 65 mins

½ cup olive oil or vegetable oil
1kg peeled brown onions, sliced
8 cloves garlic, sliced
1 bunch spring onions, chopped
1 bunch parsley, chopped
400ml can tomato puree
Salt & pepper
¾ cup water
12 medium potatoes, peeled, sliced & par-boiled
2 lemons, sliced
4-6 leatherjackets, or any firm-fleshed fish

Preheat oven to 180°C. Pour oil into a large pot or large frypan. Sauté onions over medium heat until soft and golden. Add garlic and shallots and cook for 3 mins. Add parsley, tomato puree and salt and pepper to taste. Stir well. Add water and cook or 10 mins until sauce thickens.

Place potatoes in sauce and cook for another 5 mins or so. Arrange lemon slices over base of a baking dish. Place fish on top of lemon. Pour sauce over top of fish. Bake for 45 mins or until cooked to your liking.

– Koula (and Nia McAneney)

Notes: *Psari plaki* needs to be aromatic and crispy in parts, not swimming in sauce.

paella

Serves 6-8 | Prep 20 mins | Cooking approx 55 mins

2 tbsp olive oil
1 chorizo sausage, sliced
500g chicken thigh fillets, cut into approx 3cm cubes
Pinch saffron threads
750ml hot chicken stock
½ red capsicum, thinly sliced
½ green capsicum, thinly sliced
2 garlic cloves, finely chopped
1 onion, halved, finely sliced
1 tsp paprika
400g can tomatoes, chopped
300g arborio rice (Japanese short-grain sushi rice also works well)
Salt & black pepper, to taste
8 fresh raw prawns, heads & shells removed, tails left intact, deveined
1 calamari tube, cleaned, scored, cut into large chunks
12-16 mussels &/or clams, debearded, scrubbed
½ cup frozen peas
½ cup chopped parsley
Crusty bread, to serve
2 lemons, quartered, to serve

In a large paella pan (approx 30cm) or similar-sized heavy-based frypan, heat oil and gently fry chorizo slices until starting to colour at edges. Transfer chorizo to a plate (keeping as much oil in the pan as possible). Add chicken to pan and gently fry until golden – it doesn't need to be fully cooked at this stage. Put chicken with chorizo and keep warm.

Add saffron to hot stock and leave to steep for at least 5 mins.

Meanwhile, add capsicum, garlic, onion and paprika to pan and stir over medium heat until capsicum is coated with paprika and garlic is starting to cook (see Notes). Add rice and stir to coat well. Add chorizo and chicken. Season with salt and pepper. Stir to combine.

Add about half the stock, trying to ensure an even coverage of the rice mixture. Simmer, uncovered, over a medium heat for 20 mins, adding more stock and stirring gently as required to stop mixture from sticking to pan and burning. Don't worry if a dark crust develops – just try not to let it burn.

After 20 mins, reduce heat to low and add whatever stock remains. Place prawns, calamari, mussels and peas on top of rice mixture and cover lightly with foil. Cook a further 5-10 mins. Taste and add salt and pepper if required. Sprinkle with parsley and serve with crusty bread and lemon wedges. – Gregan McMahon
(and with thanks to Terese Mellado, Erwan le Pechoux's grandmother)

Notes: Capsicum, tomato, garlic, onion and paprika cooked in oil is called the *sofrito*. Remove the capsicum skins before cooking, if you like. If you have time, cook the capsicum down for 30 mins, then add tomatoes and cook for another 30 mins to make an almost jam-like sauce. You can perform this step well ahead of time.

crown street cooks

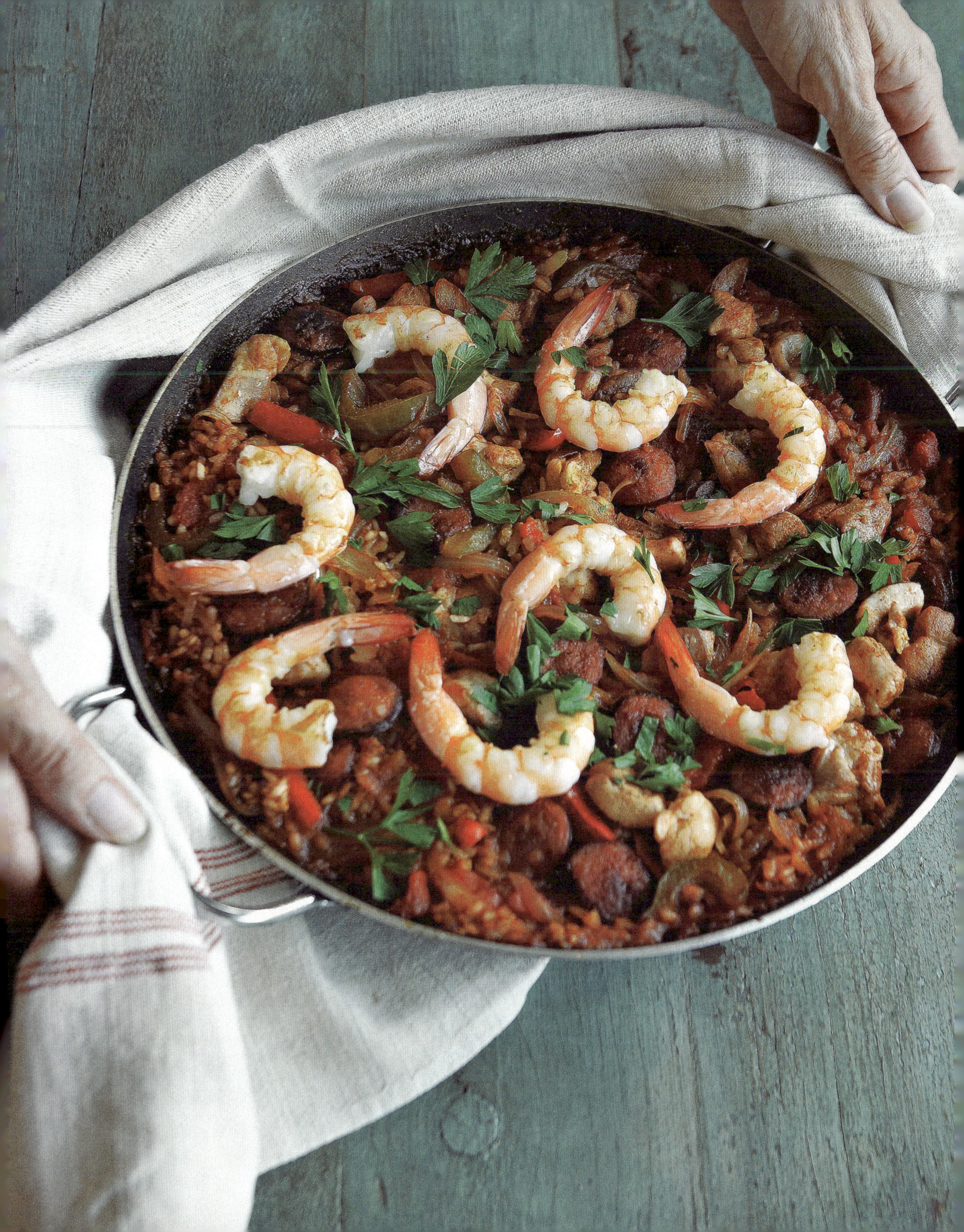

sweet & sticky chicken wings

Serves 4 | Prep 25 mins | Cooking 15-20 mins

CHEF'S RECIPE

24 free-range chicken wings
Salt & freshly ground black pepper, to taste
MARINADE
300ml Portuguese style piri-piri oil
150ml extra virgin olive oil
200ml fresh lemon juice
1 tsp salt
12 cloves garlic, chopped
6 tsp piri-piri powder
OR, FOR A QUICK MARINADE...
250ml bottle Nando's Sweet & Sticky Marinade or Portuguese BBQ Marinade

Preheat oven to 220°C. In a large bowl, mix together marinade ingredients and toss with chicken wings to coat well (or pour bottled marinade over wings and toss to coat). Season with salt and pepper, cover and place in fridge to marinate for 20 mins.

When ready to cook, shake excess marinade from wings and arrange on a rack over a large baking dish or baking sheet. Set excess marinade aside. Bake wings for 15-20 mins, turning and basting with reserved marinade every 5 mins or as required. Serve with a fresh garden salad. — *Nando's, Surry Hills*

Notes: You can marinate wings overnight if desired.

beijing pie (olympics fare)

Serves 4 | Prep 20-30 mins | Cooking 45 mins

2 chorizo sausages, cut into 3-4mm slices (medals!)
2 large Spanish onions, peeled & chopped
6 tbsp olive oil, plus extra for pie dish & pastry
400g-500g eggplant, peeled & cubed
2 cloves garlic, finely chopped
Handful chopped fresh (or dried) Italian herbs, such as oregano, parsley, thyme, basil
Salt & pepper, to taste
350ml tomato puree or passata
2 sheets frozen puff pastry, thawed
100g grated parmesan

In a large, heavy-based pan, fry chorizo in 2 tbsp oil until crispy. Remove chorizo and set aside. Add onion to pan and cook in 2 tbsp oil until soft. Add rest of oil and cook eggplant until soft. Add chorizo, garlic, herbs and salt and pepper. Stir in tomato puree and cook, covered, on low, for 15 mins. Preheat oven to 190°C.

Oil a square pie or baking dish. Roll out 1 sheet of pastry to fit inside dish with a 4mm gap. Sprinkle parmesan over pastry base. Spoon eggplant filling evenly across base. Roll out second pastry sheet just enough to form a loose lid for the pie. Cut a hole or small cross in centre of lid. Brush a little oil (or beaten egg) over pastry. Bake for 30-35 mins until golden brown. Cut into squares and serve. — *Cassy Cochrane*

Notes: This pie was a fave during the Beijing Olympics.

psari marinato (greek marinated fish)

Serves 4-5 | Prep 10 mins | Cooking 15-20 mins

5 firm-fleshed whole fish, such as blue-eye trevalla
Olive oil
5 cloves garlic, sliced
1 cup tomato puree
½ cup white vinegar
3 bay leaves
Rosemary – a handful, dry or fresh, chopped
½ cup water

In a frypan, fry fish on both sides until cooked through. Place fish in a single layer in a ceramic or glass dish.

Add some oil to frypan and gently fry garlic over medium heat. Add rest of ingredients to deglaze the pan. Stir to mix well.

Bring to boil and then reduce heat to a simmer until sauce reduces and thickens. This takes about 10 mins. Pour sauce over fish. Leave to marinate for at least half an hour before serving.

— *Koula (and Nia McAneney)*

eggplant parmigiana

Serves 4 | Prep 20 mins | Cooking 30 mins

1 large eggplant
Table salt
Olive oil
400g can peeled, crushed tomatoes
3 cloves garlic, finely chopped
Handful finely torn fresh basil
1½-2 cups grated parmesan

Preheat oven to 200°C. Cut eggplant into 1cm-thick slices. Arrange eggplant on paper towel. Sprinkle with salt (this will make it less bitter). Leave for 15 mins or so, then rinse in a colander under cold running water. Pat eggplant slices dry. In a large frypan, shallow-fry eggplant in batches, on both sides, in a couple of tbsp of olive oil for each batch.

Grab a small, round casserole dish or similar. Cover base of dish with crushed tomatoes and a sprinkling of garlic and basil. Lay eggplant slices over top and repeat until eggplant is all used. Make sure you save enough tomato for the top. Do not overlap slices in each layer. You may need to slice eggplant pieces to fit. Finish final layer with tomato and top with parmesan. Bake for 20 mins.

Remove from oven and let sit for 10 mins or so before serving.

— *Georgia Hawkins*

black chicken

Serves 5 | Prep 5 mins | Cooking 40-50 mins

10 chicken drumsticks
5 garlic cloves, peeled
5 bay leaves
Some whole peppercorns
½ cup soy sauce
½ cup *kecap manis* (sweet, thick soy sauce)
⅓ cup vinegar (red or white – it really doesn't matter)

Place chicken in a large pot with garlic, bay leaves and peppercorns. Pour over soy, *kecap manis* and vinegar. Cook on high with lid on until liquid boils, then turn down heat and leave to simmer until chicken is cooked and sauce reduced. That's it!
　Serve with rice, salad or seasonal vegetables.

— *Griffiths family*

ragù (italian meat sauce)

Serves 10-12 | Prep 1 hr | Cooking 3 hrs

SOFRITO
Olive oil
2 large brown onions, finely diced
3-4 carrots, peeled, very finely diced
4 large celery sticks, finely diced
4-8 cloves garlic (depending on size
   & your taste), chopped
2 anchovy fillets, finely chopped
2 star anise
MEAT
1.5kg chuck steak (you could also include
   a little oyster blade), cut into 1.5cm cubes
750g pork neck, cut into 1.5cm cubes
TO FINISH
1 cup red wine
½ cup white wine
3 fresh (or dried) bay leaves
3 tbsp tomato paste
1½ bottles tomato passata
1 tbsp good-quality dried oregano
½ tbsp brown sugar or maple syrup
Sea salt & pepper

Preheat oven to 120°C.
   To make the *sofrito*, heat a good splash of olive oil in an oven-safe pot and add onions, carrots, celery, garlic, anchovies and star anise. Fry over medium heat until onions become transparent and carrots soften.

   Meanwhile, heat a frying pan and brown the meat, a handful at a time, in a little oil. Transfer browned meat to a bowl as you go. When you have browned half the meat, remove star anise from *sofrito* and discard. Add browned meat to *sofrito* with red wine and turn up heat. Keep browning rest of meat in batches, adding to *sofrito* as you go. When all meat is browned, add white wine to meat-frying pan and stir to make a thin gravy. Add wine gravy to pot. Add in all the other ingredients – including a good pinch of salt and some fresh cracked pepper – and put on the lid.
   Place in oven for 2½-3 hrs. The meat should fall apart once cooked. Serve with pasta, rice, as a pie filling, on toast…
   – *John Colette*

Notes: To make in a pressure cooker, bring machine to full pressure and cook *ragù* for 45 mins.

> "This is a bit of a favourite at our place. It's great for kids and you can dress it up for grown-ups using pappardelle."

crown
street
cooks
51

crown street eats

Nando's
535 Crown Street, Surry Hills, NSW 2010
T 02 9698 0138 | F 02 9698 0179
| E nandos_surryhills@pacific.net.au
www.nandos.com.au | Open 7 days, 11am-10pm

Fire up your senses with their Portuguese-style flame-grilled free-range peri-peri chicken. Bring your family and friends to enjoy Nando's' famous hospitality in their fully licensed restaurant, or buy a peri-peri marinade and try Nando's at home.

Photo: Michael Fotoulis

chimichurri (argentinian marinating sauce)

Makes 1 cup | Prep 10 mins | Marinating 2 hrs

½ cup olive oil
2 tbsp fresh lemon juice
1 tbsp good quality red wine vinegar
⅓ cup finely chopped fresh parsley
4 cloves garlic, minced
2 spring onions, finely chopped
1 tsp finely chopped fresh basil, thyme or oregano, or a mixture
1 bay leaf
Chilli flakes (optional)
Salt & pepper, to taste

Combine all ingredients and let sit for at least 2 hrs before using. You can mince the ingredients by hand or use a food processor, which is faster and easier.

– Leo Arias

Notes: In Argentina (and Uruguay), *chimichurri* is the classic accompaniment to grilled meats. Use it as a marinade and also serve it on the side. It also goes very well with chicken and seafood.

PHOTO: MICHAEL WEE

malaysian-inspired chicken curry

Serves 4-5 | Prep 30 mins | Cooking 25 mins

2 tbsp fresh galangal, peeled, finely chopped
1 clove garlic, chopped
1 spring onion, finely chopped
1 lemongrass stalk, finely sliced
6 kaffir lime leaves (stems removed), finely sliced
½ long red chilli, seeded, finely sliced
  (leave the seeds in if you like it really hot)
2 Chinese eggplants, sliced into bite-size pieces
  (or use ½ a large eggplant, sliced, quartered)
Handful cherry tomatoes, halved or quartered
Olive oil
Salt
Zest & juice of 1 lime
250ml coconut milk
2 tbsp *tamari* (Japanese soy sauce)
1 tsp caster sugar
450g organic chicken thighs, washed, cut (across the grain) into strips
Peanut oil, for frying
2 tbsp finely chopped fresh ginger
Steamed jasmine rice or sticky rice, to serve
Nyonya achar (Malaysian pickled vegetables), to serve

Preheat oven to 180°C. In a small bowl, mix together galangal, garlic, spring onion, lemongrass, kaffir lime leaves and chilli and set aside.

Place eggplant and cherry tomatoes in a baking dish, drizzle with olive oil and toss with a little salt. Bake for approx 15-20 mins. Remove from oven and set aside.

In another bowl, mix together lime zest and juice, coconut milk, *tamari* and caster sugar. In a wok, heat some peanut oil and add reserved galangal mix. After a couple of mins, add chicken and cook for 2-3 mins. Once nearly cooked through, add zest, juice, coconut milk, *tamari* and sugar. Lower heat and simmer slowly to let flavours infuse, about 10-15 mins.

Add roasted eggplant and cherry tomatoes and finally the ginger. Cook for 2-3 mins. Serve with rice and accompany with *Nyonya achar* (pickled vegetables), if desired.

– Sarah Clapshaw

crown
street
books
54

bangladeshi chicken curry

Serves 8-10 | Prep 20 mins | Cooking 45 mins

6 tbsp olive oil
1 large onion, finely diced
1 tbsp salt
6 cloves garlic, peeled, crushed
1 tbsp ground turmeric
1 tbsp ground cumin
1 tbsp sweet Hungarian paprika
½ tsp ground chilli, or to taste
3 dried bay leaves
8 split cardamom pods
1.5kg chicken thigh fillets, each diced into 6 even pieces
3-4 cups hot water or hot chicken stock
8 baby potatoes, cut in half (peel them if you like)
Boiled rice, to serve
Small bunch coriander, to garnish

Heat oil in saucepan over medium heat. Fry onions with a pinch of the salt until soft, about 3 mins. Add garlic and cook until golden brown. Add all the spices, bay leaves, cardamom pods and rest of salt. Stir, cooking, for about 1 min.

Add diced chicken and toss to coat in spices. Pour in 3 cups hot water or stock. Stir, then cover and let simmer on low heat for about 15 to 20 mins. Do not let sauce dry up completely.

Wash baby potatoes and add to curry. Add remaining 1 cup hot water or stock (if needed) then let simmer, uncovered on low heat, for a further 10 mins or until potatoes are cooked through. Taste curry at this point and add more salt if needed.

Serve hot on a bed of boiled rice and garnish with coriander.

— *Danny Khan*

winter lamb casserole

Serves 6 | Prep 15 mins | Cooking 2 hrs

Olive oil
1 large brown or red onion, chopped
1 large carrot, peeled, chopped
2 cloves garlic, chopped
6 forequarter lamb chops (you can use other lamb cuts if you prefer)
1 large tin (820g) good-quality tomato soup
½ cup Worcestershire sauce
3 bay leaves
1 small sprig rosemary
1 tbsp brown sugar, or to taste
Salt & pepper
350ml water
Some diced peeled potato
Frozen peas

Preheat oven to 180°C. In a large flameproof casserole dish, heat some oil and sauté onion, carrots and garlic until soft. Transfer mixture to a bowl. Brown chops on both sides. Return onions, carrots and garlic to casserole dish and stir so flavours mingle. Add tomato soup, Worcestershire sauce, bay leaves, rosemary and sugar. Season with salt and pepper to taste, and add water. Bake for 90 mins. Stir casserole occasionally to prevent sticking, and add more water if necessary.

Add diced potatoes to casserole and return to oven for 25 mins – make sure potatoes are tender. Add frozen peas for final 5 mins of cooking.

— *Joanne Mulvay*

roast pumpkin & pea risotto

Serves 4-6 | Prep 10 mins | Cooking 45 mins

300g pumpkin, peeled, chopped into 3cm chunks
2 tbsp olive oil
Salt & black pepper
125ml dry white wine (use something you'd drink!)
625ml chicken stock
1 tbsp butter
1 small brown onion, chopped as finely as possible
2 cloves garlic, chopped as finely as possible
400g arborio rice
150g fresh or frozen shelled peas
Freshly grated parmesan cheese

Preheat oven to 180°C. Place pumpkin in roasting dish and toss with 1 tbsp olive oil and little salt. Roast for 20-25 mins or until soft. Heat wine and stock in a saucepan until hot (don't boil). In a large heavy-bottomed saucepan, heat butter and rest of oil and gently fry onion and garlic until soft and translucent. Add rice and stir to coat in butter/oil. Increase heat to medium. Ladle about $\frac{1}{3}$ of stock to rice; stir with a wooden spoon until liquid has all but evaporated (about 5-7 mins). Repeat until all of the stock is gone.

When you add last of stock, add peas and pumpkin and stir over medium heat until risotto is creamy, rice is firm but not chewy and peas are cooked.

Check for seasoning and serve risotto in shallow bowls, with parmesan on the side. — *Gregan McMahon*

spicy indonesian fried chicken

Serves 4 | Prep 20 mins | Cooking 30 mins

8 candlenuts
2-3 cups water
1 whole chicken, cut into pieces
1 tsp ground turmeric
4 cloves garlic, minced
2 medium brown onions, sliced roughly
2 pieces *daun salam* (Indonesian bay leaf)
½ can coconut cream (or to taste)
¼ tsp grated fresh ginger
1 tbsp ground coriander
Salt, to taste
1 cup plain flour
1L vegetable oil
Rice & green salad or Asian vegetables, to serve

Grate candlenuts to make a fine powder; set aside. In a large saucepan, bring water to boil. Add chicken pieces and all ingredients except for flour and oil. Cook until chicken is tender, about 20 mins. Remove chicken from liquid and drain. Heat vegetable oil in a deep pan or wok. Dust each piece of chicken with flour and deep-fry until golden. Drain on paper towels. Serve with rice and green salad or Asian vegies.

— *Latifah Alwiny, Crown Street After School Care*

Notes: Candlenuts and *daun salam* (these are not curry leaves!) can be found at Asian grocers. Add vegetables and/or noodles to the leftover cooking liquid for a soup.

pilau ya nyama (east african pilaf)

Serves 6 | Prep 30 mins | Cooking 30 mins

2 cups white rice
2 tbsp vegetable oil
2 medium onions, chopped
1 tsp each cumin seeds, cardamom pods & garlic paste
3 cinnamon sticks
½ tsp cloves
2 tsp garam masala
⅓ cup each cashew nuts & raisins
1 cup chicken stock
800g goat or lamb leg, diced
1 cup coconut milk
3 cups boiling water
Salt, to taste
Fresh parsley or coriander, chopped, to serve

Soak rice in water for 30 mins. Heat oil in a deep flameproof casserole dish and sauté onion over medium heat. Add all spices, garlic paste, cashews and raisins and fry for 5 mins. Add stock, meat and coconut milk and simmer over a medium heat for 5 mins.

Add drained rice and cook for a few mins. Add boiling water and cook, uncovered, for 10 mins. Turn heat down to low, cover dish tightly and simmer for 10-15 mins (or place in a moderate oven for 15-20 mins). Sprinkle with chopped parsley or coriander. Serve with *kachumbari* (East African onion, tomato and chilli salad; see page 84) and plain yoghurt.   – *Raaijmakers family*

prosciutto-wrapped chicken with polenta

Serves 4 | Prep 15 mins | Cooking 20 mins

2 tbsp dried sage leaves (or to taste)
1 tbsp grated lemon zest
1 tbsp olive oil
1 clove garlic, finely sliced
Pinch salt & pepper
4 chicken thigh fillets
4 slices prosciutto

POLENTA
3 cups water
½ tsp salt
1 cup instant polenta
50g butter

Preheat oven to 220ºC. In a bowl, combine sage, lemon zest, olive oil, garlic, salt and pepper. Cut into the side of each thigh fillet and spoon sage mixture into pocket. Wrap a piece of prosciutto around each fillet – if fillets are quite flat, spread with stuffing, roll up, then wrap in prosciutto. Secure with kitchen twine or toothpicks. Place chicken on lined baking tray and bake for 20 mins.

During last 10 mins of cooking time, prepare the polenta according to packet instructions.

To serve, divide polenta between 4 plates and top with chicken.   – *Helen Bouropoulos*

japanese miso grill sauce for bbq beef, chicken or pork

Prep 5 mins | Marinating overnight

1½ tbsp miso paste
1 tsp *mirin* (Japanese rice wine)
1 tsp sugar
1 tsp sake
Meat of your choice

Mix all ingredients in a bowl. Coat meat in sauce, cover and place in fridge overnight.

Shake excess miso sauce off meat and grill on the barbecue.

— Jun Tago, Goshu Ramen Tei

CHEF'S RECIPE

"A tasty, quick marinade, but you must remember to prepare it the day before you want to serve it."

flat roasted chicken

Serves 4-6 | Prep 20 mins | Cooking 45 mins

1 whole free-range chicken
Olive oil
Sea salt & pepper
Your choice of vegetables – roasted, steamed or both
Chicken stock & cornflour for gravy

Preheat oven to 180°C (select fan-forced grill setting).

You need a really sharp knife, or poultry scissors, to cut through breastbone. Cut chicken in half from breast to back (butterfly). Lay the 2 halves flat on a wire rack in a baking dish. Rub chicken with oil, sea salt and pepper. If making roast vegetables, put all your veg in another baking tray. Potato should be cut into small pieces or par-boiled first.

Bake chicken and vegetables for approx 45 mins. Rest chicken on rack while you make the gravy. Grab the baking tray you cooked the chicken in, pour some chicken stock over the pan juices, and bring to boil. Combine 1 heaped tsp cornflour with some water and add to the pan, stirring until thick. Cut chicken into pieces and serve with your vegetables and gravy.

— Schofield family

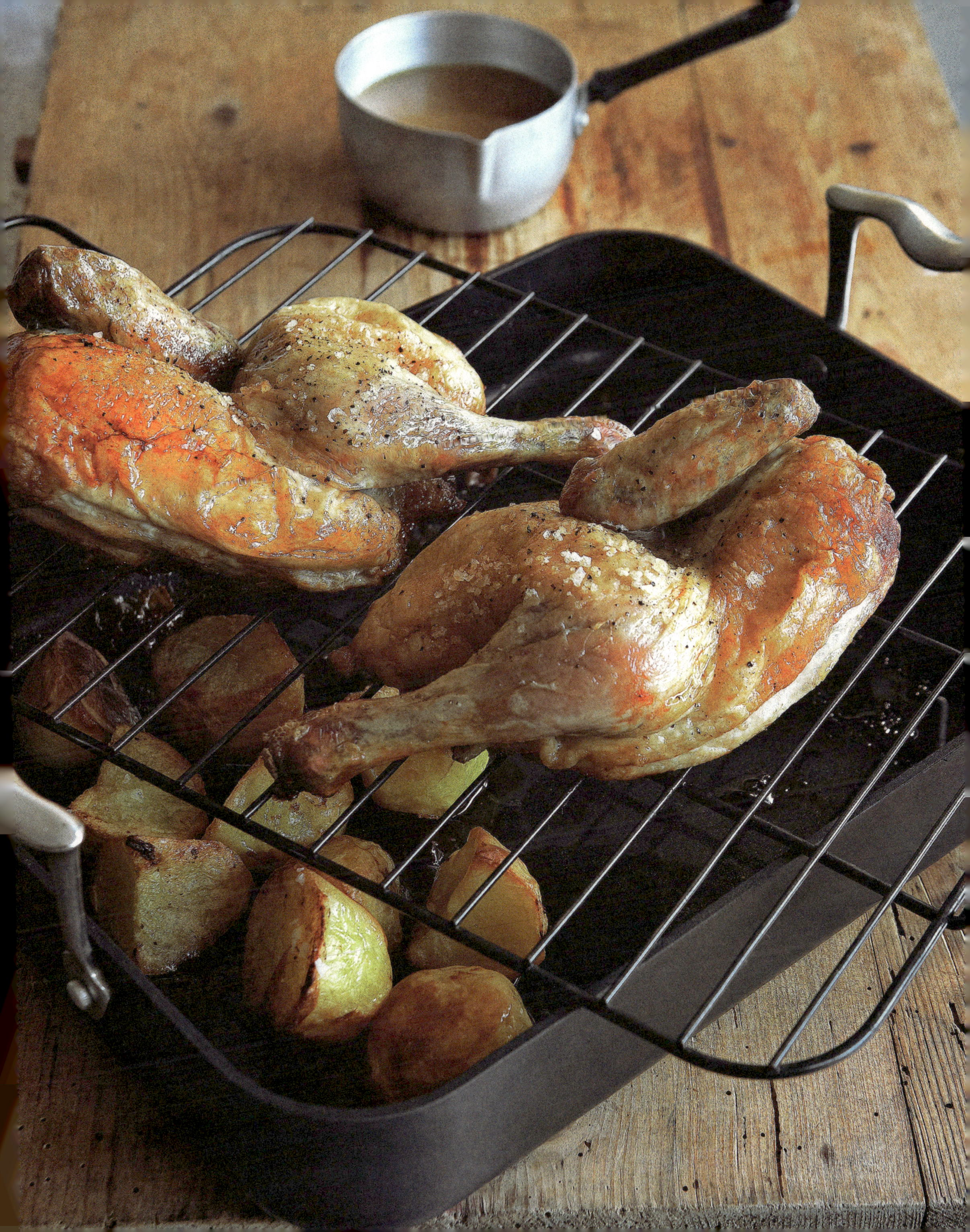

crown street eats

Crust Gourmet Pizza Bar
610 Crown Street, Surry Hills, NSW 2010
T 02 9698 9668 | www.crust.com.au

ALSO...
DOUBLE BAY: 374 New South Head Road | T 02 9328 6777
PYRMONT*: 208 Harris Street | T 02 9566 1933
ALEXANDRIA*: 486 Botany Road | T 02 9690 0233

For restaurant-quality pizza delivered to your door,
call a nearby store or order online at www.crust.com.au

All stores 7 days, 5pm-10.30pm
*Open for lunch

PHOTO : MICHAEL FOTOULIS

mui choy kau yuk
(slow-cooked cantonese pork belly)

Serves 2 | Prep & marinating 2 hrs | Cooking 55 mins

150g preserved (dried) vegetables or pickled mustard greens (found in Asian grocery stores)

MARINADE & PORK
1-2 tbsp dark soy sauce
2-3 tbsp soy sauce
1 tbsp Chinese rice wine
½ tbsp black bean paste
5cm piece fresh ginger, cut into matchsticks
5 cloves garlic, mashed
2 star anise
600g piece 3-layer pork belly with skin intact

TO FINISH
1 cup cooking oil (for frying)
2 tbsp sugar
1 tsp light soy sauce
1 tsp Chinese rice wine
1 tsp cornflour (optional)

Soak preserved vegetables/mustard greens in warm water for a few hours, changing the water several times. Drain, then chop into bite-size pieces.

Mix together marinade ingredients and marinate pork belly for at least 1 hr. Remove pork from marinade and pat dry. Set aside, keeping the marinade.

Heat oil in wok over medium heat. Fry pork until lightly browned. Remove pork from wok and leave to drain and cool. Toss preserved vegetables with sugar, light soy sauce and rice wine. Heat wok and fry vegetables for about 2 mins. Remove from wok. When pork belly is cool, slice across the grain into 1cm-thick pieces. Neatly lay pork slices, slightly overlapping, on a heatproof plate.

Pour reserved marinade mixture over pork slices. Distribute preserved vegetables evenly over top of pork. Add plenty of water to wok and bring to a simmer. Place a metal steaming rack in wok – rack should sit just above the water. Place plate on rack, cover wok and steam for 45 mins.

When pork is done and meat is soft, remove plate from wok. Drain sauce into a bowl. Plate up the pork and vegetables.

Pour sauce over pork to serve. Or, if desired, heat wok, add sauce and slightly thicken with a slurry made from 1 tsp cornflour and a little water. Pour sauce over pork. Serve warm, accompanied by plain steamed rice. — *John Croker, School Principal*

through the holes.) The *spaetzle* will swim to the top when ready. Remove with a slotted spoon. Place batch of *spaetzle* in an ovenproof bowl and sprinkle with some grated cheese. Cover bowl with foil and place in oven to keep warm. Repeat this process until there is no more dough left.

Sprinkle onions/butter and rest of cheese over *spaetzle*. Bake for 25 mins or until golden.

— Nina Smith

kaese spaetzle (german cheesy noodles)

Serves 4-6 | Prep 5 mins | Cooking 30 mins

400g plain flour (or use spelt flour for a healthier option)
4 free-range eggs
1 tsp salt, plus extra
150g-200g emmental, cheddar or gruyère cheese
50g butter
2 tbsp oil
2 Spanish onions, finely sliced
250ml water

Preheat oven to 190°C.

In a large bowl, mix flour, eggs, 1 tsp salt and water with a hand beater or whisk. Add more water if necessary. The dough should be the consistency of a brownie mixture – not too runny. Grate cheese in a separate bowl.

In a frypan, heat butter and oil and sauté onions until golden and aromatic.

Boil water in a deep pot (filled to halfway), then turn heat down to a simmer. Add some salt. Place a grater or steamer saucepan (with holes) over pot. Spread about 3 spoonfuls of dough on grater or steamer and press through holes, so that strings of dough drop into simmering water. If you have an upright grater, place dough inside grater and use a spoon to push it

butter chicken

Serves 5 | Prep 15 mins | Cooking 60 mins

1 onion, chopped
50g butter
2-3cm knob peeled ginger, grated or chopped
3 cloves garlic, crushed
1 tsp ground turmeric
1 tsp whole cumin (use ground cumin if you don't have whole cumin)
½-1 tsp salt (or to taste)
1 tbsp garam masala
1 fresh chilli, chopped, or ¼-½ tsp ground chilli (you could leave it out if the kids don't like it)
1 tomato, diced
1-2 tsp tomato paste
4 or 5 chicken thighs, diced
½ cup frozen peas (optional)
½-1 cup pouring cream (or mix of cream & yoghurt)
½ cup chopped fresh coriander (optional)
Plain Greek yoghurt, to serve (optional)
Cooked rice, to serve

In a frypan or saucepan, over a medium heat, cook onion in butter until golden, stirring regularly (about 15 mins). Add ginger, garlic, turmeric, cumin, salt and half the garam masala and cook for 2-3 mins. Add chilli and tomato and cook until nice and pulpy (about 10 mins). Add tomato paste and chicken. Coat chicken and fry, stirring, for about 10 mins. Add peas and stir.

Add cream (the amount you use will depend on how much sauce you like; you could also do half cream, half yoghurt to make it lower in fat). Stir, turn down heat and let simmer for 15-20 mins. Take off heat and stir in remaining garam masala and the chopped coriander. Serve with rice and yoghurt.

— Henrie Stride

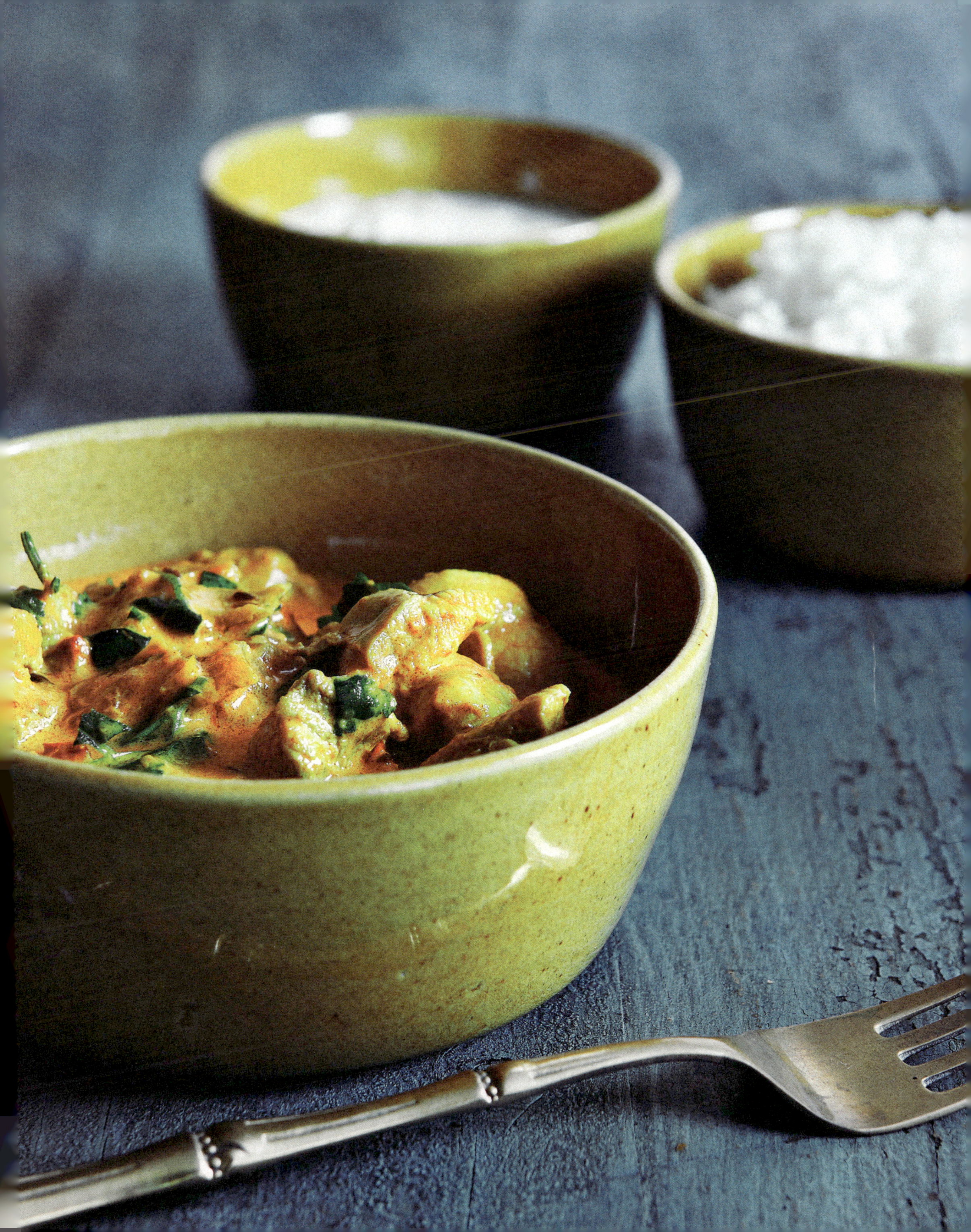

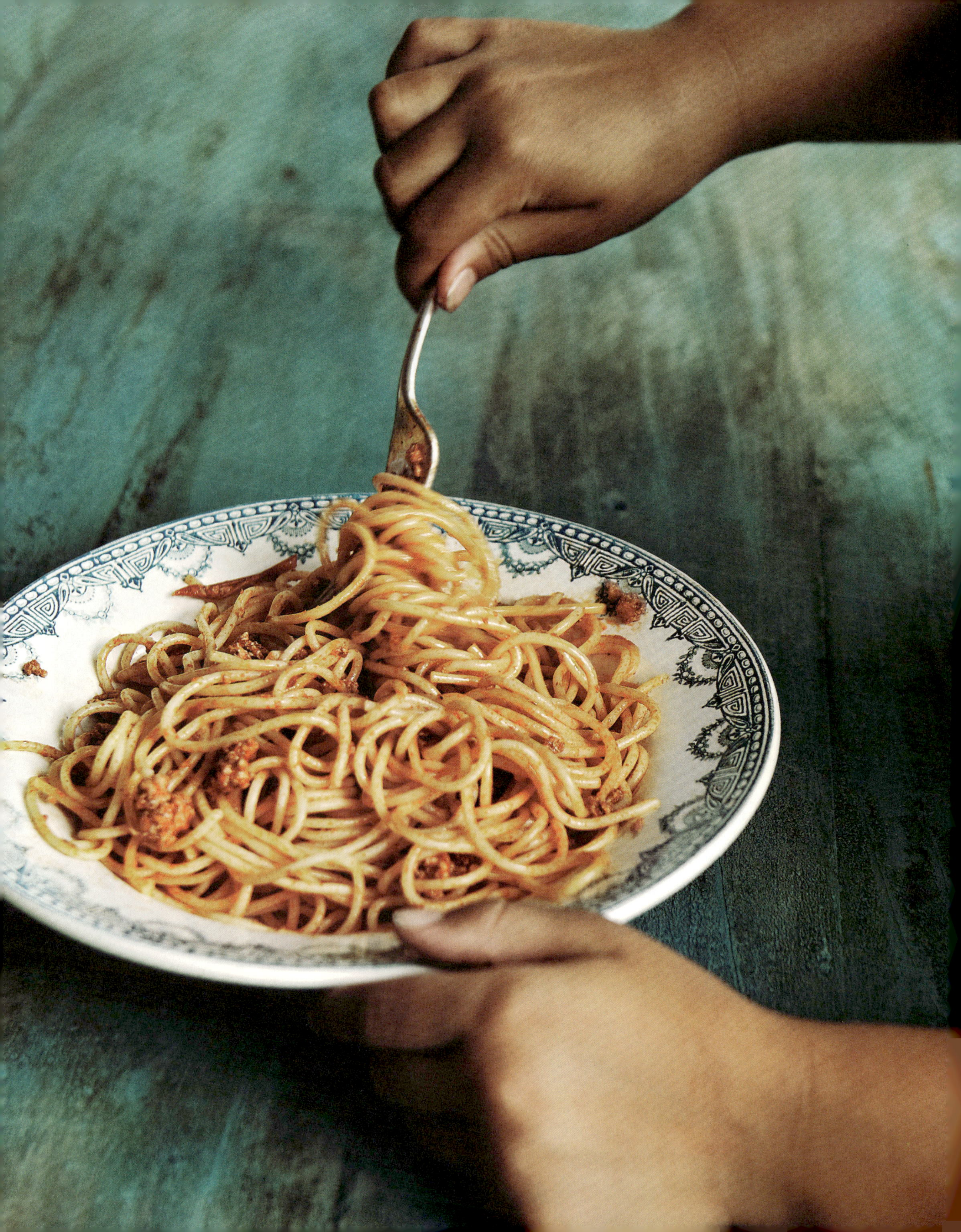

marie's greek-style bolognese

Serves 8 | Prep 10 mins | Cooking 40-50 mins

¼ cup vegetable oil
1 brown onion, grated
1kg beef or chicken mince
Salt, to taste
Cracked pepper, to taste
Chilli paste (a little)
1-2 cloves garlic, finely chopped
½ cup red wine
400g can peeled tomatoes
¼ cup tomato paste
1 cup water
4 whole cloves
1 cinnamon stick
2 x 500g packets spaghetti (size: no. 3)
1 tbsp oil
Knob of butter
Parmesan, to serve

In a large pan, heat oil and cook onion until golden brown. Add mince, stirring continuously, making sure to separate the mince. Once it has coloured, add salt, pepper, chilli paste, garlic and wine; stir.

Then add peeled tomatoes, tomato paste, water, cloves and cinnamon stick. Cook, covered, on medium heat for approx 30-40 mins. Cook on high heat, uncovered, for a further 5-10 mins or until sauce reduces.

Cook pasta, stirring occasionally, in a large pot of boiling salted water with 1 tbsp oil added. Drain, transfer to a casserole dish and add a little oil and butter. Top with sauce. Serve with parmesan.

Kali oreksi! — *Marie Apostolatos*

red velvet sauce

Serves 4-6 | Prep 15 mins | Cooking 40 mins

2 tbsp olive oil
1 medium brown onion, finely chopped
2 cloves garlic, crushed
2 x 400g cans diced tomatoes
1 cup chicken stock or water
¼ tsp mild paprika
¼ tsp dried oregano
Generous splash of white or red wine (optional)
Pasta or rice, to serve
Grated cheese to sprinkle over cooked sauce
  – a mix of fresh parmesan and cheddar is nice

Heat oil in a large frypan or saucepan over a medium heat. Add onion and garlic and sauté until soft and translucent. Add tomatoes, stock/water and wine (if using). Stir in paprika and oregano. Cook over medium heat until sauce begins to simmer. Reduce heat to low and cook for another 20 mins or until your pasta or rice is cooked.

Serve over freshly cooked pasta or rice and top with grated cheese mix.

Notes: You can sneak some vegetables into the red velvet sauce – for example, grated carrot or finely chopped capsicum – and/or add some fresh herbs at the end (such as parsley or basil). This is a great sauce to have in the freezer as it reheats easily. — *Penny Pitcairn*

crown
street
eats

The Beresford Hotel
354 Bourke Street, Surry Hills, NSW 2010
T 02 9357 1111 | E info@theberesford.com.au
| www.merivale.com | Mon to Sun, noon-1am

Now part of the Merivale family, The Beresford's had a makeover. There are lush green accents in the courtyard, a fresh mod Oz menu with an Italian twist and an impressive wine list by our master sommelier. Daily happy hours: 5pm-7pm. Drop in and enjoy the difference.

PHOTO: MICHAEL WEE

Photo: John Colette

indian beef curry

Serves 6 | Prep 50 mins | Cooking approx 2½ hrs

150ml olive oil
2 large brown onions, finely sliced
2 large knobs peeled ginger, finely julienned or grated
6 garlic cloves, peeled, finely sliced
3 bay leaves
8 cardamom pods
Sea salt & pepper
2 tbsp coriander seeds
2 tbsp fennel seeds
2 tbsp cumin seeds
Vegetable oil
1.5kg oyster blade steak, trimmed of fat, cut into 8 even pieces
400g tinned tomatoes
1L beef stock
Fresh coriander, to garnish
Rice or boiled potatoes, to serve
Yoghurt & chutney, to serve

Preheat oven to 180°C. Heat oil in a heavy-based saucepan. Add onion, ginger, garlic, bay leaves and cardamom pods. Season well with salt and pepper and cook over medium heat until soft, approx 20 mins.

Meanwhile, place fennel and cumin seeds on a baking tray and place in oven for 5 mins or until fragrant and slightly toasted. Remove from oven and allow to cool slightly. Grind to a fine powder in a mortar and pestle or coffee grinder. Sift into onion mix and cook a further 10 mins.

Meanwhile, heat a frypan over high heat. Add a little vegetable oil. Season oyster blade with sea salt and pepper. Brown meat in pan a few pieces at a time. NB: You don't want pan to lose too much heat, otherwise meat will end up stewing. The meat needs to be coloured well on all sides. Remove to some paper towel. Repeat until all oyster blade is sealed. Add meat to onion mix, along with tomatoes and stock.

Bring to boil, skim surface and allow to simmer gently until meat is tender and sauce has thickened. This will take approx 2 hrs.

Garnish with fresh coriander and serve with rice or boiled potatoes, yoghurt and your favourite chutney.

— *Jane & Jeremy Strode, Bistrode*

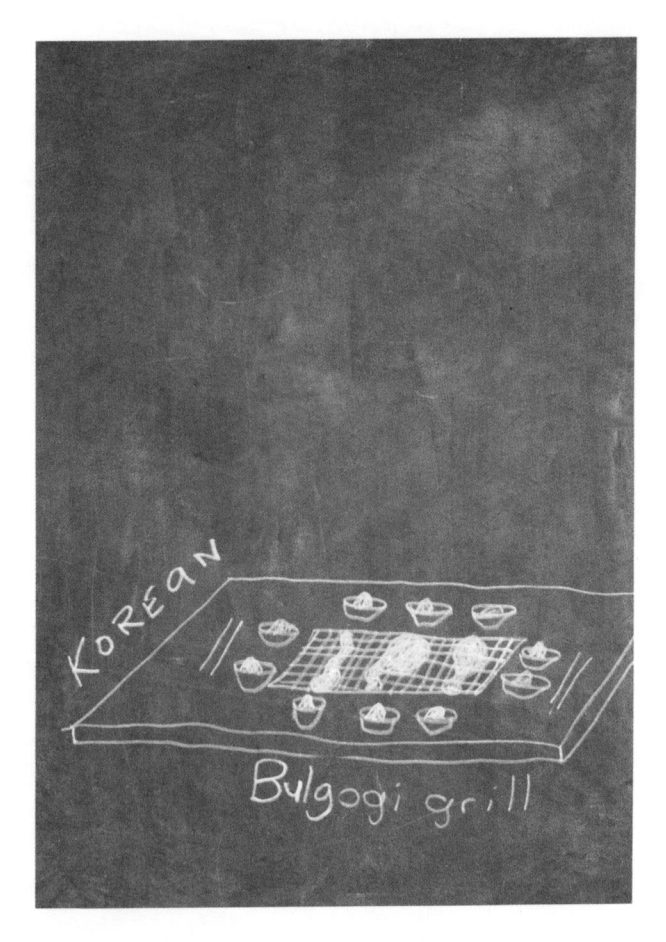

bulgogi grill (korean bbq)

Serves 4 | Prep 10 mins | Marinating 2 hrs | Cooking 3-5 mins

500g beef (not too lean)
MARINADE
2 tbsp soy sauce
1 tbsp sugar
2 tbsp sesame oil
½ tsp black pepper
4 green onions, coarsely chopped
3 cloves garlic, finely chopped
1 tsp finely chopped fresh ginger
½ cup water or white wine
Rice & green salad, to serve
1 egg per person

Cut beef into thin strips (if using stir-fry beef you need to cut it finer). In a bowl, mix together all marinade ingredients. Toss with beef strips and place in fridge to marinate for 2 hrs.

The Koreans use a special *bulgogi* grill, but a frypan is a good substitute. Heat pan to very hot, then cook beef until tender. Serve with rice, a green salad and an egg, fried thinly, and cut into strips.

Notes: Koreans serve *bulgogi* with a small side dish of cooked soybean sprouts flavoured with soy sauce. *Kimchi* (spicy fermented cabbage) adds a special touch to the meal – you can buy it at Korean supermarkets.

— *Min & Des Neil, Piper's Great Aunt & Uncle*

tandoori lamb cutlets with dahl

Serves 4 | Prep 15 mins (plus marinating time) | Cooking 25-30 mins

TANDOORI CUTLETS
Juice of 1 lemon or lime
2 heaped tbsp of tandoori paste (Sharwood's brand is best)
12 lamb cutlets
DAHL
1 tbsp olive oil
1 brown onion, finely chopped
1 garlic clove, crushed
3cm piece fresh ginger, peeled, finely grated
1 tsp ground cumin
1 tsp ground tumeric
½ tsp hot chilli powder
2 tsp ground coriander
250g dried red lentils, washed in a sieve until water runs clear, then drained
875ml vegetable stock
Salt & freshly ground pepper
Juice of ½ a lemon or lime
1 cup freshly chopped coriander
TO SERVE
Mango chutney & naan, roti or rice, to serve

For the marinade, mix juice and tandoori paste in a large bowl (use glass or ceramic as it won't stain), add cutlets and mix well to coat. Cover in plastic wrap and place in fridge – the longer the better, especially if cutlets are fatty as the lemon will break down the fat and flavours will infuse the lamb.

For the dahl, heat oil in a large heavy-based saucepan and fry onion and garlic until softened. Add ginger and spices and cook for 1 min until fragrant. Add lentils and stock, cover and bring to boil. Reduce heat and simmer, uncovered, until lentils are soft, approx 20-25 mins.

While dahl is cooking, fry, oven-bake, grill or barbecue lamb cutlets to your liking. When dahl is cooked, remove from heat. Add seasoning, lemon/lime juice and coriander just before serving.

Serve cutlets and dahl with breads and chutney (this way you can use your fingers Indian-style), or with rice and chutney.

Notes: I have made the dahl a few times for the staff of a Friday lunch club that some of us are involved in. They are always enthusiastic about it, considering it's so cheap to make, healthy and can be thrown together in 10 minutes (minus cooking time).

The dahl stores well in fridge or freezer but, when reheated, benefits from more lemon/lime juice and fresh coriander to refresh it. Just eating the dahl with brown rice is a super-healthy option.

You could use the tandoori marinade on pieces of ocean trout or chicken breast then, just before cooking, thread onto skewers. A fantastic way to liven up a barbecue.

— *Louisa Templar, teacher*

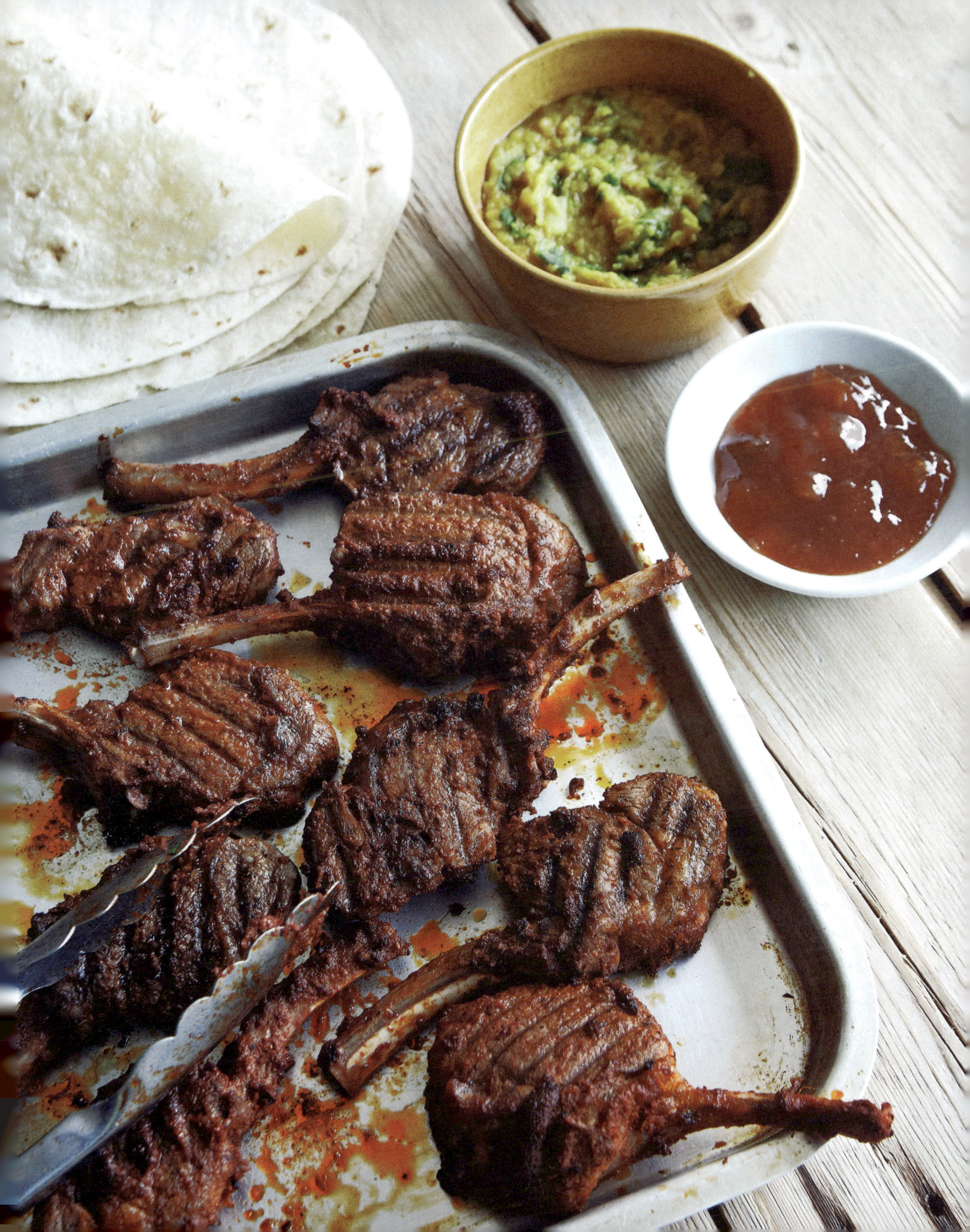

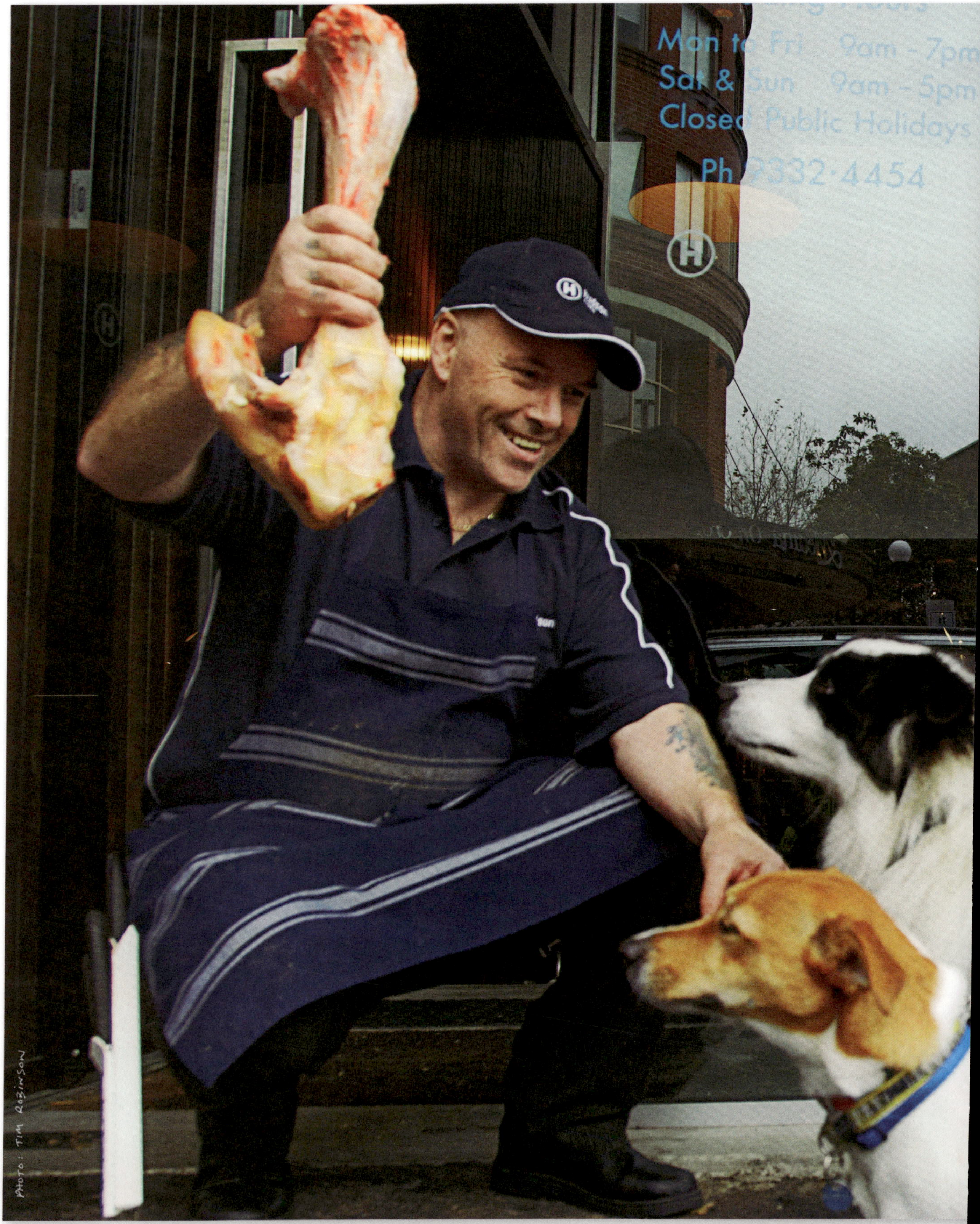

PHOTO: TIM ROBINSON

Hudson Meats

410 Crown Street Surry Hills NSW 2010
| T 02 9332 4454 | F 02 9332 4456
www.hudsonmeats.com
Mon to Fri, 9am-7pm;
Sat & Sun, 9am-5pm

Hudson Meats follows the Paddock to Plate philosophy and the Hudson team specialises in sourcing regional produce and frequently liaises directly with the farmers. Drop in for some Cape Grim grass-fed beef from Tasmania, dry-aged beef, lamb from Cowra, pork from Byron Bay, Barossa chickens, Italian prosciuttos, Spanish Jamón, artisan handmade salamis… And extra-large bones.

crown street eats

"Whether you're into tree houses or terrace houses, Walter's your man."

crown street eats

**Walter Burfitt-Williams
& Ray White Surry Hills | Alexandria**

500 Crown Street, Surry Hills, NSW 2010 | T 0402 833 566
E wbwilliams@rwdbgroup.com | www.rwdbgroup.com

Photo: Toby Burrows

ns, salads, sides

roast tomato, red lentil & cumin soup

Serves 8-10 | Prep 10 mins | Cooking 85 mins

1.5kg roma tomatoes or enough to fill a baking tray
2 heaped tsp ground cumin
¼ cup olive oil
Salt & pepper
1 red onion, sliced
2 cloves garlic, or more to taste
1½ cups red lentils, washed
1.5L water
2 small carrots, peeled & diced
1 tbsp tomato paste
Harissa (optional), to taste – 1-2 tsp to start with
1 tub Greek-style yoghurt, to serve
Freshly chopped coriander, to serve

Preheat oven to 180°C. Cut tomatoes in half. Place cut-side up on baking tray. Mix cumin with olive oil and spoon sparingly over tomatoes (there will be some left over). Season with salt and pepper. Bake in moderate oven for 45 mins to 1 hr, until they are soft and juicy.

In a large saucepan, sauté sliced red onion and garlic in leftover cumin oil. Otherwise add sufficient oil. Add washed lentils to onion mix. Cook over low heat for 5 mins. Add water and diced carrots and simmer for 30 mins. Add tomatoes and tomato paste and puree with a stick blender. Heat through. Add harissa, if using. To serve, ladle into bowls and top with a generous dollop of natural yoghurt. Sprinkle with chopped coriander. Serve with Turkish bread.

— Lesley Holden

new zealand maori fried bread

Makes 12 pieces | Prep 5 mins | Cooking 10 mins

3½ cups self-raising flour
½ tsp salt (optional, or to taste)
Cold water, to mix
Good-quality oil, for frying

In a large bowl, measure out flour, then add salt to taste. Gradually add enough cold water to make a soft dough. Mix together with a wooden spoon. Try not to over-mix as this can make them stiff and flat.

Turn dough out onto a lightly floured surface and push or roll dough out to 1.5cm thick. Cut into desired shapes and sizes. Place each piece into preheated hot oil. Fry until bread pieces are golden on both sides and twice their original size.

— Sandra Toi

aunty marina's *faki* (greek lentil soup)

Serves 8-10 | Prep 30 mins | Cooking 1½ hrs

Light olive oil
2 onions, grated
2 cloves garlic, crushed
2-3 carrots, grated
3 celery sticks, finely chopped, including leaves
2 zucchinis, grated
2 potatoes, grated
8-10 cups vegetable stock
1½ cups dried brown lentils
½ cup chopped fresh mint
½ cup chopped fresh parsley
2 tbsp chopped fresh basil
Salt & pepper
Lemon juice or vinegar, to serve (optional)

Generously coat bottom of a large saucepan with light olive oil and sauté onions and crushed garlic. Add carrots, celery, zucchini and potatoes. Then add vegetable stock. Bring to boil and cook for 30 mins, then add lentils and simmer with lid on until cooked – about 1 hr (add more stock or water if too thick). Add chopped mint, parsley, basil, salt and pepper.

To serve, add a splash of either lemon juice, brown vinegar, balsamic or red vinegar for a tangy taste.

Notes: Pronounced "F-ar-k-i" soup. If that's going to cause anxiety, refer to it as Hellenic lentil soup.

— Tiffany Cole

PHOTO: MICHAEL WEE

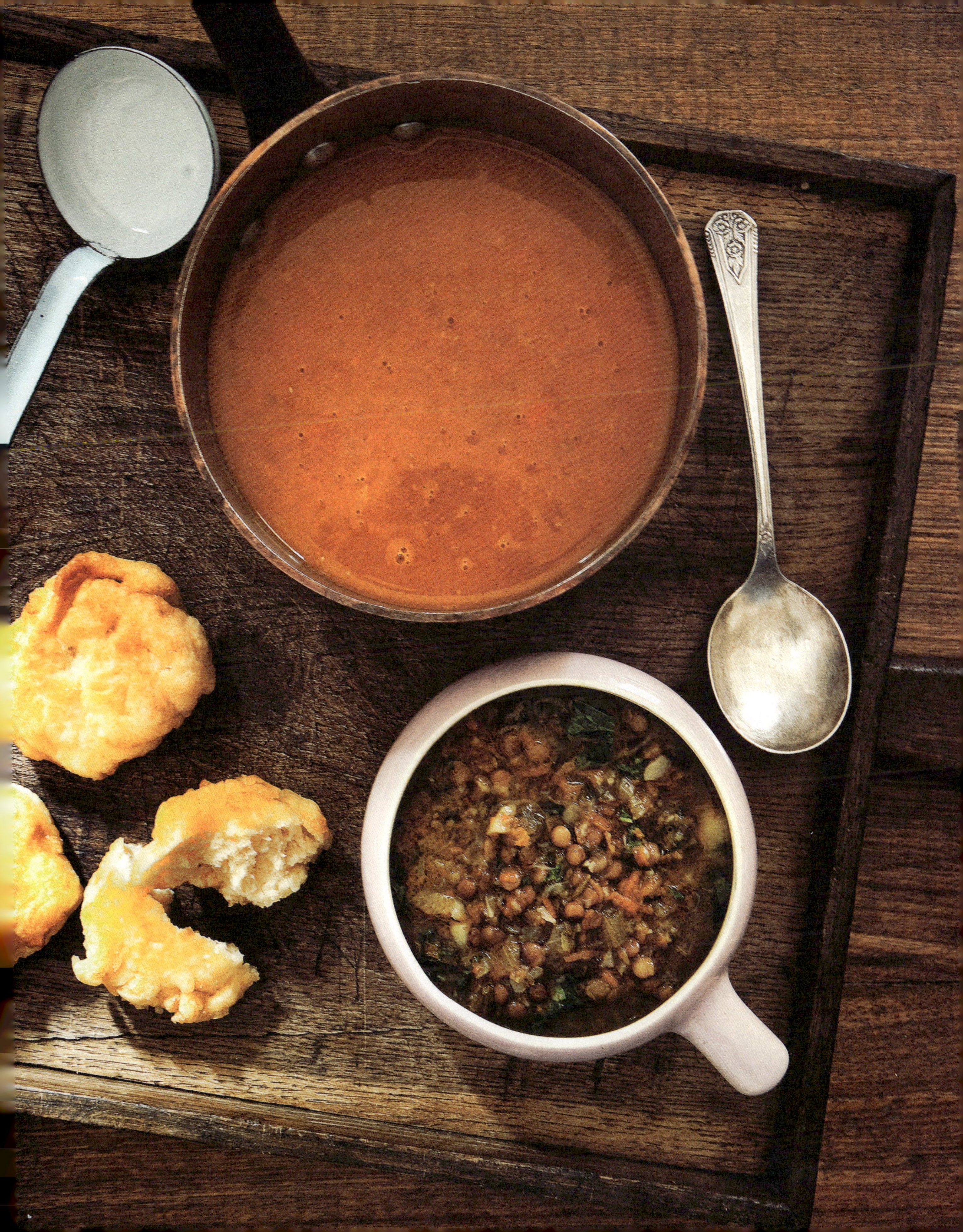

PHOTO: MICHAEL WEE

Chef's Recipe

meg's organic minestrone

Serves 4 | Prep 20 mins | Cooking approx 45 mins

1L organic vegetable stock, homemade (see below) or bought
1 medium eggplant, cut into medium cubes, salted for 10 mins, then rinsed & squeezed dry
Olive oil
1 large brown onion, diced (+ extra half if making stock)
1 carrot, cut into half moons (+ 1 extra if making stock)
2 long celery sticks, diced
2 garlic cloves, crushed or finely chopped (always organic or at least unbleached)
1 bay leaf (+ 1 extra if making stock)
A few whole peppercorns (if making stock)
1 dried shiitake mushroom (if making stock)
1 zucchini, cut into half moons
8 button mushrooms, cut in half
400g can organic diced tomatoes
400g can organic four-bean mix
Sea salt & freshly ground black pepper, to taste
Organic pasta of your choice (optional), cooked al dente – small mixed shapes are good

GARNISH
Handful flat-leaf parsley, roughly chopped (keep the stalks to make the stock)
Fresh parmesan cheese, grated (try Grana Padano)

To make the vegetable stock, wash and prepare all your vegetables (as above). Keep aside all the peelings and trimmings. In a large saucepan place carrot peelings and zucchini ends, skin and ends of onion and garlic (including brown outer skin), ends of celery (but not the leaves), some parsley stalks, a bay leaf and a few peppercorns. Roughly chop extra carrot and half an onion and add to pot. Gently brown carrot, onion and peelings, etc, in a little olive oil until the aroma is a bit like roast vegies, then add 1.2L water and a dried shiitake mushroom that has been soaked in water, along with its soaking juice. Let this simmer as you prepare rest of ingredients. When carrot is soft, pour stock through a sieve into a pot, pushing vegies down with a wooden spoon to capture all their juices.

To make the minestrone, heat olive oil in a large saucepan. Lightly brown onion, then add eggplant and cook until eggplant is golden and translucent.

Next add mushrooms, then carrot, celery, garlic and bay leaf. Sauté for a min or so to release the flavours and then add tinned tomatoes. Cook for 2 mins to infuse tomato, almost like a pasta sauce.

Now add vegie stock and four-bean mix and bring to a slow simmer. Then add zucchini and any other vegies you might like to include, one type at a time according to how much you like them cooked. When all vegies are cooked the soup is done. Season with sea salt and freshly ground pepper.

To serve, place a handful of cooked pasta (if using) into each bowl and ladle soup on top. Garnish with parmesan and chopped parsley.

— *Meg, Kawa cafe*

fig & prosciutto salad

Serves 4-6 as starter | Prep 10 mins

12 thin slices prosciutto
6 handfuls rocket leaves
6 sprigs mint, leaves torn
6 ripe green or black figs, stems removed, thickly sliced (I crisscross them ¾ of the way down & let them fall open – looks nicer)
150g fresh goat's curd
DRESSING
20ml sherry vinegar
60ml extra virgin olive oil
Sea salt
Freshly cracked black pepper

Arrange prosciutto in criss-cross fashion on a large platter. Cover with rocket and mint. Arrange figs on top in a circular pattern and add some dollops of goat's curd.

For the dressing, whisk sherry vinegar, olive oil, salt and pepper in a small bowl until well combined.

To serve, drizzle dressing over figs and take it to the table immediately.
— *Trent Chapman*

Notes: Save this dish for fig season.

pear, goat's cheese & walnut salad

Serves 5 | Prep 30 mins | Cooking 15 mins

175g walnuts
50g rocket
75g watercress
¼ savoy cabbage
500g beurre bosc pears, peeled, thinly sliced
250g goat's cheese
DRESSING
60ml walnut oil
65ml balsamic vinegar (white if possible)
Salt & pepper

Preheat oven to 180°C. Scatter walnuts on a flat tray and roast for about 15 mins or until lightly browned. Remove from oven and cool to room temperature.

Wash rocket and watercress, removing large stalks from cress. Wash and then chiffonade cabbage (that is, cut it into long, thin strips) and add to rocket and watercress. Mix until evenly combined and divide salad leaves among 5 separate bowls.

Peel pears and slice thinly. Add equal amounts to each bowl and toss salad again. Crumble goat's cheese into small pieces and add to bowls. Chop walnuts into halves and sprinkle on top of salad.

For the dressing, combine walnut oil, balsamic vinegar, salt and pepper. Drizzle over salad and serve.
— *Robert Reid*

mango & prawn salad

Serves 2 | Prep 15 mins

1 mango
8 large prawns
DRESSING
6 mint leaves, finely chopped
2 tsp fish sauce
1 tbsp Thai sweet chilli sauce
1 tbsp lime juice (lemon is OK too)

Peel mango and slice flesh into long strips. Cut heads off prawns, then shell and devein.

In a large bowl, combine mango and prawns. Blend dressing ingredients, drizzle over and serve. – *Joanne Hu*

spicy seafood dipping sauce

Serves 12 | Prep 15 mins

6 lemons, juiced
3 chillis (or more, to taste)
1 bunch coriander, finely chopped
1 stalk lemongrass, finely chopped
½ cup oyster sauce
1 tbsp fish sauce, or more to taste

In a stainless steel bowl, mix all ingredients together. Transfer to serving bowl. Great with BBQ seafood.

– *Cheryl Clarke*

beetroot & fetta salad

Serves 2-4 (main or side) | Prep 15 mins | Cooking 35-90 mins

1 bunch beetroot
100g fetta cheese
100g rocket, roughly chopped
50g pine nuts, lightly toasted
DRESSING
2 tbsp olive oil
Juice of ½ a lemon
Freshly ground sea salt & black pepper

Cut leaves off beetroot, leaving about 2.5cm of stem. Don't trim root end off – this stops juice from leaching out during cooking. Gently wash beetroot under cold running water. Carefully scrub the delicate skin with a paper towel, keeping skin intact to retain juice. Place trimmed and washed beetroot in a large saucepan with enough cold water to cover by about 5cm. Cover and bring to boil, then tilt lid to form a crack and reduce heat to medium boil. Cook 35-45 mins. NB: You could also wrap each beetroot in foil and roast up to 1.5 hrs.

They are fully cooked when easily pierced with tip of a sharp knife. When cool enough to handle, peel by rubbing gently with paper towels. Cut large beetroot into wedges. Leave small ones whole or halve them. Add rocket to salad bowl, then beetroot. To serve, crumble fetta over top then add pine nuts, lemon juice and olive oil. Season to taste. – *Katina Richards*

crown street cooks

guacamole from the texas hills

Serves 4-6 | Prep 20 mins

Zest & juice of 1 lime
1 clove garlic, finely diced
2 tbsp extra virgin olive oil
1 paper-thin slice Spanish onion
3 pinches ground black pepper
Pinch salt
1 small ripe tomato
1 bunch coriander
2 ripe avocados

In a bowl or large mortar, add lime zest, juice, garlic, 1 tbsp olive oil, paper-thin slice of Spanish onion, pepper and salt. Mix together or grind with the pestle. Set aside.

Chop tomato into 1cm cubes. Wash coriander and strip a generous handful of leaves. Cut avocados in half and get rid of the seeds. Add tomato and coriander to bowl. Stir until well mixed with the other ingredients.

Run a butter knife through avocado halves a couple times. Scoop out halves and add to bowl. NB: Do not pre-blend or mash the avocado.

Add second 1 tbsp olive oil. Mix avocado in with other ingredients but not so much that avocado becomes smooth. The texture should still be chunky – good guacamole is never a homogeneous paste.

Refrigerate if you like, or serve right away. The lime juice should help keep the avocado from browning if you refrigerate. A quick stir before serving is advised.

Serve guacamole with good-quality plain corn chips and beverage of your choice.

— Chesher family

Notes: To vary, add 1 finely chopped small hot red pepper to the initial mix in the bowl. More coriander is better than less.

moroccan orange salad

Serves 8 | Prep 10 mins | Chilling 1 hr

4-6 juicy oranges
8 dates, sliced lengthwise
8 blanched & slivered almonds
Orange flower water (or lemon juice and caster sugar if OFW is unavailable, but it won't have quite the same exotic flavour)
Pinch ground cinnamon

With a sharp knife, peel oranges and slice into thin rounds, removing the seeds. Place orange slices in a salad bowl and add sliced dates and almonds. Sprinkle orange flower water on, drop by drop, until flavour is to your taste. Refrigerate for 1 hr.

To serve, remove from fridge and dust with cinnamon.

— Louise Bickle

Notes: If you want to make this early, only add almonds and orange flower water 1 hr before so almonds stay crunchy and orange flower water doesn't overpower.

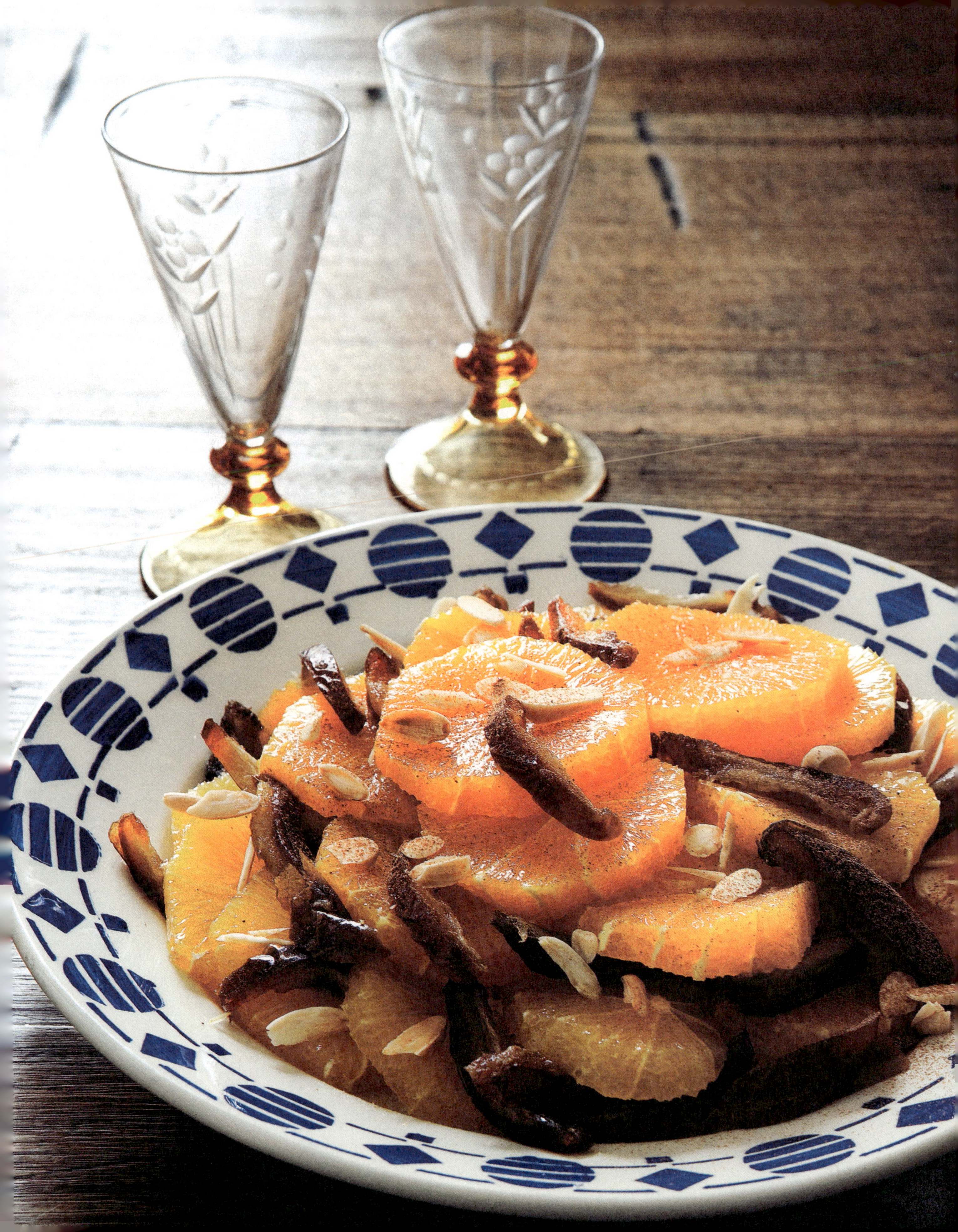

kisir (turkish cracked wheat salad)

Serves 4-6 | **Prep 20 mins**

2 cups fine bulgur wheat
1 tbsp red pepper paste (see Notes)
Salt & black pepper
Pinch ground cumin
1 cup fresh mint, chopped
1 cup chopped parsley
4 spring onions, finely chopped
½ cup olive oil
Juice of one lemon, or to taste
2 tbsp pomegranate syrup or pomegranate molasses
2 tomatoes, diced
1 cos lettuce, leaves washed, to serve

In a large bowl, pour 2 cups hot water. Add bulgur and soak for 20 mins then fluff it up with a fork. Add red pepper paste to bulgur and use your hands to mix it through. Add all spices, mix well. Then add chopped herbs, spring onions, oil, lemon juice, pomegranate syrup and mix well. Add diced tomatoes and mix.

To serve, pile some *kisir* onto small individual cos lettuce leaves.

– Keser family

Notes: You can buy Turkish red pepper paste at Turkish and Middle Eastern food stores.

aloo gobi (indian dry potato & cauliflower curry)

Serves 4-6 | **Prep 15 mins** | **Cooking 25 mins**

1 tsp oil
1 brown onion, sliced lengthways
1 tsp cumin seeds
3 potatoes, peeled, cut into eighths
1 cauliflower (florets separated)
1 tsp chilli
Salt, to taste
½ tsp powdered turmeric
1 tsp ground coriander
1 tsp grated fresh ginger
1 tsp minced garlic
2 tomatoes, diced
½ cup water
1 bunch fresh coriander, chopped

Heat oil to a large saucepan and fry onion and cumin seeds until light brown. Add potatoes and cauliflower and fry until they start to colour. Add chilli, salt, turmeric, ground coriander, ginger and garlic. Add tomatoes, fry a little, and add water and cook until potatoes are soft.

To serve, transfer to a bowl and sprinkle fresh coriander on top.

– Nuzahat Bari, Suroor Rahman's grandmother

asian lamb salad

Serves 4 as starter | Prep 20 mins | Cooking 5 mins

280g lamb backstrap
Sea salt & fresh cracked black pepper
Olive oil

DRESSING & SALAD
3 cloves garlic, peeled, chopped
2 red birdseye chillies, deseeded, chopped
3cm piece fresh ginger, peeled, roughly chopped
2 tbsp grated palm sugar or brown sugar
3 tbsp lime juice
2 tbsp fish sauce
1 bunch mint
1 bunch coriander
4 large stringless beans or 10 snow peas, shredded
3 small eschalots, thinly sliced
2 tbsp unsalted roasted peanuts, coarsely crushed

Season lamb backstrap with salt, pepper and olive oil and cook to rare on the BBQ. Allow to rest.

Put garlic, chillies and ginger in a mortar and work to a coarse paste (or whiz in a little blender). Add sugar and then lime juice and fish sauce. Stir until sugar has dissolved.

Slice lamb thinly. In a large bowl, toss lamb and dressing together so lamb is well coated. Add remaining ingredients, mix well and serve.

– MacMaster family

sumashi-jiru (japanese clear soup)

Serves 4 | Prep 5 mins | Cooking 5-10 mins

5 cups water
2 tsp or ½ pack *hondashi* (fish stock powder)
½ white onion, cut into small segments
2 tsp sake
3 tsp soy sauce
2 tsp salt
2 eggs

Add water and *hondashi* to a saucepan and bring to the boil. Add onion and boil until clear and soft. Add sake, soy sauce and salt.

In a bowl, break eggs and beat with chopsticks.

Bring soup to boil, remove from heat and stir rapidly in a circular motion to create a whirlpool. Then quickly pour in egg mix, in a thin stream. Put lid on saucepan and leave to set for 2-3 mins. When ready, soup should be clear and the egg "curdled"-looking. **NB: To keep the soup clear, heat must be high enough to set egg as soon as it is added.** Serve with rice for an easy, light dinner or as part of a Japanese meal.

– Smith family

Notes: Our old flatmate, Momo, used to make this soup for our eldest, Pearl, when she was little. We've called it Momo's soup ever since.

crown street cooks
83

kachumbari
(east african onion salad)

Serves 6 | Prep 5 mins

2 small red onions, thinly sliced
5 tomatoes, thinly sliced
1 red or green chilli, deseeded, cut lengthwise into slivers
½ cup finely chopped coriander leaves
Juice of 1 lime
3 tbsp olive oil
Salt & freshly ground black pepper, to taste

Place sliced onions, tomatoes, chilli and chopped coriander into a large serving bowl. Add lime juice and olive oil and toss mixture. Season *kachumbari* with salt and freshly ground black pepper, and serve.

– Klaas Raaijmakers

Notes: Our family has a long connection with Tanzania – my parents worked there and I was born there... Very excited to be able to share this African recipe.

north african carrot salad

Serves 4-6 | Prep 10 mins | Cooking 10 mins | Resting 2 hrs

500g carrots, cut into sticks, cores removed
½ tsp sweet paprika
½ tsp ground cumin
1 clove garlic, finely chopped or grated
2 tbsp flat-leaf parsley, chopped
1 tbsp lemon juice
2 tbsp olive oil
½ tsp salt (optional), to taste
½ tsp sugar (optional), to taste

Cook carrots in boiling salted water until just tender, approx 10 mins. Drain.

In a stainless steel bowl or serving bowl, combine all other ingredients. Add carrots and mix with your hands until carrots are well coated.

Cover and refrigerate for about 2 hrs to enable the flavours to fully develop. Serve at room temperature.

– Joanne Boufous, teacher

Notes: This recipe was given to me by my Moroccan mother-in-law. It's a winner! If you use baby carrots there's no need to core them.

organic thai-spiced chicken salad

CHEF'S RECIPE

Serves 4 | Prep 30 mins | Marinating 4 hrs | Cooking 15 mins

MARINADE & CHICKEN
1 large organic garlic clove, roughly diced
1 bunch organic coriander roots, washed well, roughly chopped
1 tbsp organic *tamari* (Japanese soy sauce)
Salt & pepper, to taste
6 organic chicken thighs, excess fat trimmed off
DRESSING
2 tbsp tamarind juice
1 tbsp organic raw sugar
2 tbsp fish sauce
½ tbsp lime or lemon juice
1 small red chilli, finely chopped
SALAD
1 organic red or green oak lettuce, washed, drained, spun
½ green mango, skin removed, flesh julienned
120g organic cherry tomatoes, cut in half
1 cup organic mint, washed, leaves picked
1 cup organic coriander, washed, leaves picked
½ small organic red onion, halved, thinly sliced

To prepare marinade, combine ingredients in a large bowl, add chicken and turn until well coated. Cover bowl and place in fridge for 4 hrs to marinate.

To make the dressing, combine all ingredients in a jug. Taste and adjust sweet/sour with lime/lemon juice and sugar.

Preheat a skillet, BBQ or heavy-based frypan. Cook chicken for 10-12 mins, turning once or twice. Set aside. Combine salad ingredients and drizzle lightly with dressing. Cut chicken into 1cm strips and toss through salad.

To serve, arrange salad on a platter and drizzle with a little dressing. Enjoy.

– O Organics Cafe

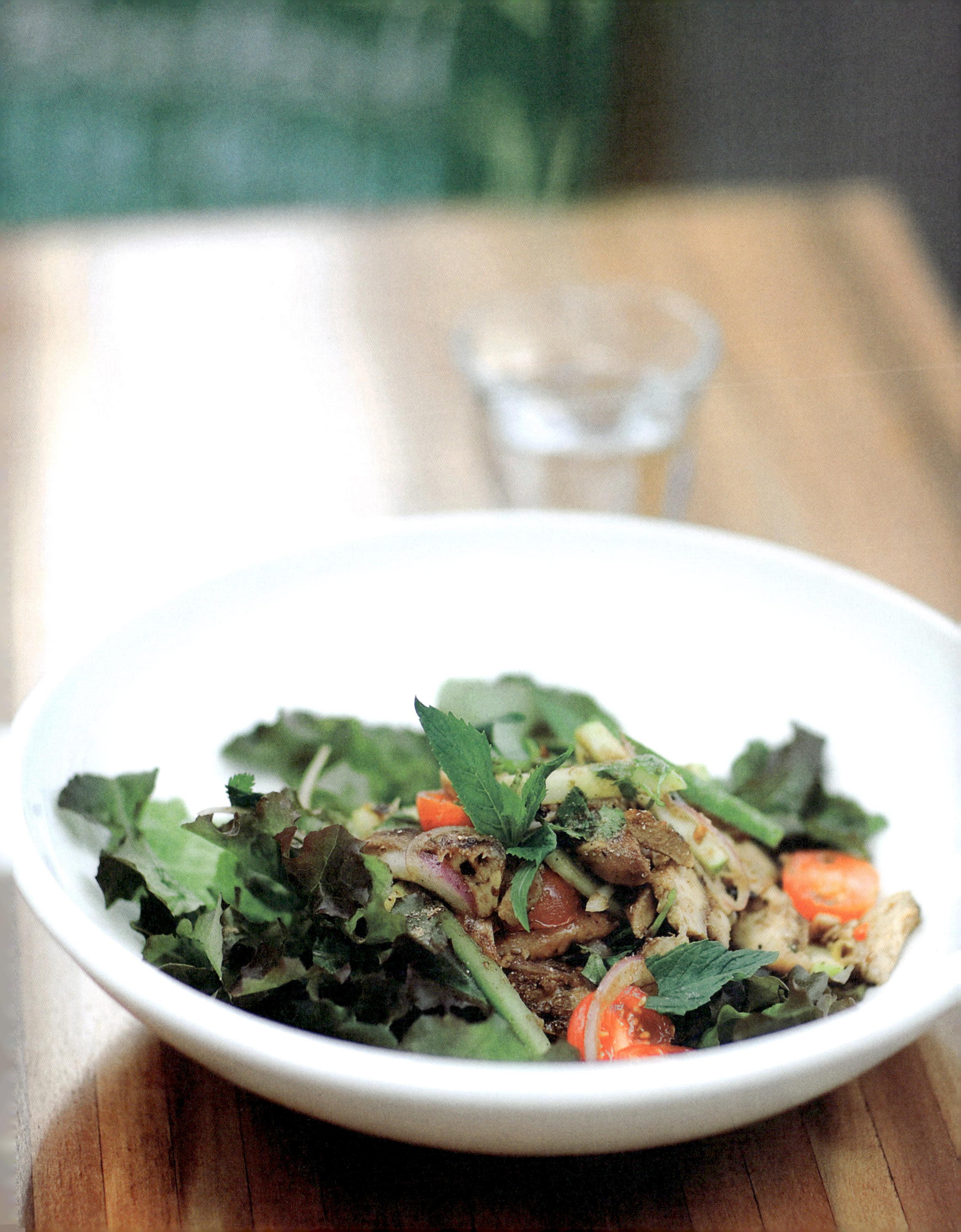

Hiscoes Fitness Club
525 Crown Street, Surry Hills,
NSW 2010 | T 02 9699 9222 |
E info@hiscoes.com.au | www.hiscoes.com.au

Part of the local community for nearly 30 years, Hiscoes understands the challenges of balancing a real lifestyle with a healthy, fit lifestyle. Our experienced and dedicated staff offer sensible, no-fuss fitness solutions.

Photo: Michael Fotoulis

dessert

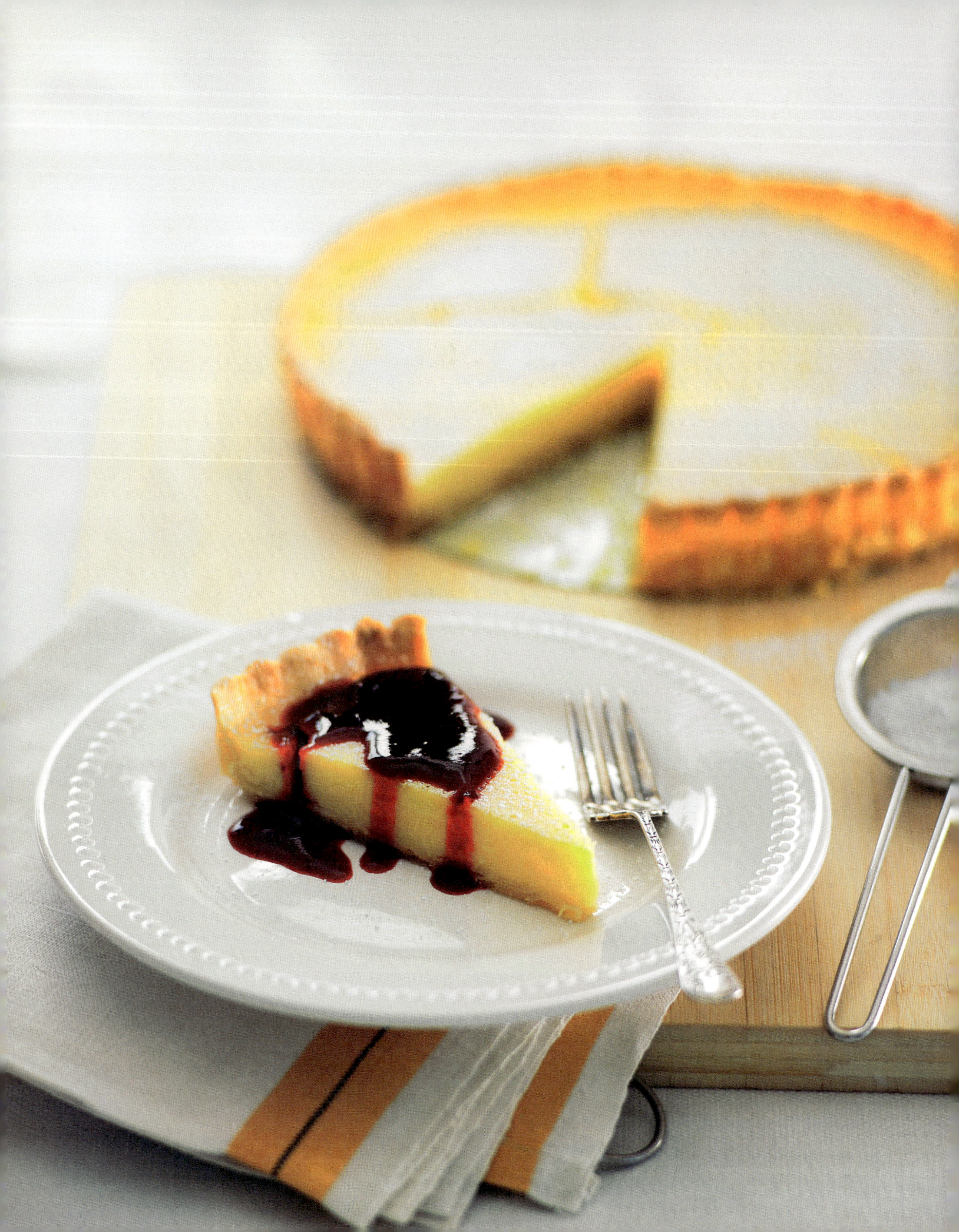

baked lemon tart

Serves 15 | Prep 20 mins | Resting 1 hr | Cooking 1 hr 15 mins

PÂTE SUCRÉE (SWEET SHORTCRUST PASTRY)
125g sugar
1 egg
125g butter, chopped
250g flour
FILLING
4 eggs
135g sugar
125ml double cream
135ml lemon juice
COULIS
60g frozen raspberries
25ml red wine
25g sugar
1½ tsp vanilla essence
TO SERVE
Double cream

For the pâte sucrée pastry, place sugar and egg in a mixing bowl and whisk until sugar has dissolved. In another bowl, rub butter into the flour with your fingertips until it resembles fine breadcrumbs. Mix sugar/eggs and flour/butter to form a paste. Place in fridge for 30 minutes. Roll out into a circle that will fit a 30cm loose-based round tart tin. Press pastry into tin, gently pressing it into the vertical grooves around sides. Refrigerate for another 30 mins.

Heat oven to 180°C. Line pastry case with baking paper and weight paper down with baking beads, or dry rice or beans such as lentils. Bake for 10 mins, remove paper and weights, then pop pastry back in oven for 5 mins – this ensures the base can withstand a liquid filling. Reduce oven temperature to 150°C.

Now make the lemon filling. During the 5 mins the pastry goes back in the oven, whisk together eggs, sugar, cream and lemon juice. Let mixture sit (it will separate), then skim the bubbly stuff off the surface with a spoon. Open oven, pour lemon mixture into pastry case and bake at 150°C for 1 hr.

While that's happening, make the coulis. Add frozen raspberries to a pan with red wine, sugar and vanilla essence. Bring to boil and reduce until a syrupy consistency. Strain and cool.

To serve, allow tart to cool. Serve in slices with a drizzle of coulis and some cream.

— Robert Reid

foolproof pav

Serves 6 | Prep 15 mins | Cooking 1-1½ hrs

4 eggwhites
Pinch salt
1 cup caster sugar
1 tsp white vinegar
½ tsp vanilla essence
2 tsp cornflour
Whipped cream
Fruit to top the pav – I've used pineapple & passionfruit, or try berries, strawberries, kiwi, mango, banana…

Preheat oven to 120°C. Line a baking tray with baking paper.

Place eggwhites and salt in a clean, dry bowl. Beat with electric beaters (make sure beaters are clean) until soft peaks form. Add sugar in small lots, beating well after each addition, until mixture becomes stiff and glossy. Gently fold in vinegar, vanilla and cornflour.

Heap mixture in a rough 20cm-diameter circle – that's dinner-plate size – on baking paper. (You could draw a circle in pencil first as a guide, and turn paper over so pencil side faces down). Shape meringue with a spatula, leaving a slight hollow in centre for topping. Bake for 1-1½ hrs or until crisp on outside.

Turn oven off and allow pavlova to cool slowly for several hrs or even overnight – put a folded tea towel in door jam to make a gap. To serve, top with whipped cream and heaped seasonal fruit.

Variation: Substitute a little of the white sugar with brown sugar. It gives it a lovely caramel colour and a slightly richer flavour. You could also add a little rosewater.

– *Andrea Healy*

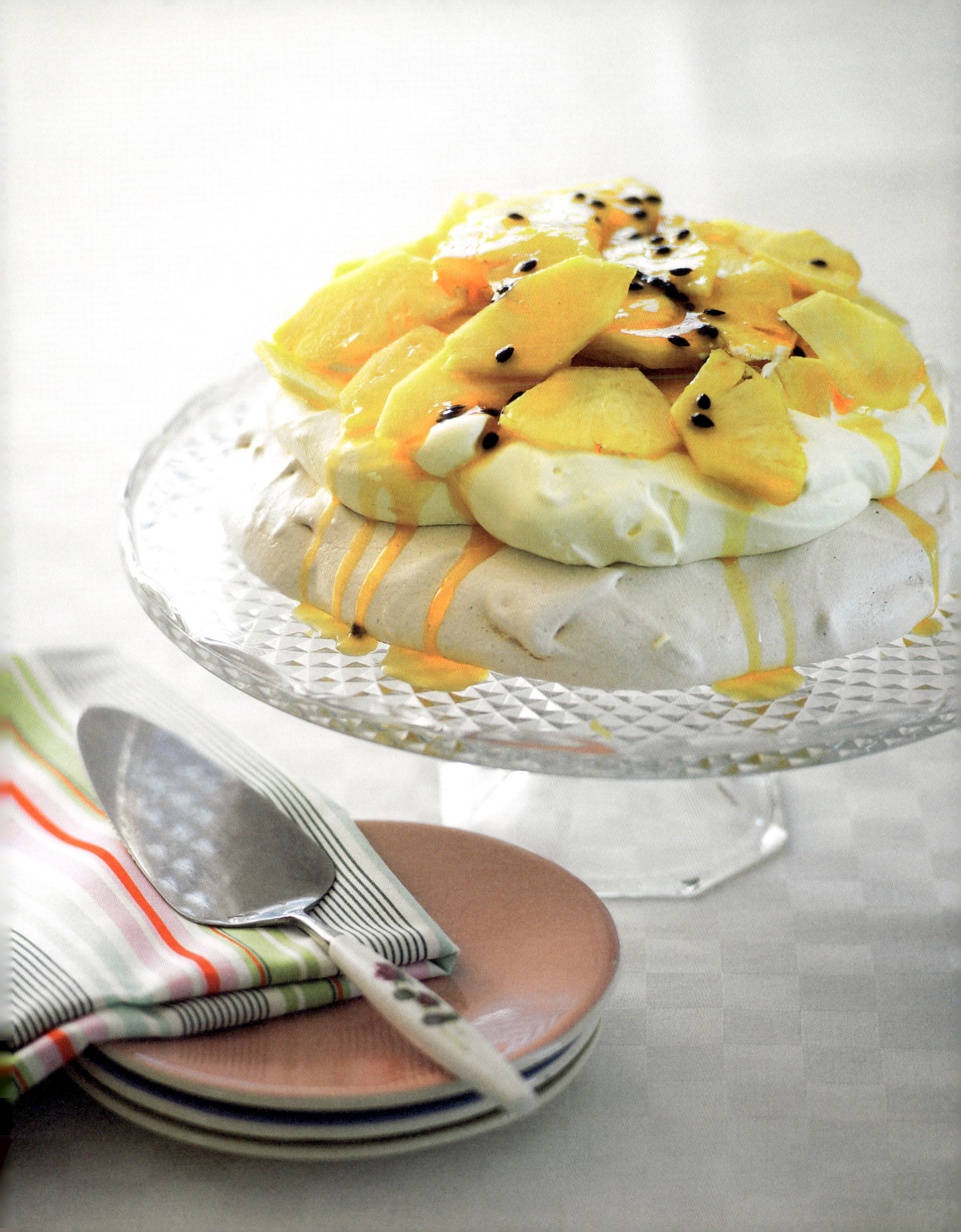

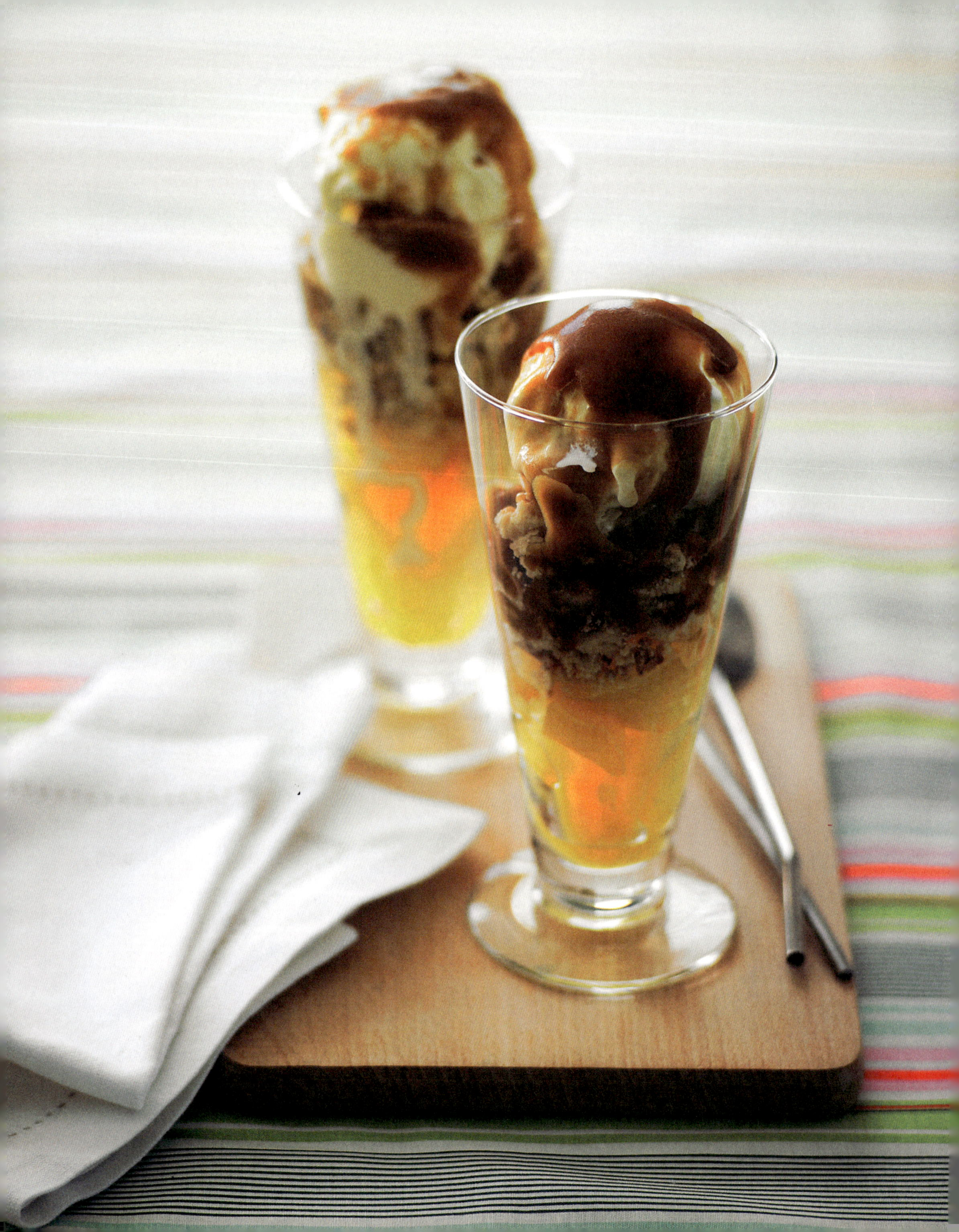

apple crumble sundae

Serves 4 | Prep 30 mins | Cooking 25 mins

TOFFEE FUDGE SAUCE
75g unsalted butter
150g light brown sugar
150ml single cream
CRUMBLE MIXTURE
100g plain flour
50g butter, diced
25g-50g demerara sugar (to taste)
Dry-roasted walnuts (a handful)
APPLE COMPOTE
3 cooking apples, peeled, cored, chopped
50g caster sugar (optional)
Juice of ½ a lemon
½ a vanilla bean
TO SERVE
4 or 8 scoops vanilla ice-cream

Preheat oven to 200°C.

For the toffee fudge sauce, place all ingredients in a pan and cook gently for 2-3 mins. Stirring continuously, bring to boil and cook for 3 mins, until thickened. Remove from heat. Set aside to cool.

For the crumble, place flour and butter in a bowl and rub together with your fingertips until mixture resembles breadcrumbs. Stir in sugar. Line a baking tray with baking paper and spread crumble mixture evenly. Bake for 8-10 mins until golden.

Meanwhile, dry-roast walnuts (either in the oven or in a small pan) for approximately 5 mins. Don't take your eyes of them – they can burn very quickly. Add walnuts to crumble mixture.

For the apple compote, place apples, sugar and lemon juice in a medium pan. Scrape seeds from vanilla bean and add, along with the pod, to apples. Cover and cook over a gentle heat for 12-15 mins, stirring now and then. Remove lid and cool.

Use a fork to break up the crumble.

To assemble, layer each parfait glass with apple compote, crumble and ice-cream and toffee sauce and pop in a long spoon.

– Zoe Porter

lemon delicious

Serves 6 | Prep 20 mins | Cooking 30 mins

3 eggs, separated
½ cup self-raising flour
Pinch salt
1½ cups caster sugar
1½ cups full-cream milk
Juice & zest of 2 medium to large lemons
Double cream or ice-cream, to serve

Preheat oven to 180°C. Grease a 5-to-6-cup capacity (approx) ovenproof casserole dish. Use a whisk or electric beaters to mix together egg yolks, flour, salt, sugar, milk, lemon zest and lemon juice.

In a separate bowl, using very clean, dry electric beaters, whip eggwhites until soft peaks form. Gently fold eggwhites into lemon mixture. Pour mixture into prepared dish and bake for 30 mins. The pudding should have a firm golden top and thick lemony syrup at the bottom. Serve with double cream or ice-cream.

Notes: It's best eaten as soon as the pudding is out of the oven as it can drop a little. The recipe can easily be doubled.

– Dimity Noble

simple berry dessert

Serves 4-6 | Prep 2 mins | Cooking 5 mins

2-3 punnets mixed fresh berries, such as blueberries, raspberries, strawberries (remove leaves & hull)
Splash of vodka (or water)
2 tsp sugar
1 dozen shortbread or vanilla biscuits (homemade or bought), or small meringues (homemade or bought)
Good vanilla ice-cream or King Island vanilla bean or honey yoghurt
Icing sugar or grated dark chocolate (optional)

In a small saucepan over a low heat, combine berries, vodka (or water) and sugar. Gently stir until a syrup forms and fruit is soft but not mushy.

Place biscuits or meringue in individual bowls with 1-2 scoops of ice-cream or yoghurt on top. Add berries and syrup, and sprinkle with icing sugar or grated chocolate and serve.

Notes: You can use frozen berries but the result will not be as good.

— Linda M. Bretherton

rich vanilla ice-cream

Serves 6 | Prep 15-20 mins | Chill 24 hrs + freezing

½ cup milk
350g caster sugar
8 egg yolks, beaten
1L cream
1 tsp vanilla extract, 1 tsp vanilla bean paste or seeds scraped from 1 vanilla bean

Place milk and sugar in a saucepan. Stir until sugar dissolves, then bring slowly to boil.

Once milk and sugar foam, immediately pour very slowly onto beaten egg yolks. Whisk continuously until mixture is cool, thick and creamy. Add vanilla. Allow to cool.

In a separate bowl, whip cream until firm peaks form, then fold into cold egg mixture. Place in fridge for 24 hrs to allow flavour to develop.

Remove mixture from fridge, transfer to a bowl and beat until well combined (about 2 mins). Return to container and freeze.

— Michelle Holmes

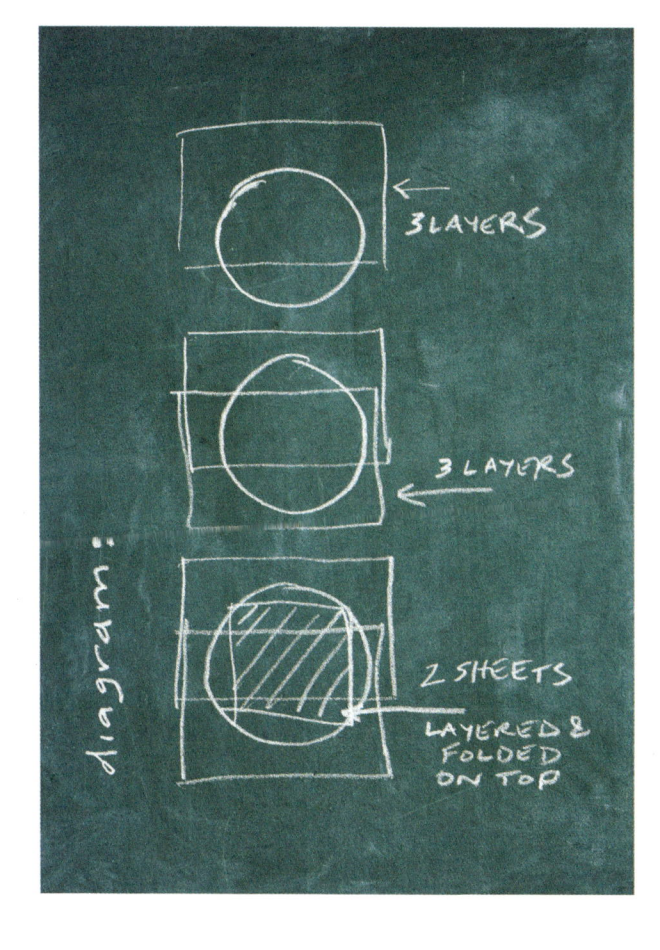

bougatsa (greek custard & filo treat)

Serves 8-10 | Prep 45 mins | Cooking 45 mins

CUSTARD FILLING
4 cups full-cream milk
¼ cup unsalted butter
1 cup fine semolina
½ tsp cornflour
⅔ cup caster sugar
2 free-range eggs
2 egg yolks
1 tsp vanilla bean paste or vanilla extract (not essence)
FILO PASTRY CASE
10 sheets filo pastry
⅔ cup unsalted butter, extra
Caster sugar, extra
Icing sugar
Cinnamon

Preheat oven to 200°C. In a small saucepan, bring milk to boil. In a larger saucepan, melt ¼ cup butter then whisk in semolina. Continue to whisk as you add cornflour.

Add milk to semolina, whisking continuously, then add sugar. Continue whisking over low heat until custard thickens. Once thickened, remove from heat and leave to cool.

Whisk eggs and yolks together, then pour over cool custard while stirring, and then add vanilla bean paste/extract. Stir to combine. Place plastic wrap on top of custard so it doesn't form a skin.

Now prepare the filo pastry. Cover filo with a moist tea towel so the pastry does not dry out while you're working. Melt extra butter and, using a pastry brush, butter 1 side of a filo sheet. Sprinkle some caster sugar all over. Repeat process by 3, stacking pastry sheets on top of each other.

Place stacked pastry in 26cm round cake tin, with 1 edge reaching ⅔ of the way across base of tin (see diagram above). Make another buttered-and-sugared stack of 3 filo pastries and place in tin, this time coming from the opposite direction so that pastry stacks overlap evenly across base. Repeat with another 2 filo pastries, then fold in half and position on centre of base.

Pour custard into filo pastry case. Put another 2 buttered-and-sugared folded sheets on top of custard. Fold all overhanging filo sheets into middle of tin. Sprinkle with caster sugar and bake for 45 mins or until golden. Before serving, dust with icing sugar and cinnamon.

— *Koula (and Nia McAneney)*

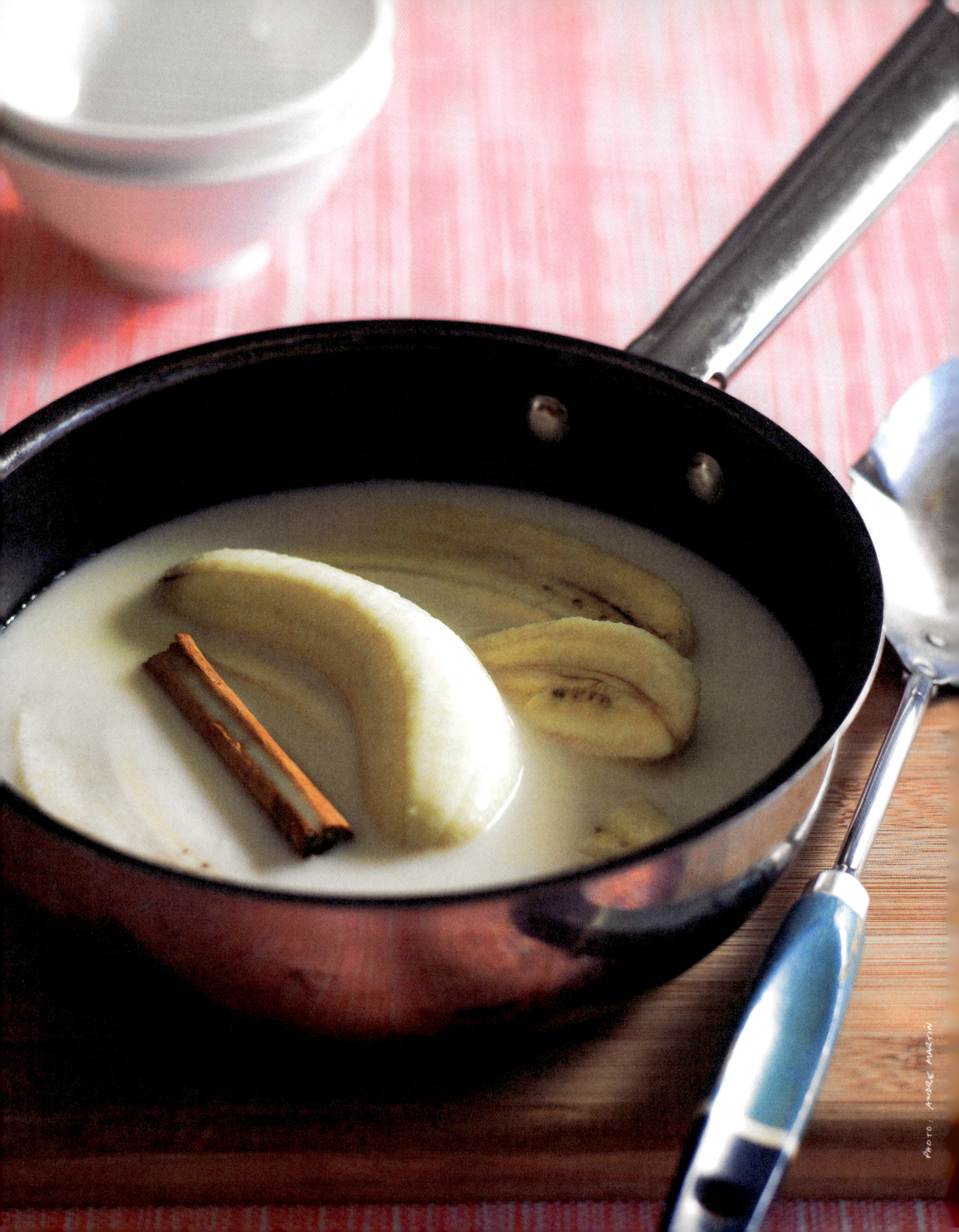
PHOTO: ANDRE MARTIN

stoff pisang (indonesian ladyfinger bananas in coconut sauce)

Serves 4-5 | Prep 5 mins | Cooking 10-15 mins

400ml can coconut cream
¼ cup water
½ cup white or brown sugar, or more or less to taste
1 cinnamon stick or ½ tsp ground cinnamon
¼ tsp vanilla sugar
¼ tsp salt
5 ladyfinger bananas, peeled, split lengthwise

In a saucepan, bring coconut cream to boil. Add water, sugar, salt, cinnamon and vanilla sugar. Taste for sweetness; add more sugar to suit your taste. Carefully add bananas and boil for another 2 mins. Remove cinnamon stick (if used). Serve hot or cold.

– Latifah Alwiny, Crown Street After School Care

kue lapis sagu (indonesian sweets)

Serves 12-14 | Prep 35 mins | Cooking 90 mins

1kg tapioca starch flour (or 750g tapioca starch flour + 250g of rice flour)
1½ tsp vanilla sugar
1½ tsp salt
750g white sugar
2.4L coconut milk
1 pandan leaf or ¼ tsp pandan paste
Oil for brushing baking tin
Food colouring (2 different colours)

In a large, deep bowl, mix tapioca flour (or tapioca + rice flours), vanilla sugar and salt. Place white sugar, coconut milk and pandan leaf/paste in a saucepan; stir and bring to boil. Set aside to cool.

Once cooled, slowly pour coconut mixture over flour and whisk until smooth. Put mixture through a sieve to remove any lumps. Divide mixture into 2 lots and add food colouring according to your preferences.

Prepare your steamer. Brush a baking tin or glass dish with oil. You need to steam each layer one after the other. The height of each layer will depend on the size of your dish and the amount of filling you add for each layer. For example, add 1 cup green mixture and steam for at least 15-20 mins. Then add 1 cup red on top of green layer, which should have set (if not, continue steaming until it does), then steam the 2 layers again for another 20 mins. Continue until all mixture has been used. NB: Do not fill dish to the top – it will overflow while steaming. Leave at least 2cm between final layer and rim of dish.

Let kue lapis sagu sit in dish overnight, then cut with a well-oiled knife.

– Yessy Tjan

Notes: Make sure your steamer does not boil dry. Check water level often. You can buy pandan leaf or paste in most Asian food shops, and tapioca starch flour (and rice flour) at health food shops.

black sticky rice

Chef's recipe

**Serves 4-5 | Soaking overnight | Prep 5 mins
Cooking 20 mins**

2 cups black sticky rice
½ cup white sticky rice
1 tin coconut milk
½ cup sugar
2 tsp salt (or less, to taste)
COCONUT SYRUP
1½ cups coconut milk
2 tbsp grated palm sugar

Soak black and white sticky rice in water overnight. Drain and put rice into steamer for 20 mins (flip rice after 10 mins).

Meanwhile, make syrup by placing coconut milk, and palm sugar in a saucepan. Cook until reduced and thickened.

When rice is cooked, place in a large bowl and mix in coconut milk, sugar and salt. Let sit for 20 mins and it's ready to serve. Serve sticky rice topped with 1-2 tbsp syrup spooned over the top.

– *Art Sukantamala, Little Bangkok*

hokey pokey

**Serves 6 | Prep 15 mins | Cooking 5 mins
Freezing 8 hours or overnight**

60g soft brown sugar
2 tbsp golden syrup
1 tsp bicarb soda
450ml double cream
400g can condensed milk
150ml single cream

Line a baking sheet with baking paper. In a saucepan, melt brown sugar and golden syrup over medium heat. Bring to boil and cook for 4-5 mins. Be careful not to burn it – you need to stir it continuously, and that means continuously! Take saucepan off heat, and add bicarb soda. Mixture will turn pale and froth up.

Pour mixture onto baking sheet and leave to cool and harden into honeycomb (approx 30 mins). Keep it away from moisture. Once it has hardened, break it into bite-sized pieces (I put it in a plastic ziplock bag and smash it with a rolling pin). Whisk double cream. You want it to be just whipped (soft peaks).

Stir in condensed milk, single cream and lastly honeycomb. It now needs to be frozen, preferably overnight (or at least 8 hours).

To cheat, you can just add the crushed honeycomb to your favourite vanilla ice-cream and mix it in.

Notes: For hokey pokey affogato – now THAT's what it's all about! – pour a shot of espresso into a chilled glass. Add two scoops of your homemade hokey pokey ice-cream. Garnish with a cinnamon stick or chocolate-covered coffee beans.   *Fiona Macneall*

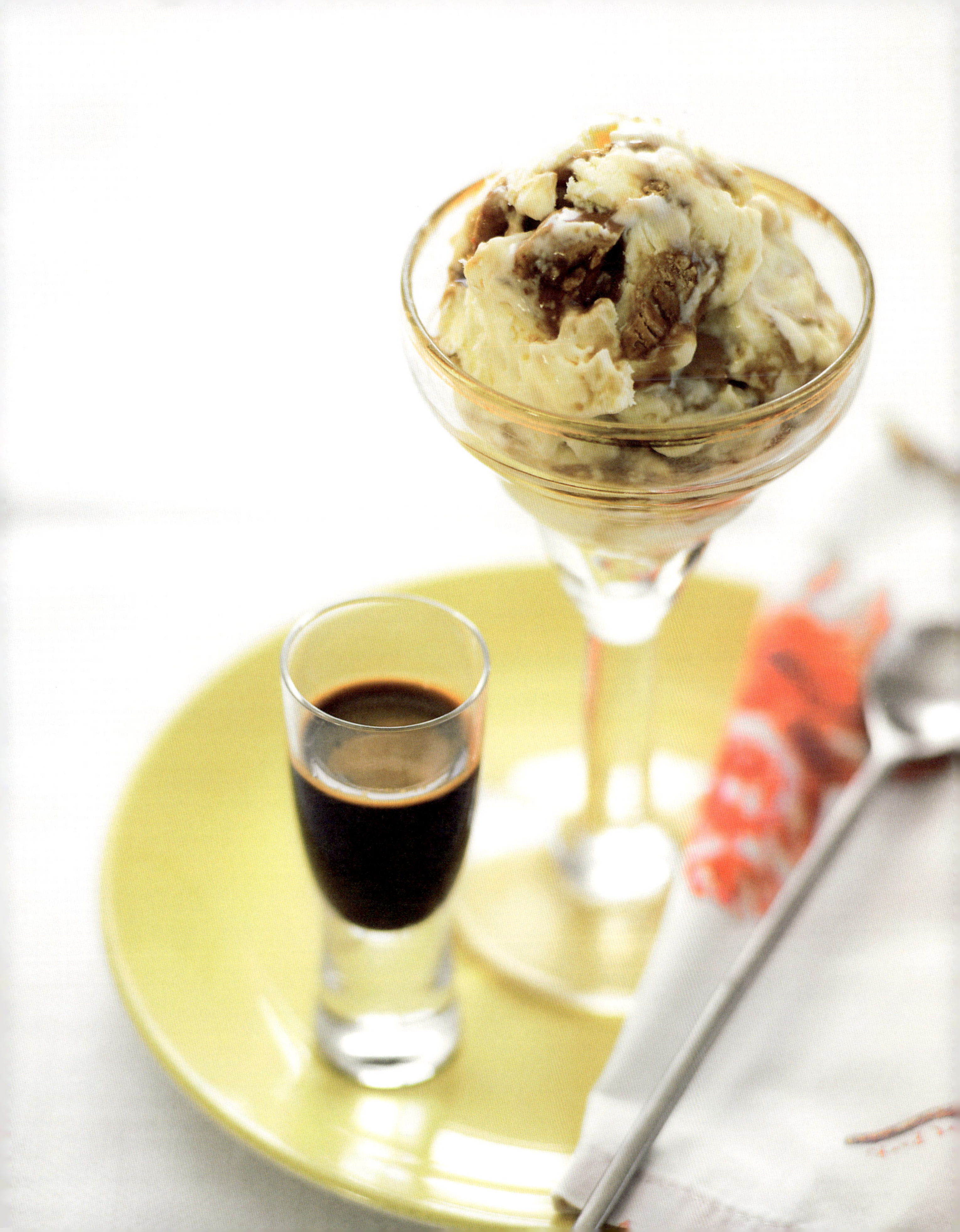

appeltaart (dutch apple pie)

Serves 8 | Prep 20 mins | Chilling 1 hr | Cooking 60 mins

SHORTCRUST PASTRY
360g plain flour
1 tsp salt
75g caster sugar
180g cold butter, chopped
1 egg yolk
3-4 tsp iced water

APPLE FILLING
800g apples
1 lemon
2 tbsp water
60g sugar
1 cinnamon stick
4 cloves
60g currants
Whipped cream, to serve

To make the pastry, blitz flour, salt, sugar and butter in a food processor until it resembles breadcrumbs. Add egg yolk and just enough water for mixture to form to a ball. Be careful not to overwork. Place dough on plastic wrap, wrap and flatten. Chill in fridge for 1 hour.

Cut ¼ of the pastry off and set aside. Roll out larger piece of pastry on a floured work surface until 3-5mm thick. Line base and sides of a 22cm springform tin (3-4cm high). Roll out remaining pastry until 3mm thick and cut into 1cm-wide strips ready for decorating top of apple. Put pastry-lined tin and additional strips of pastry in fridge.

Preheat oven to 160°C.

For the filling, peel, core and slice apples. Cut apples into wedges. Peel zest from lemon with a vegetable peeler. In a heavy-based saucepan, put water, sugar, lemon zest and juice from half the lemon, cinnamon and cloves. Simmer gently for a few mins.

Add apples and currants to sugar syrup and gently cook until apples are softer. Remove apples and currants, dispose of lemon zest, cinnamon stick and cloves and reduce remaining liquid until syrupy. Pour syrup over apples and currants and leave to cool.

Remove prepared pastry-lined tin from fridge and immediately fill with apple and currant mixture. Crisscross strips of remaining pastry across top of apple and attach to pastry at sides. With a pastry brush, coat pastry with milk and sugar.

Place tart in oven and bake until light brown (approx 50 mins). Remove from oven and allow to cool before removing from form. Serve with whipped cream.

Notes: There is nothing more Dutch than an apple pie served with whipped cream. The traditional way to make an apple pie is with a decorative pattern of pastry woven in a diagonal pattern across the top revealing the apple and currant filling. Visit any cafe in Amsterdam and you will find it on the menu.

— *Emma Rees-Raaijmakers*

Crown Street Grocer
Shop 1, 365 Crown Street Surry Hills NSW 2010
T 02-8668 5326 | E crownstgrocer@optusnet.com.au
Family owned and operated; 6am-8pm, 7 days

Photo: Michael Fotoulis

Photo: Michael Wee

crown street eats

Cafe Mint
579 Crown Street Surry Hills NSW 2010
T 02 9319 0848 | E cafemint@optusnet.com.au
Mon 7am to 3.30pm; Tues-Fri 7am to 7.30pm;
Sat 8am-10.30pm

Photo: Toby Burrows

Clock Hotel
470 Crown Street, Surry Hills, NSW 2010
T 02 9331 5333 | E clock@solotel.com.au
www.clockhotel.com.au
BISTRO OPEN
Mon to Fri, noon-3pm; 5-10pm
Sat & Sun, noon-10pm

Photo: Tim Robinson

Room Nine

crown street eats

289 Crown Street, Surry Hills, NSW 2010 | T 02 8353 2809 | E reservations@citycrown motel.com.au | www.citycrownmotel.com.au

Come and get to know the people of Sydney. Wonderful staff, stunning coffee and beautiful food at a great price.

PHOTO: MICHAEL WEE

cake stall

"A favourite childhood recipe. My mother would undercook them a little so they remained a bit chewy."

pat stride's choc chip cookies

Makes 24 | Prep 10 mins | Cooking 10-12 mins

Pinch salt
85g butter, softened
85g caster sugar
85g brown sugar
½ tsp vanilla extract
¼ tsp water
1 egg
170g self-raising flour
60g coarsely chopped walnuts (optional)
120g dark choc drops

Preheat oven to 190°C. Grease 2 baking trays or line them with baking paper.

In a large bowl, beat butter, sugars, vanilla and water with an electric mixer until creamy. Beat in egg until combined. Stir in sifted flour. Fold in nuts and chocolate drops. Spoon 12 evenly spaced teaspoonfuls of dough onto each baking tray – cookies will spread out as they bake and you don't want them to join up. Bake for 10-12 mins. Remove from oven and cool on wire racks.

– Henrie Stride

marcia's apple chocolate cake

Serves 8 | Prep 30 mins | Cooking 1 hr

Approx 6 small apples, cored, peeled, diced
125g butter
1 cup sugar
1 tsp bicarb soda
2 cups self-raising flour
1 tbsp cocoa
1 tsp cinnamon
½ tsp mixed spice
Whipped cream (for filling)
Chocolate icing (optional)

Preheat oven to 175°C. Grease and flour a 22cm round cake tin. Cook apples in saucepan until soft and pulpy – you'll need about 1½ cups of stewed apples. In a bowl, beat butter and sugar with electric beaters until pale and creamy.

Stir bicarb soda into hot apples and combine with creamed butter. Sift other dry ingredients and fold into mixture. Pour into prepared tin. Bake for 1 hr, or slightly longer if necessary (test by inserting a metal skewer into centre: if it emerges clean, cake is cooked).

Cool cake in tin. Turn out and cut through centre to create 2 layers. Fill with whipped cream – enough to make it ooze out when cut! Ice with your favourite chocolate icing, or serve warm with cream for dessert.

– Marcia Holden, Jack's grandmother

fig & pecan cake

Serves 8 | Prep 20 mins | Cooking 45 mins

200g butter, softened
1½ cups caster sugar
3 tsp grated lemon zest
3 eggs, at room temperature
1½ cups chopped dried figs
¾ cup chopped pecans (or almonds)
1¾ cups self-raising flour
¾ cup milk
Orange zest, to garnish (optional)
SYRUP (OPTIONAL)
2 tbsp honey
2 tbsp sugar
Juice of 1 lemon

Preheat oven to 180ºC. Beat butter, sugar and lemon zest until pale and fluffy. Add eggs one at a time, beating well after each. Add figs and nuts and mix thoroughly. Fold in flour alternately with milk to make a batter. Pour into 2 greased 20cm bundt tins (like one photographed), or 1 larger bundt tin or a greased and lined 23cm round springform tin. Bake for 45 mins. Once cool, turn out of tin.

For syrup (optional), in a small saucepan over medium heat, cook honey, sugar and juice until sugar dissolves.

To serve, pour syrup over cake and garnish with orange zest, if desired.

— Smith family

> "We were raised on my grandmother's pikelet recipe and now I make them with my kids. We do pikelets in all sizes, then stack them high. It's fun!"

cherry smith's pikelets

Makes a tall stack | Prep 5 mins | Cooking 10-15 mins

1 cup self-raising flour
½ tsp bicarb soda
4 tbsp caster sugar
1 egg
1½ cups milk (more or less to suit)
4 tbsp golden syrup
Butter & raspberry jam, to serve

In a large mixing bowl, combine flour, bicarb soda and sugar. Make a well in centre and add egg and a splash of milk. Using a whisk, mix in egg and add milk gradually until mixture is smooth and lump-free. Stir in golden syrup. Mixture should now be about the consistency of thickened cream.

Transfer to a jug. Heat a heavy-based non-stick frypan and pour rounds of batter in any sizes you like. Bubbles will form on surface of each pikelet; when they have all popped, turn pikelets with a spatula and brown the other side.

Serve with butter and raspberry jam.

— Georgie Hawke

cherry smith Pikelets

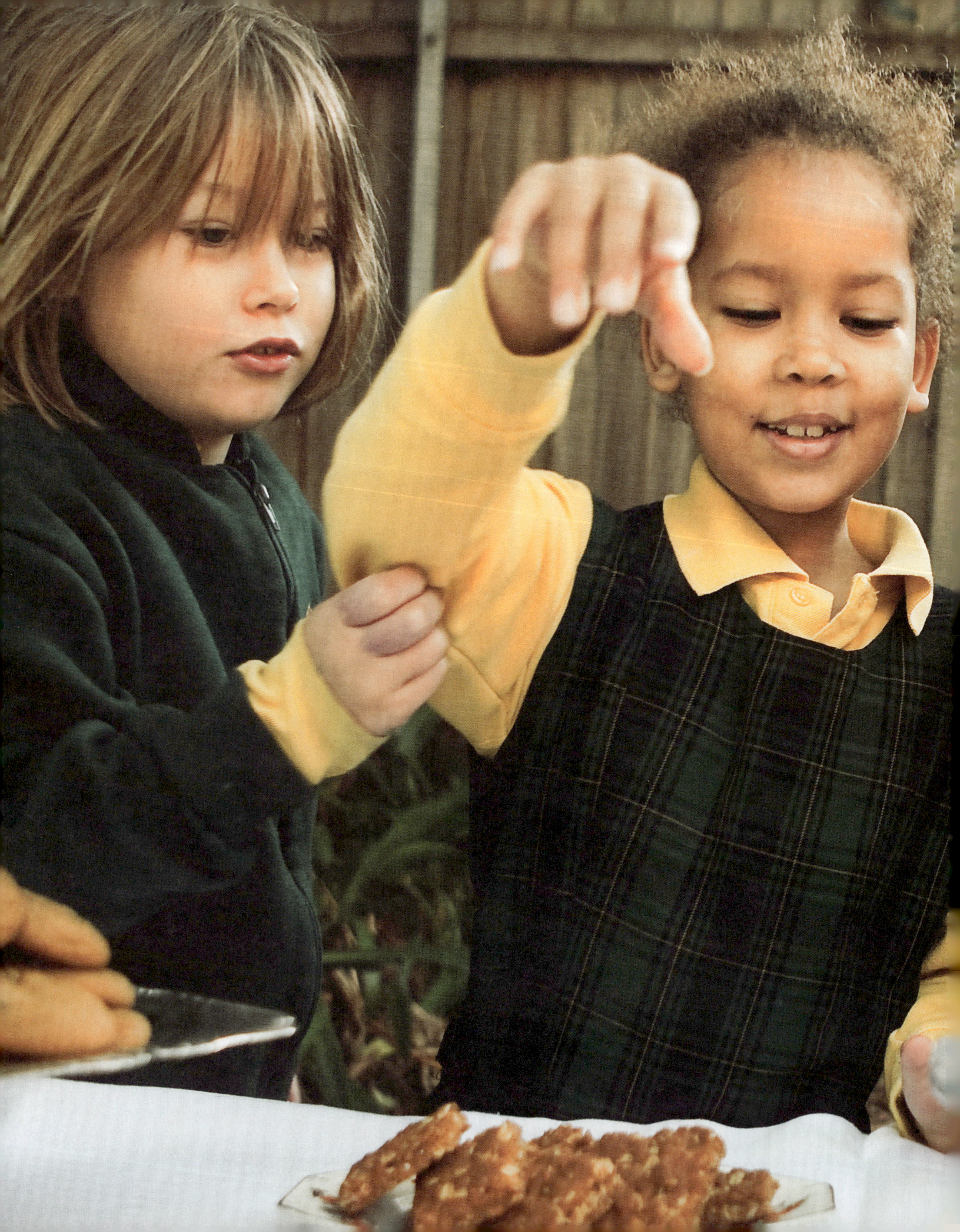

PHOTO: PAUL MCMAHON

LOAF TIN

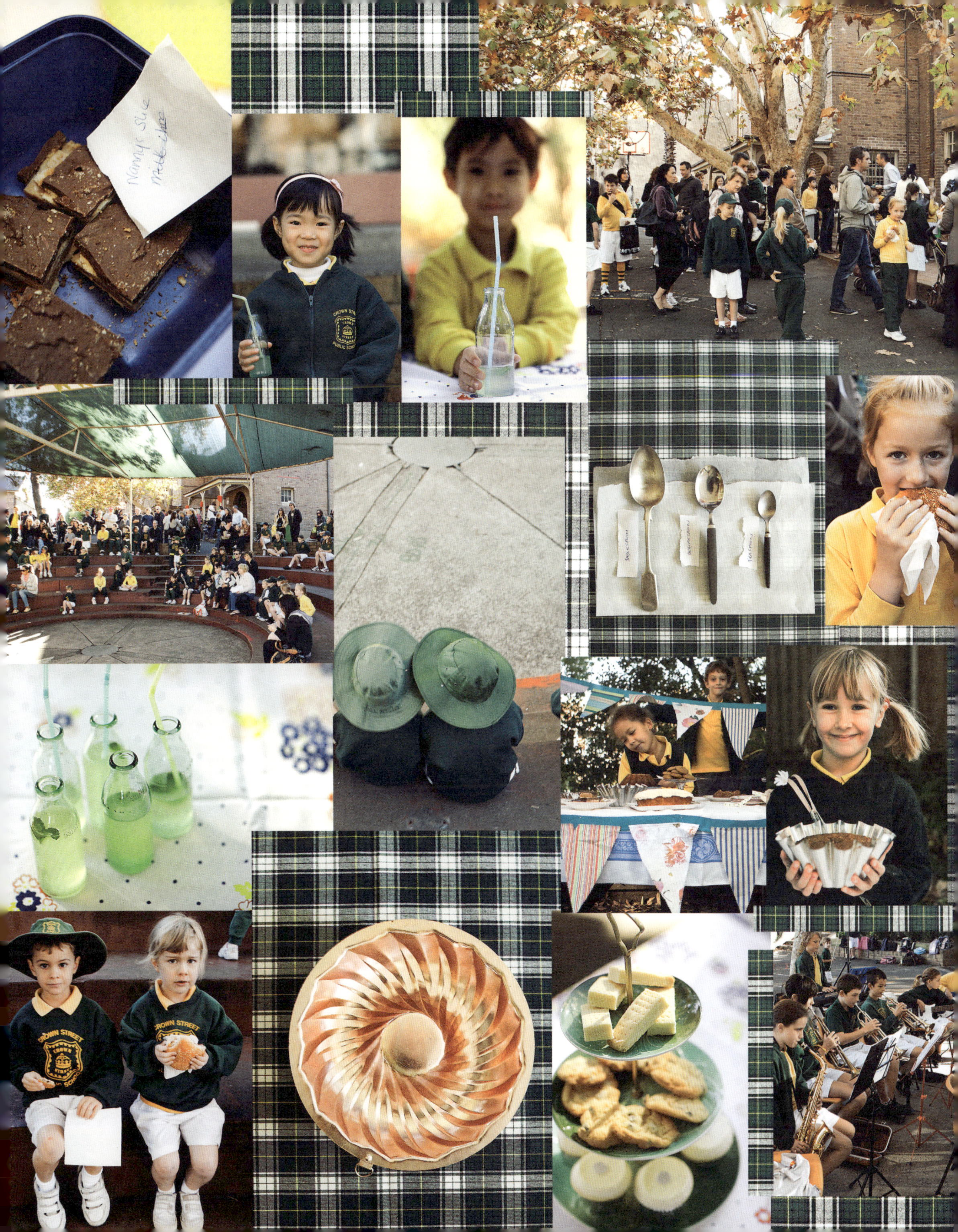
CROWN STREET

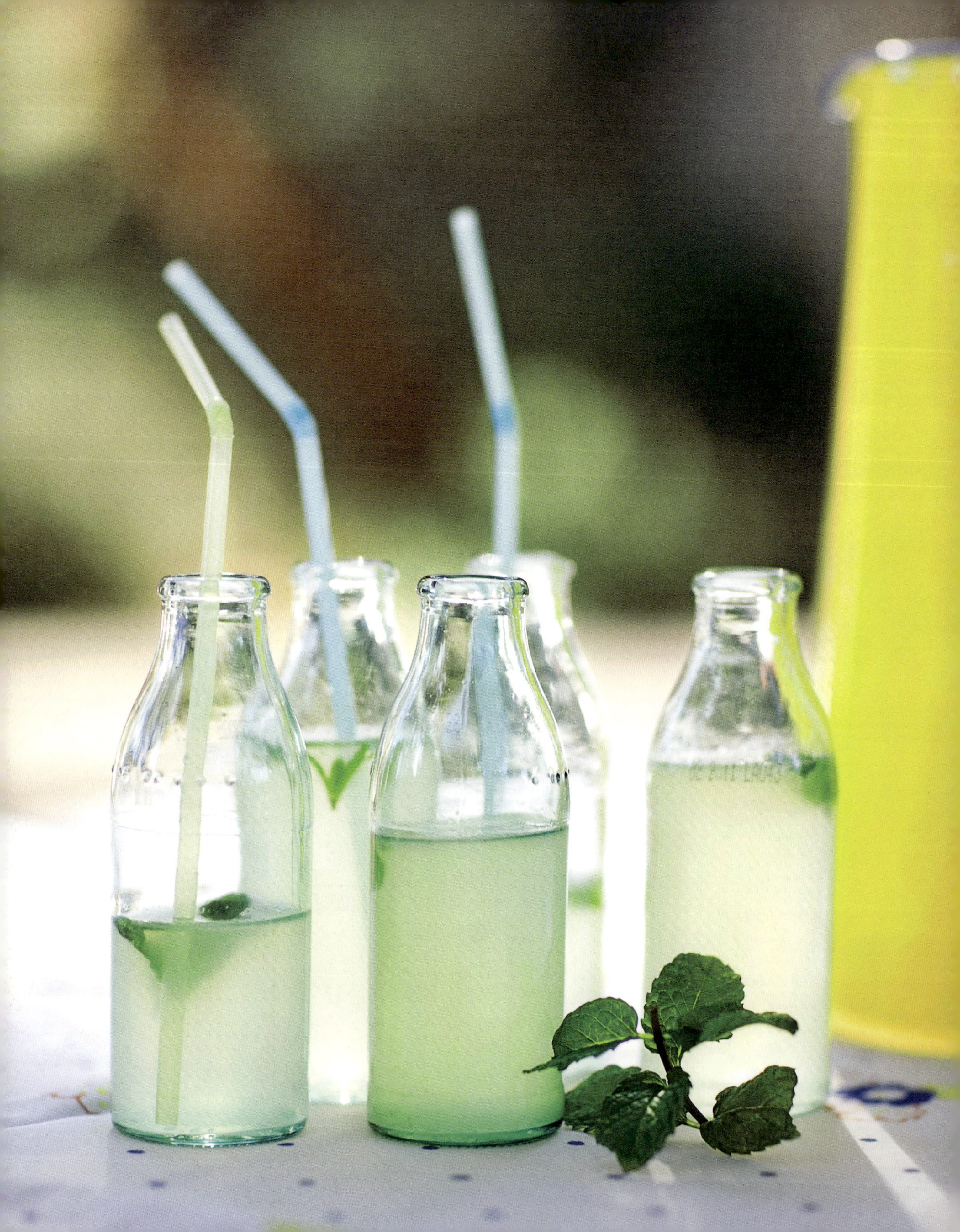

PHOTOS: TOBY BURROWS

fresh lemon cordial

Makes 1L | Prep 10 mins

3 juicy lemons
1L water
500g sugar
1 tbsp citric acid
1 tbsp tartaric acid
1 tbsp Epsom salts

Wash lemons, then heat in microwave on high for about 20 secs – this will maximise the amount of juice they release. Finely grate rind of each lemon, then juice them, keeping fleshy bits from juicer. Place about ½ the water in a saucepan, then add sugar and heat until dissolved. Remove from heat and add citric acid, tartaric acid and Epsom salts. Stir until dissolved, then add lemon juice plus any flesh, the grated rind and rest of water. Cool and bottle. Can be stored in fridge for about 2 weeks. Use just like bought cordial, diluting to taste. — *Lynne Johnson, Ella Kirby's Grandmother*

Notes: You can buy citric acid and tartaric acid (in the baking section) and Epsom salts (in the health and beauty section) of the supermarket.

chinese apple pear drink

Makes 2L | Prep 10 mins | Cooking 75 mins

3 Ya pears (Chinese white pears; or use nashi pears)
3 Red Delicious apples
20g plump dried apricots
5-10 dried dates
Sugarcane juice or sugar, to taste
2L-3L water

Cut each pear and apple into 4 pieces and remove cores. Wash pears, apples, apricots and dried dates and put them into a big pot. Add water and boil for 20-30 mins, then reduce heat and simmer gently for another 30 mins.

Add sugar and stir to dissolve. Strain mixture through a sieve and retain liquid. Discard the solids. Store drink in fridge. — *Yim Ha Chan*

Notes: Enjoy this drink hot or cold. It is great for chasing away the flu.

middle-eastern lemonade

Makes 1.4L | Prep 15 mins

1½ cups lemon juice (from approx 16 lemons)
1½ cups caster sugar
3½ tsp orange blossom water
½ cup chopped fresh mint
Ice, preferably crushed
4L water, soda water or mineral water

In a jug or punchbowl, mix together lemon juice, sugar, orange blossom water and mint. Add ice and water. Stir gently, then serve.

Notes: Limes can be used instead of lemons – or use a mixture of the two. Decant the lemonade into little bottles for the cake stall.

— *Kate Flynn, Piper Macneall's godmother*

CHEF'S RECIPE

sparkle's vanilla cupcakes

Makes 16 lge | Prep 20 mins + 10 for icing | Cooking 30 mins

260g butter
1⅓ cups caster sugar
4 eggs
3 cups plain flour
3 tsp baking powder
½ cup milk
2 tsp vanilla bean paste

TOPPING
115g butter
2½ cups pure icing sugar
1 eggwhite
½ tsp lemon juice
1½ tsp vanilla extract

Preheat oven to 150°C. Sift together flour and baking powder. Cream butter and sugar on high speed in mixer for between 5 and 20 mins, depending upon butter's softness. Add eggs, one at a time, allowing to combine and not curdle. Add ½ the sifted flour and baking powder and ½ the milk and vanilla bean paste. Add remaining sifted flour and baking powder, then remaining milk and vanilla bean paste. Mix through to combine to a smooth batter.

Use an ice-cream scoop to put mix into cupcake foils. Bake for 30 mins on 140°C to 160°C (oven temperature may vary, depending upon type) turning once during cooking.

To make topping, cream butter and icing sugar on high speed in mixer for between 5 and 10 mins, depending upon softness of butter. Add eggwhite, lemon juice and vanilla extract. Cream an additional 3 mins. Use to ice cooled cupcakes.

— *Kathryn, Sparkle Cupcakery*

crown street cooks

PHOTO: TOBY BURROWS

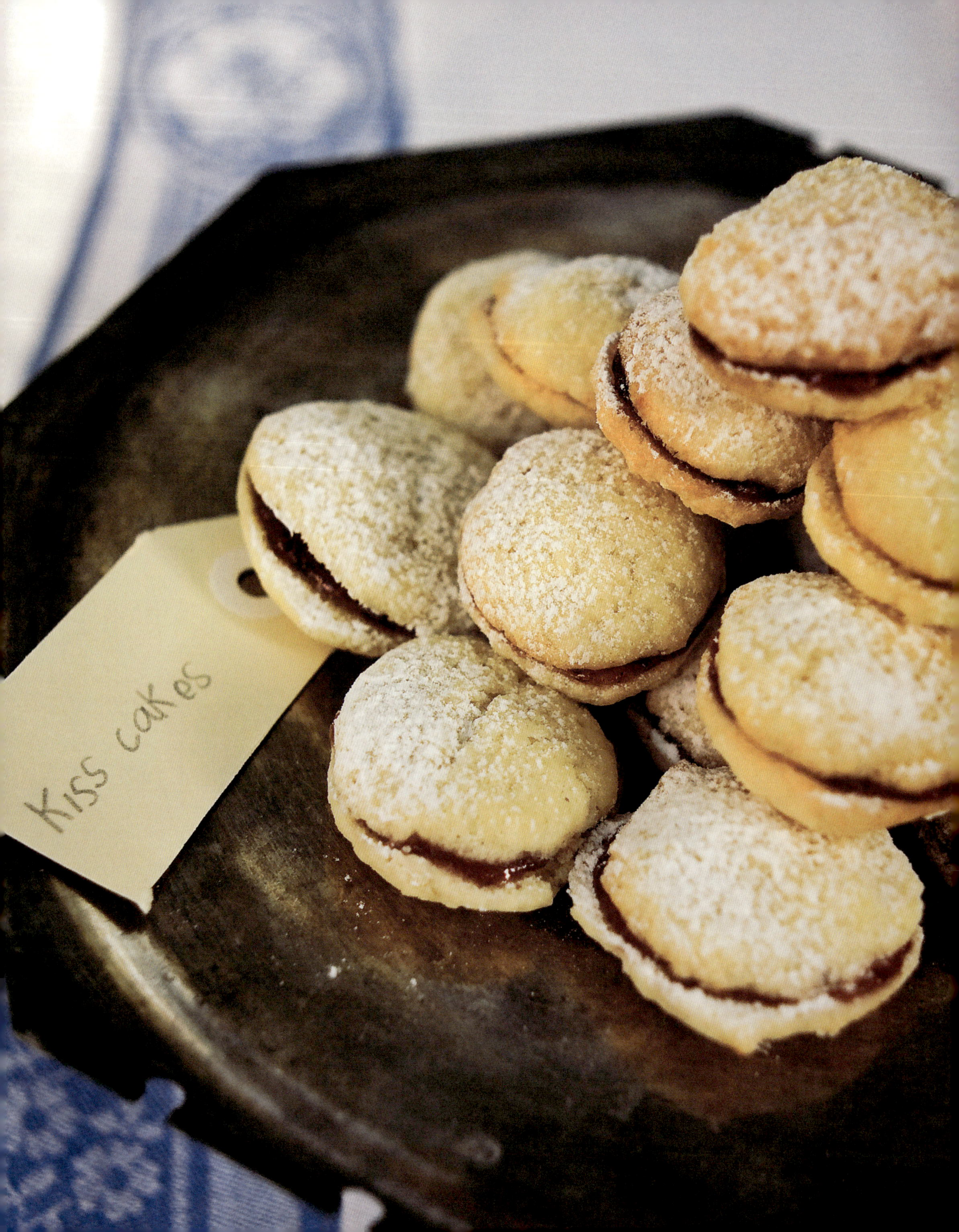
Kiss cakes

grandma melville's kiss cakes

Makes 24 | Prep 40 mins | Cooking 8 mins

120g butter
½ cup sugar
2 eggs, beaten
1 cup plain flour
1 cup cornflour
2 tsp baking powder
Jam
Icing sugar

Preheat oven to 160°C-180°C. Beat butter and sugar until pale and fluffy. Mix in well-beaten eggs. In a separate mixing bowl, sift together flour, cornflour and baking powder. Lightly fold dry ingredients into wet mixture, adding extra flour if necessary, to make a stiff dough. Put half-teaspoonfuls of mixture on a greased baking tray, 2cm apart.

Bake for 8 mins. Turn onto cooling rack. When cool, join together with jam. Sprinkle tops with icing sugar.

— Melville family

coconut cake

Serves 10 | Prep 15 mins | Cooking 30 mins

1 cup self-raising flour
¾ cup sugar
¾ cup coconut
115g butter, melted
2 eggs, beaten
½ cup milk
Vanilla or coconut icing

Preheat oven to 180°C. Grease a 30cm loaf tin and line with baking paper. In a large bowl, mix together dry ingredients. Add butter, eggs and milk and mix well. Pour mixture into tin. Bake for 30 mins. Let cool, turn onto rack and ice with vanilla or coconut icing.

— Margaret Cox, Harry Prodes' godmother

> **"This old favourite can be used for many occasions, including birthdays."**

> "This coconut ice recipe was brought to us by Aunt Rosie, who knows it by heart."

pineapple fruitcake

Serves 8 | Prep 20 mins | Cooking 1¾-2 hrs

440g can crushed pineapple
125g butter
1 cup sugar
500g mixed dried fruit
1 tsp mixed spice
1 tsp bicarb soda
1 cup self-raising flour
1 cup plain flour
Pinch salt
2 eggs, beaten

Preheat oven to 180°C. Grease and line a 21cm square cake tin with brown paper. Drain pineapple and put in a saucepan with ½ cup of the juice. Add butter, sugar, fruit, spice and bicarb soda. Bring to the boil and simmer for 3 minutes. Cool completely. Sift flours and salt together and stir into mixture with eggs. Bake in moderate oven for 1¾-2 hrs. Test with a skewer.

Notes: This cake is great to cut up and freeze in single serves – perfect for kids' recess snacks. It also freezes whole very well. My great-grandmother always made this cake when she had visitors coming.

— *Joanne Boufous, teacher*

aunt rosie's no-cook coconut ice

Makes 16 small squares | Prep 10 mins | Cool 15 mins

½ tin sweetened condensed milk (approx 200g)
2 cups icing sugar
2 cups desiccated coconut
1 tsp vanilla essence
Dash raspberry essence (for pink colour)

Place all ingredients into a mixing bowl, except for raspberry essence. Mix together thoroughly. The mixture will become tough, so knead with your hands until it forms a stiff ball. Divide mixture in half. Grease a square or rectangular baking dish or slice tin. Press ½ the mixture (about 1.5cm in height) down into base of tin. Knead a dash of raspberry essence into other half of mixture. Press pink layer on top of white. Refrigerate coconut ice for approximately 15 mins and – voila!

Notes: Keep refrigerated (otherwise it will lose its shape) and eat within a couple of days. The condensed milk and lashings of coconut give this a creamier, less sugary consistency than regular fudge-style coconut ice. It's a great recipe for kids to make as there is no cooking involved. However, the mixture gets really stiff – we once broke a wooden spoon.

— *Cassy Cochrane*

traditional scottish shortbread

Makes about 25 pieces | Prep 10 mins | Cooking 30 mins

200g butter
85g sugar
250g plain flour
60g rice flour
Just under 1 tsp baking powder
Pinch salt

Preheat oven to 180°C. In a mixing bowl, beat butter and sugar with electric beaters until almost white in colour. In a separate bowl, sift in flour, rice flour, baking powder and salt. Return to sifter then gradually sift into butter and sugar mixture. Knead mixture with hands in bowl until it stays together, then remove from bowl and "thump" mixture onto work surface several times. Roll dough out onto a lightly buttered baking tray, to a thickness of about 1.5cm. Cut into fingers in tray and prick with fork. Bake for 30 mins.

When cool, store in an airtight container lined with backing paper until you're ready to serve. — *Louise Bickle*

Notes: Get the kids in on the act. They can roll the dough and use biscuit cutters to make fun shapes. Decorate with choc chips, raisins or edible sparkles. Or dip one end in melted chocolate for a domino effect.

lemon-crusted tea cake

Serves 4-6 | Prep 20 mins | Cooking 35 mins

2 cups self-raising flour
30g butter
2 tbsp sugar
½ cup raisins, chopped
1 egg
⅔ cup milk
TOPPING
60g butter
1 tbsp grated lemon rind
¾ cup sugar

Preheat oven to 180°C. In a large mixing bowl, sift flour then rub in butter until mixture resembles breadcrumbs. Stir in sugar and raisins and mix well. Make a well in the centre of mixture. Add egg and milk. Mix until combined, then turn out and knead lightly on floured board. Cut dough into 16 even-sized pieces and roll into balls or scones. Place scones into a greased, deep cake tin (approx 30cm).

To make the topping, melt butter in a saucepan. Add sugar and lemon rind, and stir until sugar almost dissolves. Spoon over balls of tea cake and place tin in ven. Bake for 30-35 minutes. When done, cool in tin for 5 mins then turn onto rack. To serve, break into 16 scones and slice if desired. — *Kristen Bettridge, teacher*

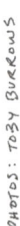

hazelnut cake

Serves 8-10 | Prep 15 mins | Cooking 40 mins

125g self-raising flour
125g sugar
50g hazelnut meal
3 or 4 eggs, beaten
125g butter, softened
Dash vanilla essence
1 green apple, grated
Icing sugar & sliced green apples, to garnish

Preheat oven to 180°C. Grease and flour a round cake tin. In a mixing bowl combine flour, sugar and hazelnut meal. Stir in beaten eggs, then softened butter and vanilla. Add grated apple and mix well. Pour mixture into tin and bake for 40 minutes.

To serve, sprinkle with icing sugar and decorate with some sliced green apple, if desired.

— Bruce Strath, teacher

ma stibbard's chocolate coconut slice

Makes about 15 squares | Prep 15 mins | Cooking 20-25 mins

1 cup self-raising flour
1 tbsp cocoa
½ cup brown sugar
1 cup desiccated coconut
125g unsalted butter
ICING
½ tsp butter
Approx 2 tbsp hot water
1 cup icing sugar
1 tbsp cocoa
2 tbsp desiccated coconut

Preheat oven to 180°C. Grease a 16cm x 26cm slice tin and line with baking paper. Sift flour and cocoa into a mixing bowl. Add brown sugar and coconut and mix well.

Melt butter and add to dry ingredients. Mix well with a fork. Press mixture evenly into a slice tin with fork. Bake for 20-25 mins (exact time will depend on your oven). Remove from oven and ice while hot.

For the icing, heat butter and hot water in a small saucepan until butter melts. Stir in icing sugar and cocoa. Stir constantly over low heat until it takes on a pouring consistency. Pour over hot slice and sprinkle with coconut.

— Terina Stibbard

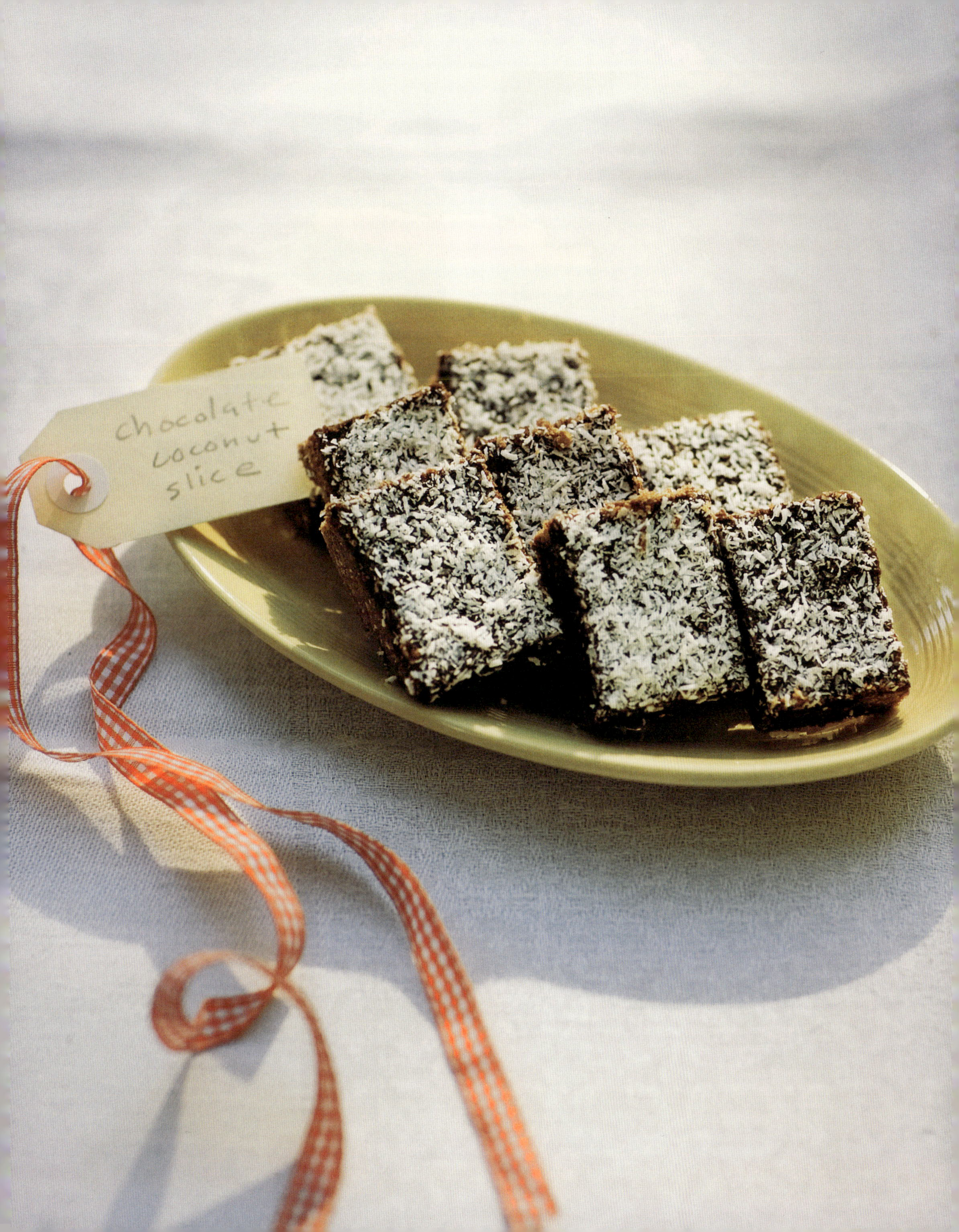
Chocolate
coconut
slice

double gingernut biscuits

Makes 32 | Prep 30 mins | Cooking 12 mins

90g butter
⅓ cup brown sugar
⅓ cup golden syrup
1⅓ cups plain flour
¾ tsp bicarb soda
1 tsp ground cinnamon
1½ tbsp ground ginger
¼ tsp ground cloves (optional)
½ cup crystallised ginger, finely chopped

Preheat oven to 180°C. Place butter, sugar and golden syrup in a saucepan and stir over low heat until melted. Remove from heat, then stir in sifted dry ingredients. Next, stir in crystallised ginger, then allow to cool slightly (about 10 mins) until mixture is warm to the touch.

Grease 2 oven trays and line with baking paper. Make balls of mixture (2 tsp for each ball). Place on trays, allowing space for them to spread.

Bake for about 12 mins or until slightly browned. Cool slightly on trays, then transfer to wire rack. Store in an airtight container.

— Fiona Macneall

best-ever chocolate cake

Serves 12 | Prep 20 mins | Cooking 1 hr

2 cups plain flour
½ cup cocoa
1 tsp bicarb soda
1½ cups caster sugar
1 tsp vanilla extract
2 eggs
125g butter, very soft
1¾ cups milk
CHOCOLATE GLAZE
⅓ cup cream
30g butter
250g dark or milk chocolate

Preheat oven to 180°C. Grease a 22cm round cake tin and line with baking paper. Sift dry ingredients into a bowl. Add vanilla, eggs, butter and milk and mix together. Beat with electric beaters for 4 mins. Pour into tin and bake for 1 hr. Remove from oven and let cool for 5 mins, then turn onto a cake rack to cool completely. Cake may flatten somewhat as it cools.

For the chocolate glaze, place cream, butter and chocolate in a saucepan. Stir over a gentle heat until melted and smooth. Pour over top and sides of cake while it's on the rack, allowing excess to drain off. Dust with a little cocoa to finish off.

— Sarah MacMaster

Notes: For an adult version, swap the milk for alcohol.

oaty coconut slice

Makes 16 squares | **Prep 10 mins** | **Cooking 35 mins**

1 cup rolled oats
1 cup plain flour, sifted
¾ cup desiccated coconut
¾ cup raw sugar
125g butter
2 tbsp honey
2 tbsp water
½ tsp bicarb soda

Preheat oven to 180°C. Grease a 25cm x 30cm swiss roll tin and line with baking paper. In a large mixing bowl, combine oats, flour, coconut and sugar. In a saucepan, heat butter, honey and water over gentle heat until butter is melted. Stir in bicarb soda, mix well, then pour over dry ingredients and stir until combined. Turn mixture out into prepared tin and press down evenly. Bake for about 25 mins. Cut into squares before it cools completely. — *Margaret Cox*

Notes: Great for school snacks.

carrot cake

Serves 8-10 | **Prep 15 mins** | **Cooking 50-60 mins**

4 eggs
2 cups brown sugar
1½ cups vegetable oil
2 cups plain flour
2 tsp bicarb soda
2 tsp mixed spice
1 tsp salt
3 cups finely grated carrot
Lemon icing, to finish

Preheat oven to 180°C. Grease a 30cm square cake tin, then line with baking paper. In a large bowl, mix together eggs, sugar, oil and sifted flour, bicarb soda, mixed spice and salt until smooth. Pour mixture into tin and bake for 50-60 mins or until it has risen and a skewer inserted into centre comes out clean. Ice when cold. — *Briony Schofield*

Notes: I've made this as a birthday cake, baked in a large lamington tin with lemon icing and sprinkles on the top. It fed 20-plus kids. You can also use to make muffins. Add sultanas or chopped walnuts for something different.

moist orange cake

Serves 8-10 | Prep 5 mins | Cooking 50-60 mins

1 whole orange, chopped (including peel; remove pips)
180g unsalted butter, melted
3 eggs
1 cup caster sugar
1½ cups self-raising flour
ICING
2½ cups icing sugar
2 tbsp melted butter
Orange juice
Finely grated orange rind & sliced orange, to garnish

Preheat oven to 180°C. Grease and flour a deep 20cm loaf tin, or grease a springform tin and line with baking paper.

Place whole orange, including peel (no pips), in food processor and puree. Add remaining ingredients and mix until just combined. Spoon into tin. Bake for 40-50 mins. Turn onto cake rack. Cool before icing.

For icing, beat icing sugar with butter and enough orange juice to make a icing consistency. Ice cake and decorate with orange slices and grated rind.

— MacMaster family

Notes: Omit the peel for a fluffier cake. For syrup instead of icing, squeeze an orange, add 2 tbsp sugar and heat to form syrup. Pour over the cake. You can also substitute lemons for oranges if you like.

oma's *gemberkoek* (dutch ginger cake)

Serves 8-12 | Prep 20 mins | Cooking 40-45mins

150g unsalted butter (although my great-grandmother preferred margarine!) plus extra to grease tin
1 large egg
100g white sugar
25g self-raising flour
125g plain flour
2 heaped tbsp stem ginger, plus a little of the syrup from the jar (see Notes)

Preheat oven to 175°C. Grease a round springform tin with butter and line with baking paper (or butter and flour a fluted flan dish). Melt butter in a saucepan over very low heat – don't let butter turn brown.

Lightly beat egg. Keep a little egg aside for brushing cake at the end. Pour melted butter into a bowl with sugar and flours. Add ginger, syrup and beaten egg. Mix well. Spoon mixture into tin or dish and spread evenly. Brush with remaining egg. Bake for approx 40-45 mins, until golden.

— Raaijmakers family

Notes: Stem ginger in syrup (such as Buderim Ginger brand) comes in jars; Maloneys Grocer stocks it.

Oma's gemberkoek

crown
street
eats

Toko Surry Hills
490 Crown Street, Surry Hills, NSW 2010
T 02 9357 6100 | www.toko.com.au
| www.toko.com.au/tokonoma
LUNCH Tue to Fri
DINNER Mon to Sat

Take the opportunity to experience the informal style of Japanese *izakaya* dining at Toko, or lounge with friends next door in Tokonoma. Showcasing Australia's world-renowned fresh produce and complemented by stunning contemporary design, the Toko dining experience lingers long after you have left the restaurant.

celebration

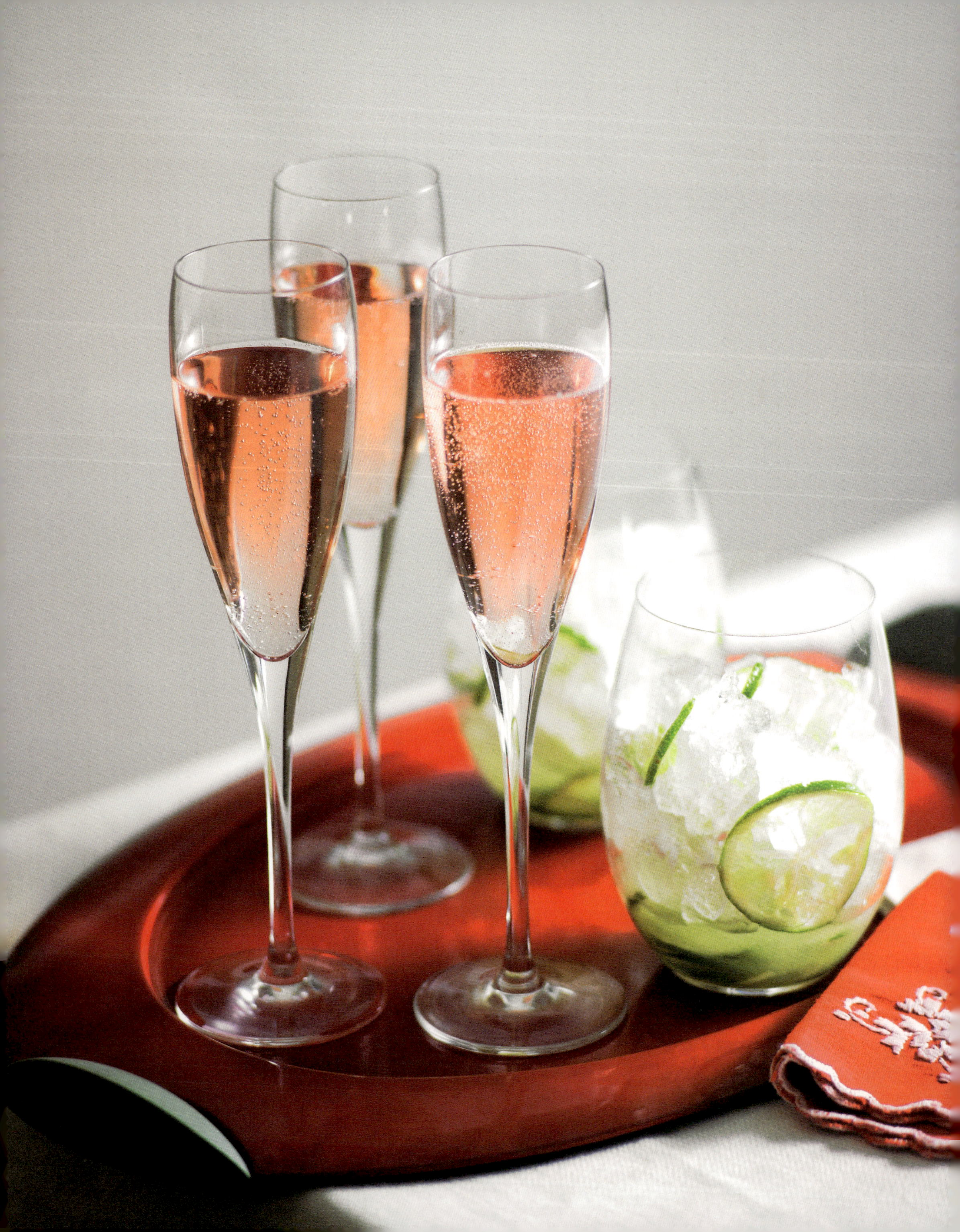

rhubarb sparkling (berry bubbly)

Makes 4.5L | Prep 15 mins | Settle 48 hrs | Rest 2 weeks

875g rhubarb, chopped
875g sugar
1 lemon, chopped
200ml white wine vinegar or cider vinegar
4.5L cold water

Combine rhubarb, sugar, lemon, vinegar and water in a food-safe bucket, cover loosely with a clean tea towel and leave for 48 hrs. Strain and pour into very clean bottles and seal.

The rhubarb sparkling will be ready in 2 weeks. Chill well before serving. Open carefully. – *Whittaker family*

Notes: This recipe is from our country cousins at Berry. It's super easy. The longer it rests the better it gets. It's non-alcoholic.

caipirinha (brazil's national cocktail)

Makes 2 | Prep 5 mins

2 limes
2 tbsp sugar (or adjust to taste)
Ice
½ cup *cachaça* or vodka (see Notes, below)

Cut limes into thin slices, removing central core and end bits. Divide lime slices between 2 sturdy glasses and add 1 tbsp sugar to each (or to your taste). Mash sugar and lime with a muddler until sugar starts to dissolve and you have a good amount of juice in each. Fill glasses with ice. Pour ½ cup cachaça or vodka into each glass.

– *Claudia de Souza*

Notes: The authentic Brazilian *caipirinha* is made with *cachaça* (sugarcane spirit). You can substitute with vodka if *cachaça* is not available.

molly's christmas cake

Serves 20 | Prep 30 mins | Cooking 2 hrs

675g mixed dried fruits (sultanas, raisins, currants, glacé cherries, peel)
30ml whisky, rum or brandy
300g self-raising flour
3 tsp mixed spice
1 tsp cinnamon
1 tsp ground ginger
Pinch salt
215g butter, softened, plus extra to grease tin
215g soft brown sugar
3 eggs
3 tbsp milk
35g chopped almonds
Apricot jam, marzipan, white icing (to decorate)

Preheat oven to 180°C. Grease and line a 20cm cake tin. Soak mixed fruits in whisky, rum or brandy. Leave to plump up. In a large bowl, sift flour, spices and pinch of salt. In another deep bowl, cream butter and sugar. Add eggs 1 at a time, beating well after each addition. Add milk and keep beating. Fold in sifted flour and spices. Add fruit and mix. Transfer to cake tin and bake for about 2 hrs or until cooked through (test with skewer before removing from oven).

When cool, remove from tin, smear all over with apricot jam then cover with marzipan and white icing. Stick on icing shapes, if you like. – *Kirwan family*

oyster shooters

Makes 1 dozen | Prep 10 mins | Standing overnight

2 tsp wasabi
Juice of ½ a lemon
1 tsp very finely fresh grated ginger
½ clove garlic, very finely chopped
½ tsp very finely chopped red chilli
Salt & black pepper, to taste
1 tbsp chopped coriander leaf
Tamari (Japanese light soy sauce), a few drops
1 dozen freshly shucked oysters
¼ cup vodka, grappa or sake
Crush ice, to serve

In a stainless steel bowl, dissolve wasabi in lemon juice, then add ginger, garlic, chilli, salt and pepper. Allow to stand in fridge overnight (or as long as possible) so flavours infuse dressing.

To serve, remove dressing from fridge. Once it reaches room temperature, stir in coriander and a few drops of *tamari*. Take freshly shucked oysters and spoon a little vodka, grappa or sake onto each one, followed by dressing – no more than 1 tbsp liquid per oyster. Arrange oysters on a platter of crushed ice and serve immediately.

– John Farnan, Mietta & Evie's Pop

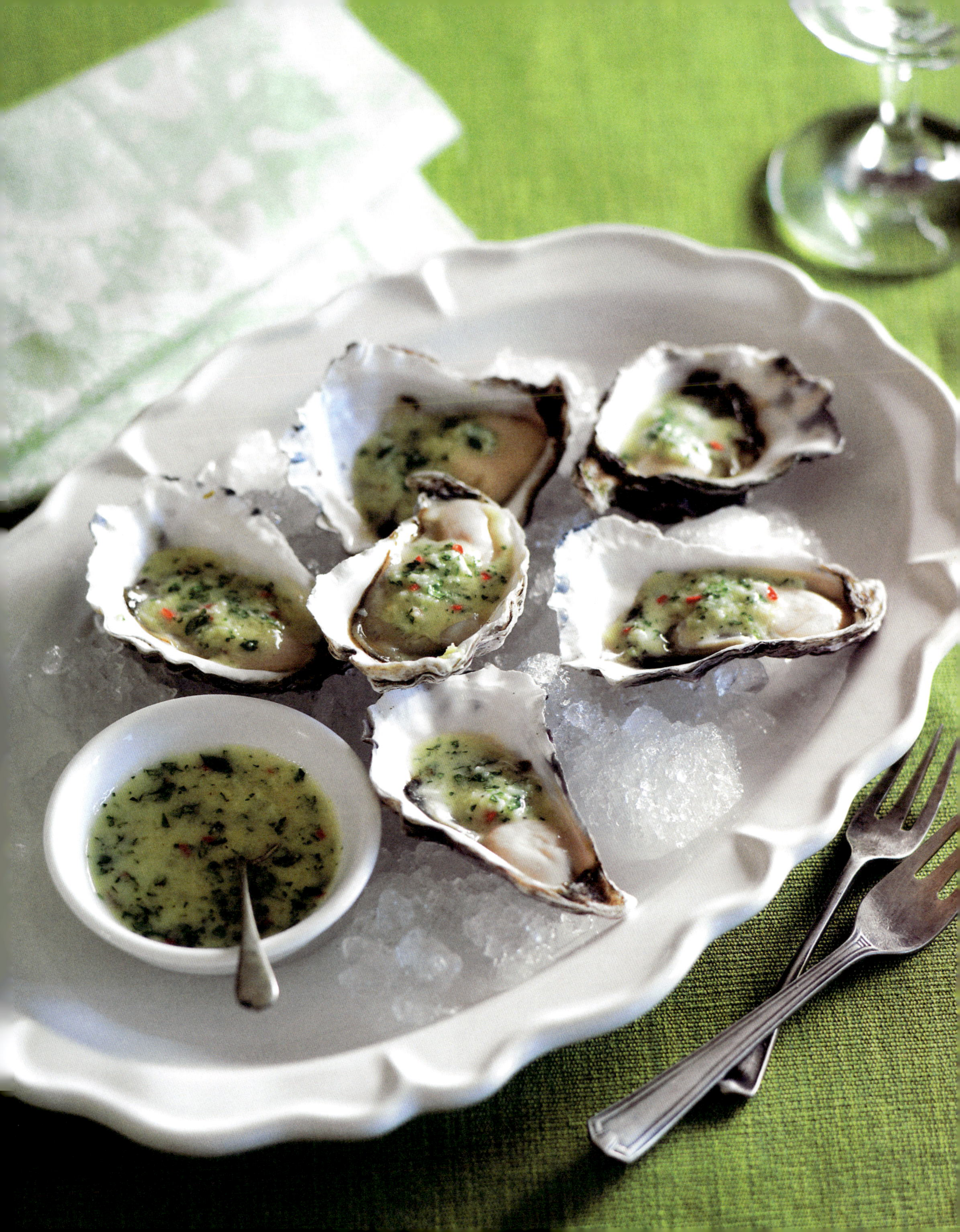

yiouvetsi (greek baked lamb & pasta)

Serves 6 | Prep 10 mins | Cooking 1-1½ hrs

2kg leg of lamb, fat trimmed (or try shanks or chops)
1 tbsp tomato paste
1 whole garlic clove, peeled
Salt & pepper
3 tbsp olive oil
Water, at room temperature
500g pasta – flat square noodles (*hilopites*) or rice-shaped pasta (*kritharakia*, also known as orzo or risoni)
5 cups boiling water
Pecorino or parmesan cheese, grated, to serve

Preheat oven to 180°C. Place meat in a deep roasting dish. In a bowl, mix together tomato paste, garlic, salt and pepper and add to dish. Drizzle olive oil over meat.

Pour room temperature water into dish to halfway up sides of meat. Place dish in oven and cook until meat is tender – 30-60 mins depending on cut. (Add more water during cooking to ensure meat stays moist.)

Remove roasting dish from oven and, leaving lamb in, add pasta and cups boiling water. Remove garlic clove, season pasta and return dish to oven. Cook for 30-40 mins, stirring occasionally, until pasta is cooked. Top up boiling water as needed.

To serve, spoon pasta onto warmed plates and place sliced lamb, shanks or chops on top and sprinkle with percorina or parmesan cheese. 　　　– *Helen Bouropoulos*

teurgoule (french rice pudding)

Serves 6-8 | Prep 20 mins | Cooking 20 mins + 8 hrs oven rest

120g round-grain rice (short-grain or pearl)
150g sugar
Pinch salt
1 vanilla bean, split
2 tsp cinnamon
1 bay leaf
1.5L full-cream milk

Preheat oven to 240°C. Place rice in a large porcelain bowl with sugar, salt, vanilla bean, cinnamon and bay leaf. Pour cold milk on top of ingredients.

Place bowl in hot oven and cook for 20 mins.

Turn oven off and leave bowl there for 8 hours without opening door.

Once cooked, the *teurgoule* should be kept at room temperature. 　　　– *Le Pechoux-Mellado family*

Notes: This countryside dish is from Normandy. It's a traditional Sunday dessert and is also made on special occasions such as christenings and weddings.

pork chop with fennel-seed crust, fennel & pear puree

CHEF'S RECIPE

Makes 4 | Prep 15 mins | Cooking 45 mins

1 small brown onion, sliced
25g butter
Salt & pepper
1 large fennel bulb, trimmed, sliced
1 pear, peeled, chopped
250ml chicken stock
1 tbsp whole white peppercorns
2 tbsp fennel seeds
½ tbsp sea salt
½-1 tbsp grated lemon rind
4 pork chops, trimmed (scrape tails clean)
Olive oil
Salad leaves & roast potatoes, to serve

Gently cook onion in butter until soft, approx 15 mins. Season. Add fennel, pear and chicken stock. Simmer until fennel is very soft and stock has reduced by half, approx 30 mins. Blend to a smooth consistency in a blender or with a stick blender.

Preheat oven to 180°C. Place peppercorns, fennel seeds and salt in a coffee grinder or mortar and pestle. Grind to a coarse consistency. Add grated lemon rind.

Coat chops with spice mixture. Pan-fry on medium heat in a little olive oil, both sides, until golden brown. Place in oven for 8-10 mins. Serve with warm fennel puree, salad and potatoes.   — *Jane & Jeremy Strode, Bistrode*

baked pineapple ham

Serves 8-10 | Prep 15 mins | Cooking 1½ hrs

500g brown sugar
440g can crushed pineapple
½ cup dry sherry
Coca-Cola (a splash)
Whole ham, any size
1 small jar hot English mustard
2 tsp ground cloves (+ whole cloves for decoration)

Preheat oven to 150°C. In a small saucepan put sugar, crushed pineapple (see Notes), dry sherry and splash of Coke. Stir until syrupy. Set aside.

Ease the skin off the ham, remove excess fat and score the remaining fat in a crisscross pattern. Smother ham with mustard and sprinkle with ground cloves. Decorate with whole cloves if you like. Place ham on a baking tray and bake for 1½ hrs. Remove from oven.

Carve ham into thin slices and arrange on a platter. Pour reduced syrup over the top. Serve hot or cold.
    — *Nancy Shannon, James & Hugh Vermeesch's great-grandmother*

Notes: This recipe is adapted from the late, great Joan Campbell's first cookbook and has been made for every Christmas and family get-together since. You can heat some of the canned pineapple juice in the baking pan first and use to baste ham while cooking if you like.

gravlax crostini

Serves 4-6 as a starter | Prep 30 mins | Curing 24-36 hrs

GRAVLAX
1½ tbsp caster sugar
6 white peppercorns, crushed
3 tbsp chopped dill
2 tsp salt
250g-300g skinless ocean trout (or salmon), pin-boned & trimmed of any dark meat
DRESSING
½ cup sour cream
2 eschalots (French shallots), finely chopped
2 tbsp chopped dill, plus extra for garnish
6 cornichons (pickled mini cucumbers), finely chopped
Juice of 1 lemon
Salt & pepper
CROSTINI
1 baguette, thinly sliced, toasted
Extra lemon wedges, to serve

For gravlax, combine sugar, white peppercorns, dill and salt in a bowl. Select a container large enough to fit the fish. Line container with plastic wrap, leaving plenty of overhang. Sprinkle ½ the sugar/dill mixture over the cling wrap. Place fish on top. Sprinkle with remaining mixture. Enclose fish tightly with plastic wrap, cover with a sheet of cardboard (to protect it) and weigh down with something heavy like cans or a brick. Place in fridge for 24 to 36 hrs to cure.

Remove fish from plastic wrap and rinse and pat dry with paper towel. NB: At this point, fish can be refrigerated for 2 to 3 days, so it's ideal for making ahead if you're having a party.

Prior to serving, use a sharp knife to slice fish, very thinly, across the grain. It can now be covered and refrigerated for up to 2 hrs before serving.

To make the dressing, combine sour cream, eschalot, dill and cornichons in a bowl. Add lemon juice, and salt and pepper to taste. Mix well, adding a little water if too thick.

To serve, spread a little sour cream mixture onto each crostini and top with gravlax. Garnish with ground black pepper and freshly chopped dill. Serve with extra lemon wedges. — Rebecca Ritchie

Notes: You can double the recipe for larger crowds. Tell them it's raw fish after they've tried it.

crown street cooks

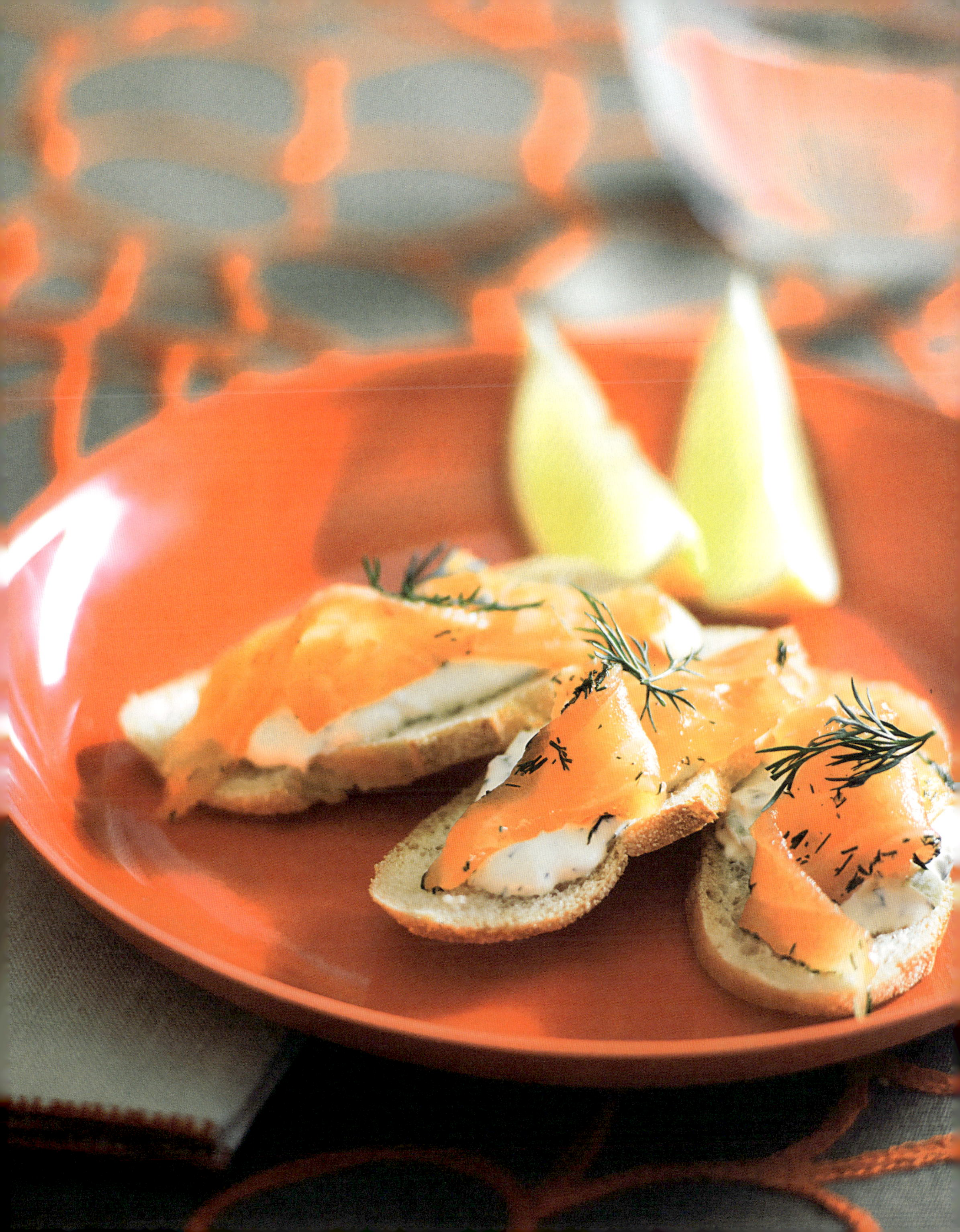

"Our family passes the servings around the table and keep passing until they get the slice they like the look of – either the size or because it might have a lucky coin."

scottish christmas pudding

Serves 12 | Prep 1 hr + 24 hrs resting time
Cooking 6 hrs (+ 2 hrs prior to serving)

225g currants
450g seeded raisins
225g sultanas
225g mixed peel (orange & lemon)
Zest of 1 orange and 1 lemon
115g blanched almonds, chopped
3 tbsp whisky
3 tbsp rum
225g butter
225g brown sugar
5 eggs
1 tbsp treacle or golden syrup
225g plain flour
½ tsp bicarb soda
1 tsp mixed spice
½ tsp salt
1 cup milk
225g breadcrumbs (don't use packet crumbs – grate 1- or 2-day-old white bread, crust cut off)

Place fruits, fruit zest and almonds in a large bowl. Sprinkle whisky and rum over, cover and leave overnight or 2-3 days if you can, turning occasionally. Next, cream butter and sugar. Add eggs one at a time, beating well. Add treacle/golden syrup. Sift flour, bicarb soda, spice, salt and add to creamed mixture. Mix until smooth. Stir in milk, breadcrumbs and prepared fruit mixture. Mix well. Transfer to a greased pudding bowl (this mix is enough for 1 large 8-cup bowl or 2 medium bowls). NB: Bowl should have a "lip" to tie a string around.

Pack the pud bowl full of mixture and press down to prevent air pockets. Cover top with foil or buttered paper and use kitchen string to tie under lip of bowl. Take a strong cotton or calico square – about the size of a dinner napkin – and place over foil or paper-covered bowl. Use kitchen twine to secure tightly under lip of bowl. Now lift corners of the cloth and tie them in a knot on top of bowl, creating a "handle" to use for moving pud in and out of boiling water.

Put an old saucer or plate on bottom of a large saucepan and add about 2 cups of water. Bring to a fast boil. Plunge pudding bowl into boiling water, which should reach no more than half the height of pudding bowl. Boil quickly for 10 mins, then lower heat and boil slowly for 6 hrs (or 4 hrs if you make 2 smaller puddings). NB: The water *must* be boiling rapidly when pudding is added and pud must boil steadily for duration of cooking time. Top water up if necessary.

When cooked, store pudding, still in cloth-covered bowl, in a cool dry place. It will keep for 3 months, so you can make it well ahead of the Christmas madness.

Before serving pudding on Christmas day, boil for a further 2 hrs. When ready to enjoy, untie cloth and foil and turn pudding out onto a serving plate.

Notes: For appreciative "oohs" and "aahs" at serving time, enlist an assistant and try the following. Turn the pudding out onto a flameproof serving plate. Heat extra brandy in a saucepan. When brandy is hot, carry pudding to the dining room door and have your helper pour brandy over and light with a match. You then carry the flaming pudding to the dining table – all very exciting, especially if lights are turned off.

My mother always hid a couple of silver threepences and sixpences to the mixture (look for them in antiques & collectables stores because it's unsafe to use today's currency) to bring the finder good luck for the following year. If you use lucky coins, make sure you sterilise them just prior to using next time.

To serve, cut the pudding into slices or wedges from the centre and pour hot custard over the top.

– *Margaret Bickle, Harry Prodes' grandmother*

lena's rum roll

Makes 4 rolls | Prep 20 mins

250g Arnott's Choc Ripple biscuits
150g marshmallows, regular size
100g glacé cherries
½ cup walnuts
½ cup desiccated coconut, plus extra for coating
1 cup sweetened condensed milk
1 tbsp rum, sherry, or brandy

Crush biscuits in food processor or similar until fine. Roughly cut marshmallows in half. Halve cherries. Break walnuts roughly, so there are still large pieces – quarters and halves.

In a large bowl, mix together all ingredients to arrive at a gooey mess, then divide mixture into 3 or 4 portions. Generously sprinkle a board with extra coconut and roll each portion to form a log shape. The outside should be well coated in coconut. Wrap in foil and keep in fridge. Cut into slim rounds for serving.

— Lisa Green

Notes: I was given one of these rolls last Christmas and requested the recipe. (Thank you, Anna-Marie B!) An easy-to-make rich, sweet treat.

vanilla bavarois with toffee shards

Serves 8 | Prep 1 hr | Cooking 30 mins

BAVAROIS
400ml full-cream milk
1 vanilla bean, split
4 egg yolks
200g caster sugar
20g powdered gelatine or 4 sheets gelatine
400ml cream
TOFFEE SHARDS
215g caster sugar
125ml water

To make the bavarois, in a saucepan, slowly heat milk with vanilla bean. Remove from heat, set aside and allow to cool. In a bowl, whisk together egg yolks and caster sugar until smooth. Remove vanilla bean from milk and discard. Pour warm milk onto egg mixture, whisking constantly until well combined. Pour mixture into clean pan; heat until mixture is thick enough to coat the back of a wooden spoon but do not allow to boil or the custard will curdle.

Remove from heat and cool slightly. Dissolve powdered gelatine in a little water (see packet instructions), then stir through custard. If using gelatine sheets, soak them in cold water for a few mins to soften, squeeze well, then mix squeezed sheets with 2 tbsp boiling water to dissolve. Mix some custard into gelatine mixture, then fold this back into custard.

In a separate bowl, whip cream. When custard is completely cold, fold through whipped cream until combined. Pour into 8 x 150ml ramekins or dariole moulds and refrigerate until set.

To make the toffee shards, line a baking tray with baking paper. Place sugar and water into a small saucepan over a low heat. Cook, stirring until sugar dissolves. Increase heat to high and bring to boil, brushing sides of pan down with pastry brush dipped in water for 10-12 mins or until toffee is pale golden in colour. Pour onto baking paper and tip mixture into tray to evenly cover surface. Allow to cool before breaking into shards.

Turn out bavarois onto serving plates and decorate with toffee shards.

— Robert Reid

Notes: Use gelatine sheets for a more even consistency.

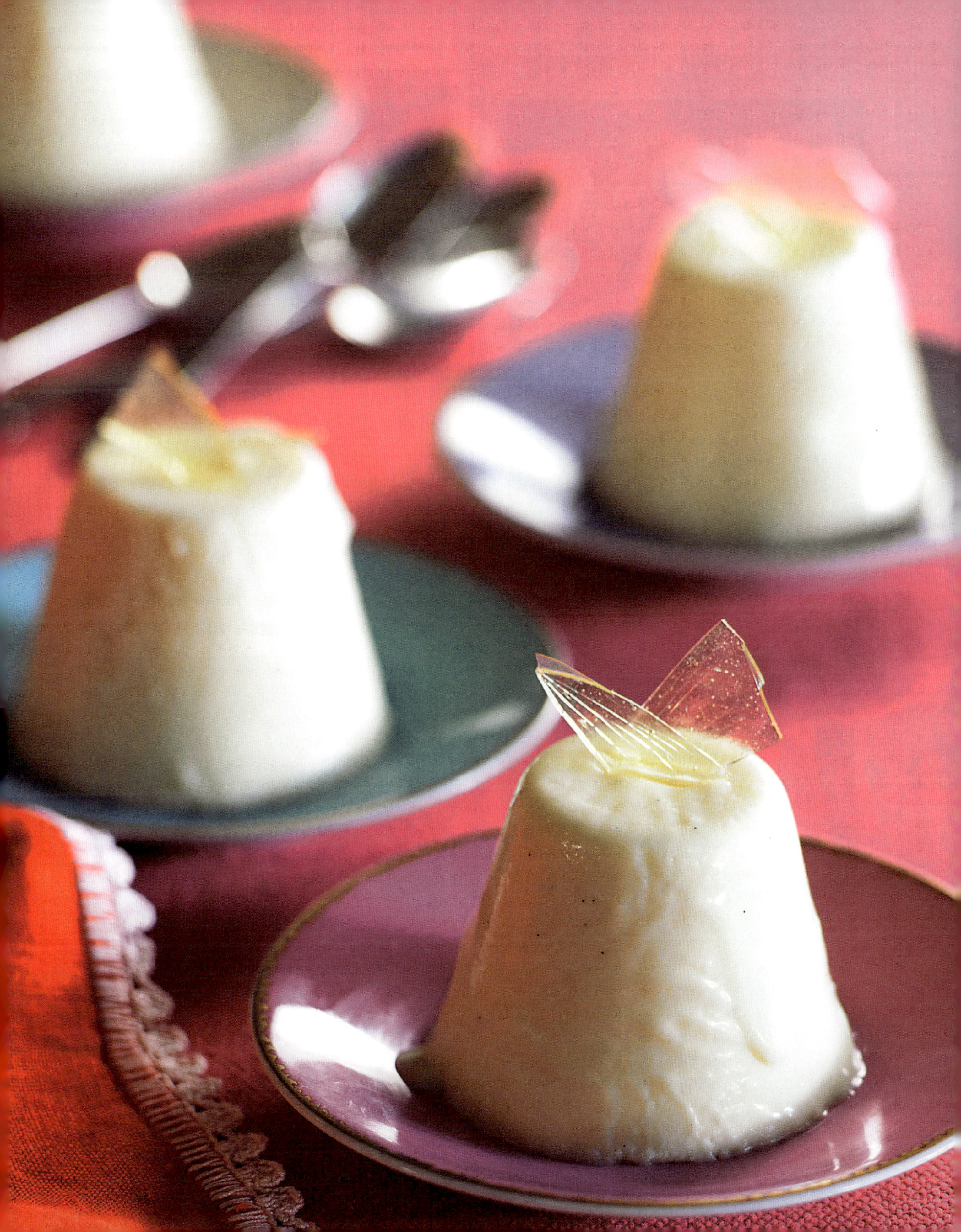

crown street eats

Pazzo Restaurant
583 Crown Street Surry Hills
NSW 2010 | T 02 9319 4387
E pazzorestaurant@optusnet.com.au
www.pazzorestaurant.com.au
| DINNER Mon to Sat
from 6pm | BYO

Photo: Michael Wee

Tabou
527 Crown Street Surry Hills NSW 2010
| T 02 9319 5682 | E info@tabourestaurant.com.au
www.tabourestaurant.com.au
LUNCH Mon-Fri, noon to 2.30pm
DINNER Sun-Fri, 6.30pm 'til late; Sat 6pm 'til late

Photo: Toby Burrows

Trinity Bar
505 Crown Street, Surry Hills, NSW 2010
| T 02 9319 6802 | www.trinitybar.com.au

Photo: Tim Robinson

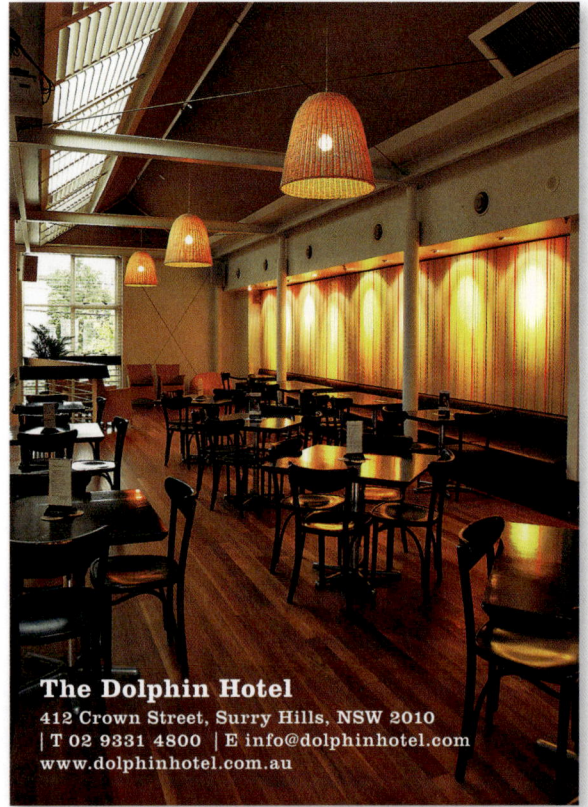

The Dolphin Hotel
412 Crown Street, Surry Hills, NSW 2010
| T 02 9331 4800 | E info@dolphinhotel.com
www.dolphinhotel.com.au

Photo: Michael Wee

kokkina avga (traditional greek red eggs for easter)

Serves 10-12 | **Prep 15 mins** | **Cooking 1 hr 20 mins**

Skins from 20 red onions
2 tbsp white vinegar
4½ cups water
1 dozen eggs, fresh & uncooked (50g eggs work best as they have the thickest shells)
Olive oil
FOR LEAF MOTIF
12 flat, nicely-shaped leaves – parsley or another herb
Old stockings
Cooking string

To make the dye, in a stainless steel saucepan, place onion skins, white vinegar and water and bring to boil. Lower heat and simmer, covered, for 30 mins.

Strain dye into a glass bowl, and let cool to room temperature. It will look orange in colour. (Or you can purchase "Egg Colouring" dye from your local Greek cake store or fruit shop.)

To dye the eggs, first clean the eggs of dirt/feathers if using organic eggs direct from the farm. In a stainless steel saucepan (approx 20cm diameter), add cooled strained dye and eggs at room temperature or put eggs in hot (not boiling) water for 10 mins. The eggs should be in 1 layer and covered by dye. Bring to boil over medium heat. When boiling, reduce heat to low, cover and simmer.

Dyeing time will be affected by the natural colour of the egg shells. Start checking for colour at 12-15 mins. Do not simmer longer than 20 mins.

When eggs are the right colour, remove from dye with a slotted spoon and cool on racks. NB: If eggs are not red enough after 20 minutes, leave in pot and remove from heat. When pot has cooled, place in refrigerator and let sit until desired colour is reached.

When eggs are cool enough to handle, coat lightly with olive (or other edible) oil and polish with paper towel. Refrigerate until time to use.

To create leaf motifs, before dyeing, wash and place leaves from parsley or other herb flat over each egg. Carefully tie a layer of stocking around each egg to keep leaf in place and tie off very tightly with string. Then continue with all dyeing steps. When cool, untie stockings and remove leaves.
– *Prodes family*

Notes: Ask your local fruit shop to save some onion skins for you – give them some notice and they won't mind. At home, save onion skins in a plastic bag in the refrigerator until ready to use.

twice-baked gruyère soufflés

Makes 3 | Prep 10 mins | Cooking 50 mins

FOR 1ST BAKING
Melted butter & plain flour, for coating moulds
35g butter
3 tbsp plain flour
250ml-300ml warm milk
45g grated gruyère cheese
1 tsp chopped fresh thyme
2 eggs, separated
Salt & freshly ground black pepper
Pinch freshly grated nutmeg
FOR 2ND BAKING
3 tbsp thickened cream
40g grated gruyère cheese
TO SERVE
Salad leaves, fresh figs & fresh crusty bread

Preheat oven to 160°C. Rub 3 x 1-cup capacity moulds or coffee cups with butter, then dust with flour.

The 1st stage of baking can be done well in advance.

To make the roux, melt the 35g butter in a saucepan over medium heat. Add flour and stir continuously for 1-2 mins. Remove from heat and add milk a little at a time, whisking constantly until smooth. Return to heat and cook, stirring with wooden spoon until smooth, adding more milk if sauce is too thick. Add cheese and stir until melted. Remove from heat. Stir in thyme.

Stir egg yolks into cheese sauce and season with salt, pepper and nutmeg. Cool to room temperature.

Whisk eggwhites and pinch of salt together until soft peaks form. Fold ⅓ of eggwhites into cheese mixture to loosen it, then carefully fold in remaining ⅔. Spoon filling into moulds until ⅔ full, then tap on bench to remove any air bubbles. Place moulds into a roasting pan lined with a clean tea towel to prevent moulds from slipping. Pour in enough boiling water to come halfway up sides of moulds, and bake uncovered for 20-25 mins until set. Remove soufflés from water bath and leave to cool slightly. They will collapse a little, so don't worry.

If not serving until later, leave to cool completely, then place soufflés, still in their moulds, in the fridge.

For 2nd stage of baking, preheat oven to 160°C. Turn soufflés out onto a tray lined with a sheet of baking paper. Top each soufflé with 1 tbsp cream and extra gruyère cheese and bake for 15 mins until golden.

Serve with a mixed leaf salad with fresh figs and some fresh crusty bread.
— *Tim Ritchie*

Notes: This dish is also great for dinner parties as most of the work can be done beforehand.

chocolate mousse

Serves 6 | Prep 40 mins | Chill 1 hr

170g dark chocolate (such as Lindt)
60g butter
3 large eggs
1 small orange
2 tbsp orange juice
60g caster sugar

Melt chocolate in a small basin over a pan of hot water (on the stove). Cut butter into small pieces. When chocolate has melted, remove from heat and mix in butter. Allow to cool slightly. Separate eggs, put whites into a large, clean bowl and place in fridge to chill.

Finely grate rind from half the orange. In another bowl, whisk egg yolks with half the sugar until fluffy. Add grated orange peel. Now slowly add chocolate mixture with the 2 tbsp orange juice. Remove bowl of eggwhites from fridge and whisk until stiff, then gradually add other half of sugar. Fold ⅓ of eggwhites through chocolate mixture, then fold in remaining whites. Pour into 6 individual ramekins. Cover with plastic wrap (my mother's recipe says "in case you have anything in the fridge which could taint the flavour") and chill for at least 1 hr.

Serve with fresh cream and berries.
— *Henrie Stride*

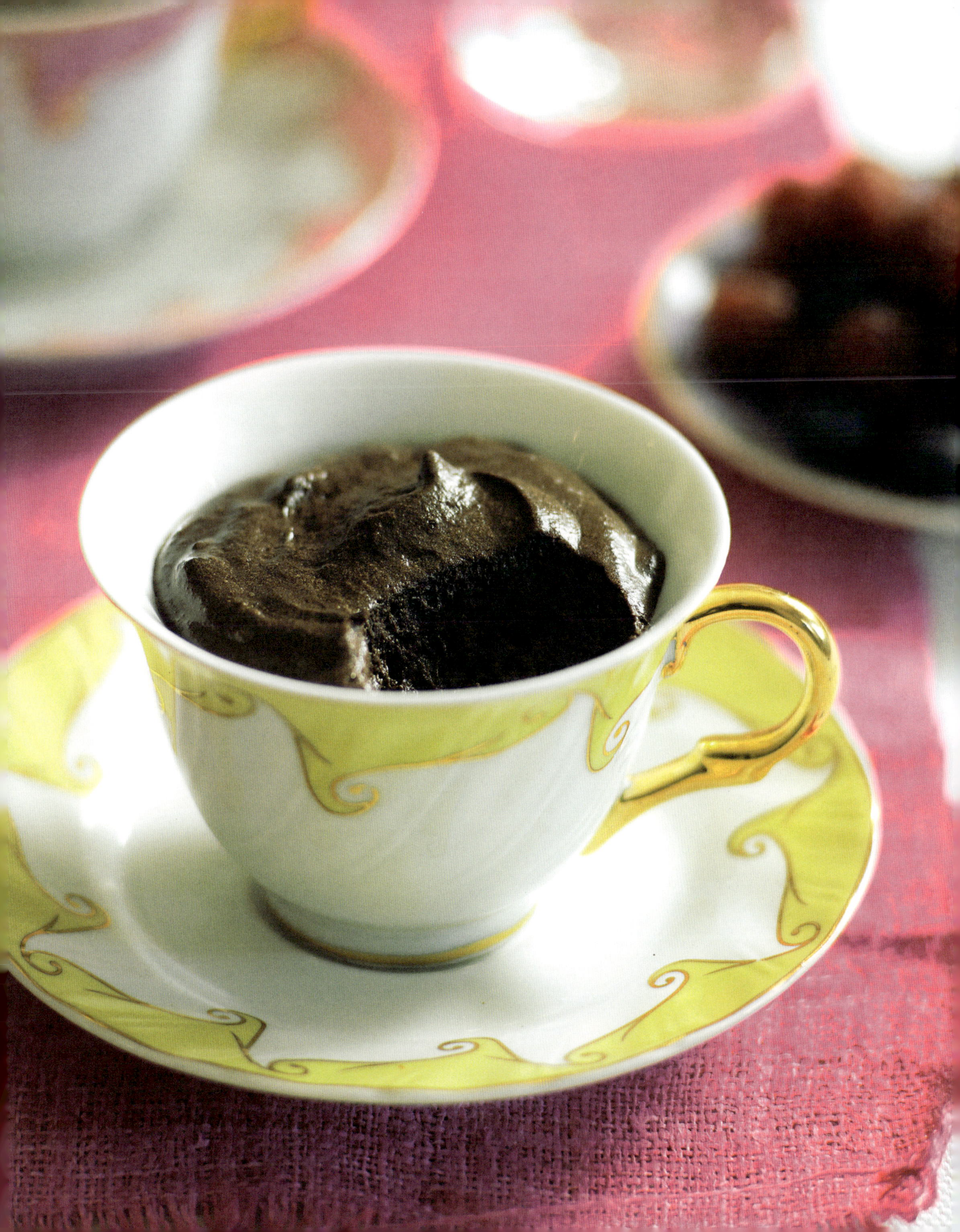

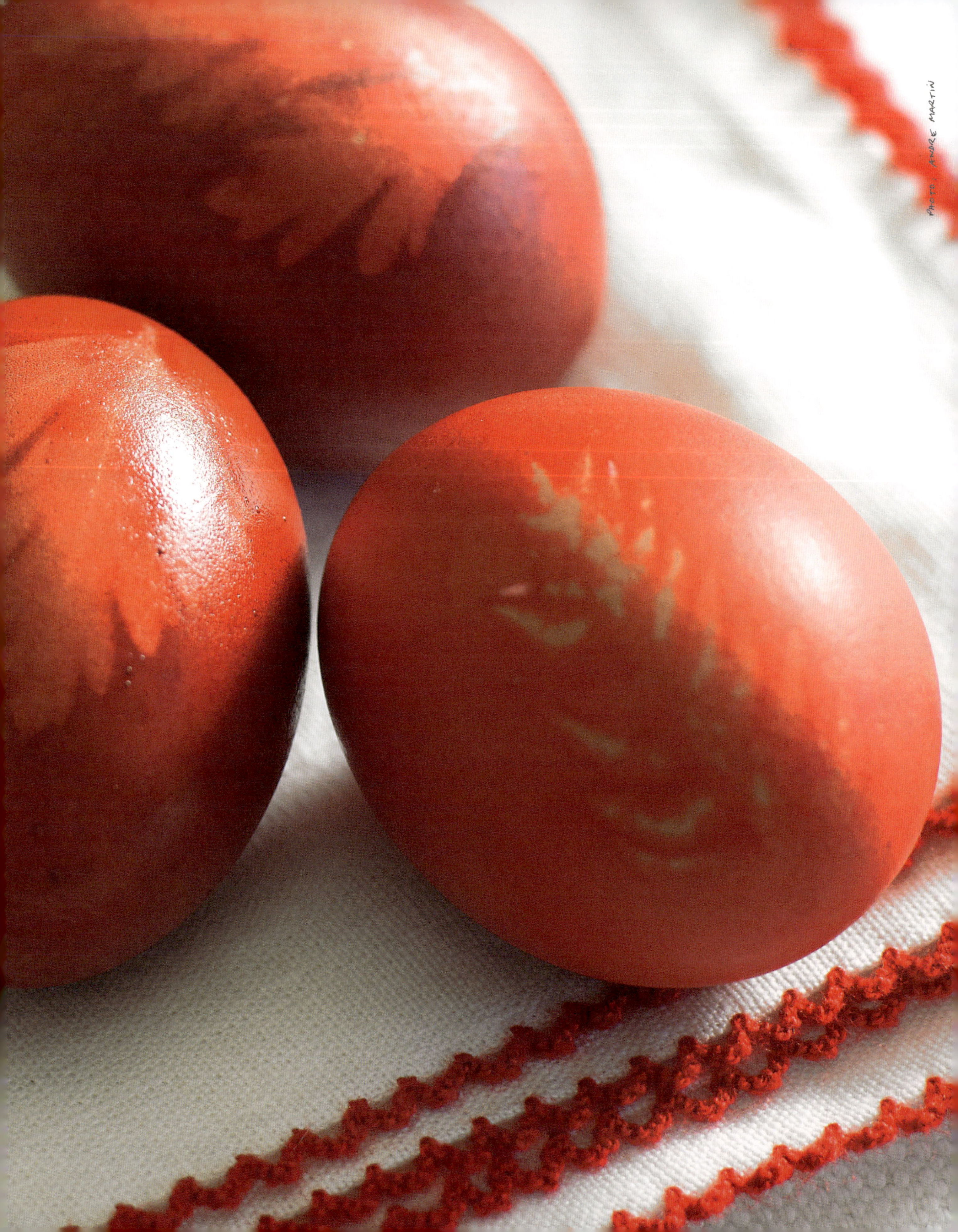
PHOTO: ANDRE MARTIN

PHOTO: MICHAEL WEE

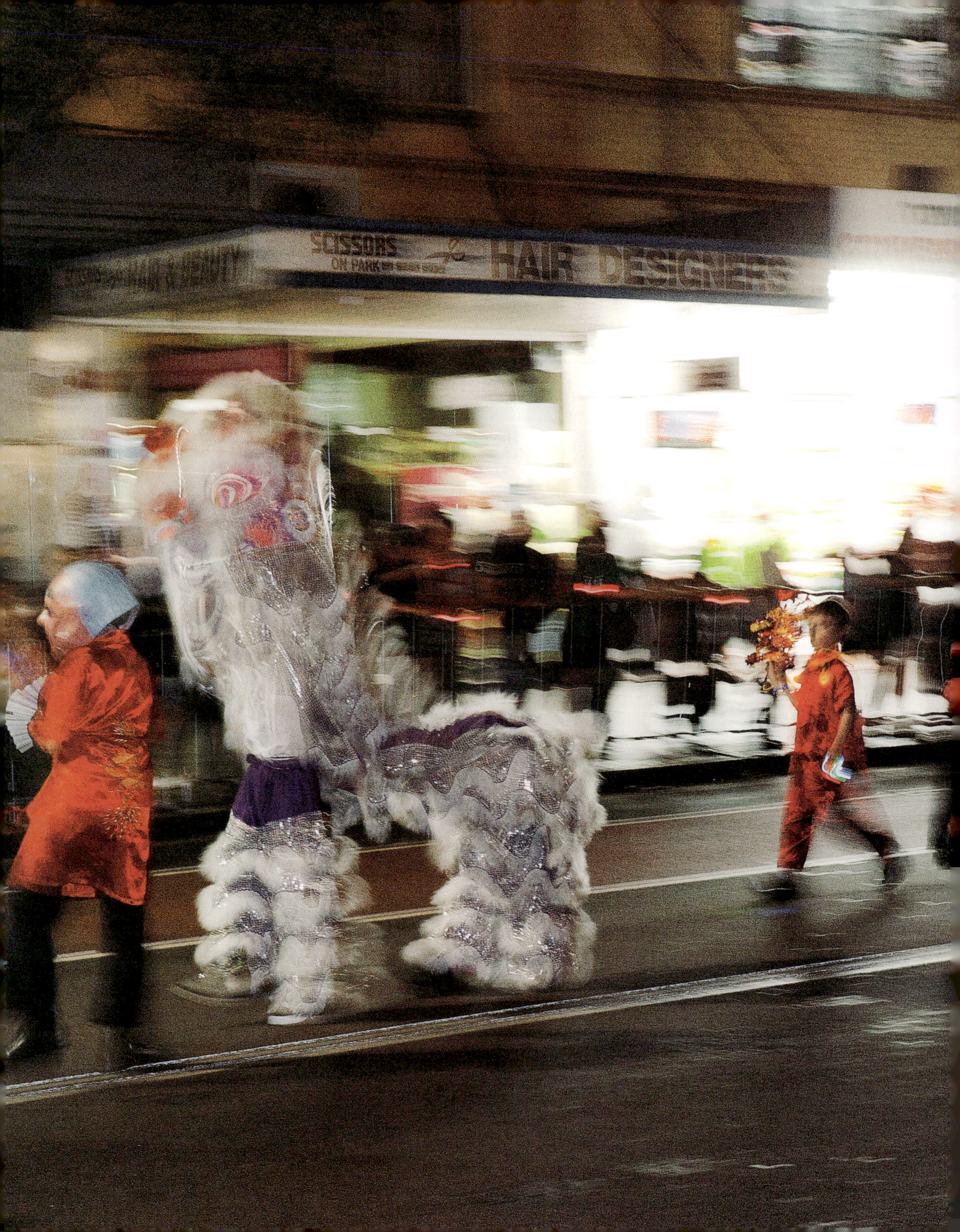
SCISSORS
ON PARK
HAIR DESIGNERS

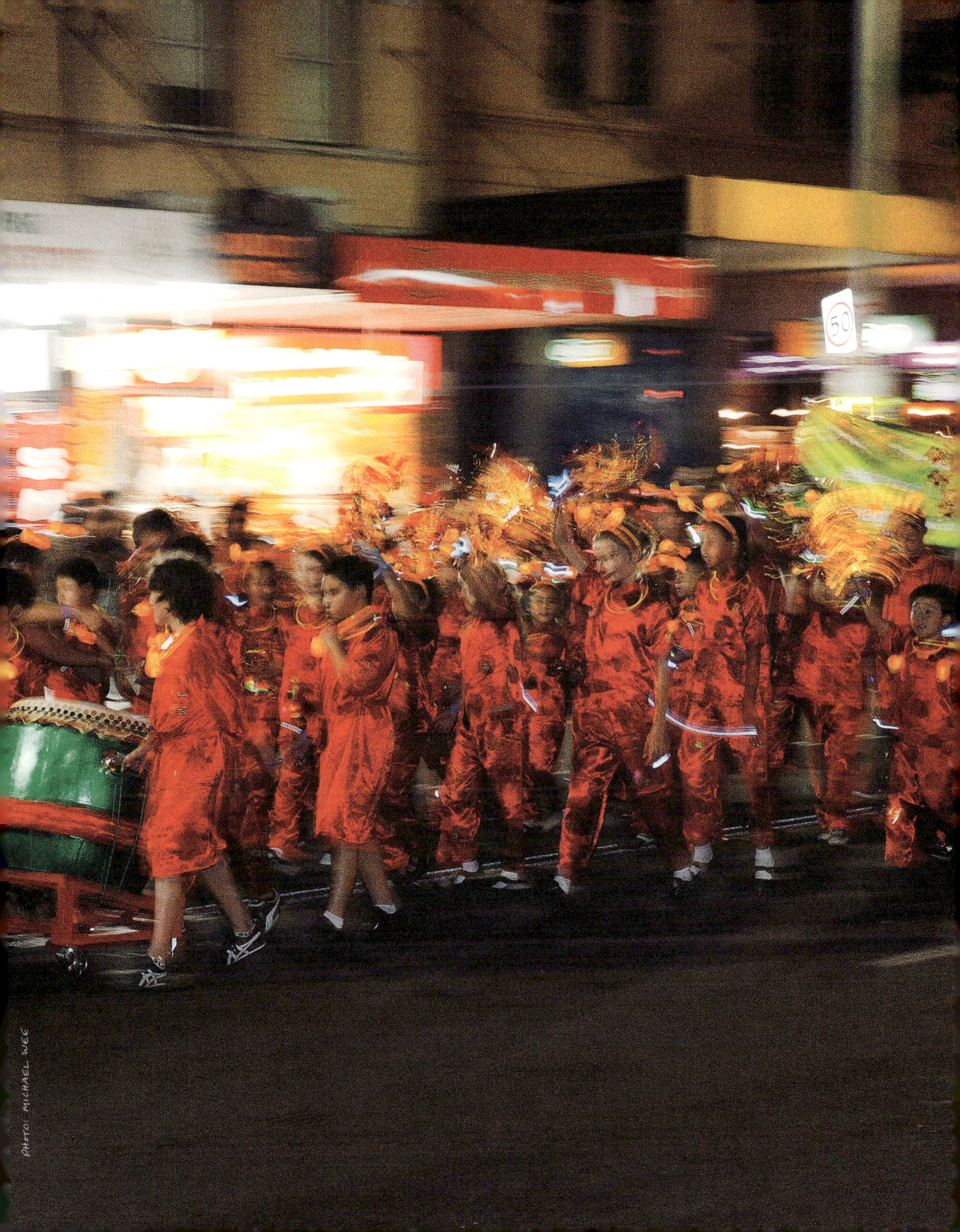

PHOTO: MICHAEL WEE

crown street
eats

The Book Kitchen
255 Devonshire Street, Surry Hills, NSW 2010
| T 02 9310 1003 | E info@thebookkitchen.com.au
| www.thebookkitchen.com.au
7 days for brekkie & lunch, 8am-3pm.
Dinner from 6pm, Wed to Sat

Browse or buy from our selection of new and used cookbooks in our cafe by day, restaurant by night. We use local suppliers and the freshest of produce – organic and sustainable where possible.

PHOTO: TIM ROBINSON

crown street eats

chef's recipes from the Crown Street strip

organic mushroom salad

Serves 4-6 | Prep 15 mins

400g button mushrooms, stems discarded, caps finely sliced
150g red radish, trimmed, finely sliced
50g flat-leaf parsley
3 spring onions, cut into julienne
½ cup finely shredded mint leaves
⅓ cup organic extra virgin olive oil
¼ cup lemon juice
2 tbsp organic *tamari* (Japanese soy sauce)
½ tsp sea salt flakes
Pinch ground white pepper

Combine salad ingredients in a large bowl. Mix together oil, lemon juice, *tamari*, salt and pepper. Pour over salad and toss to combine. Serve as a side dish or main.

— Billy Kwong

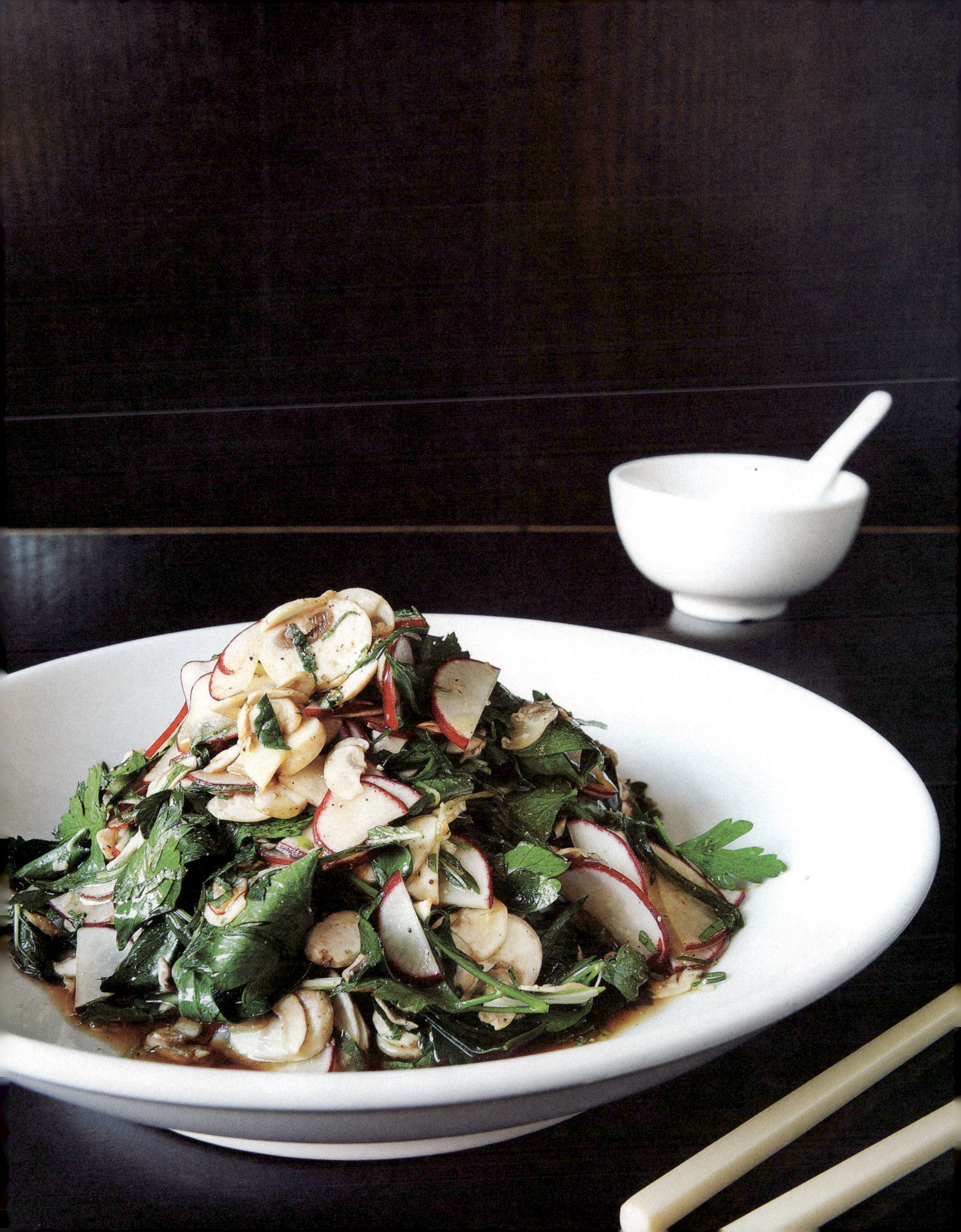

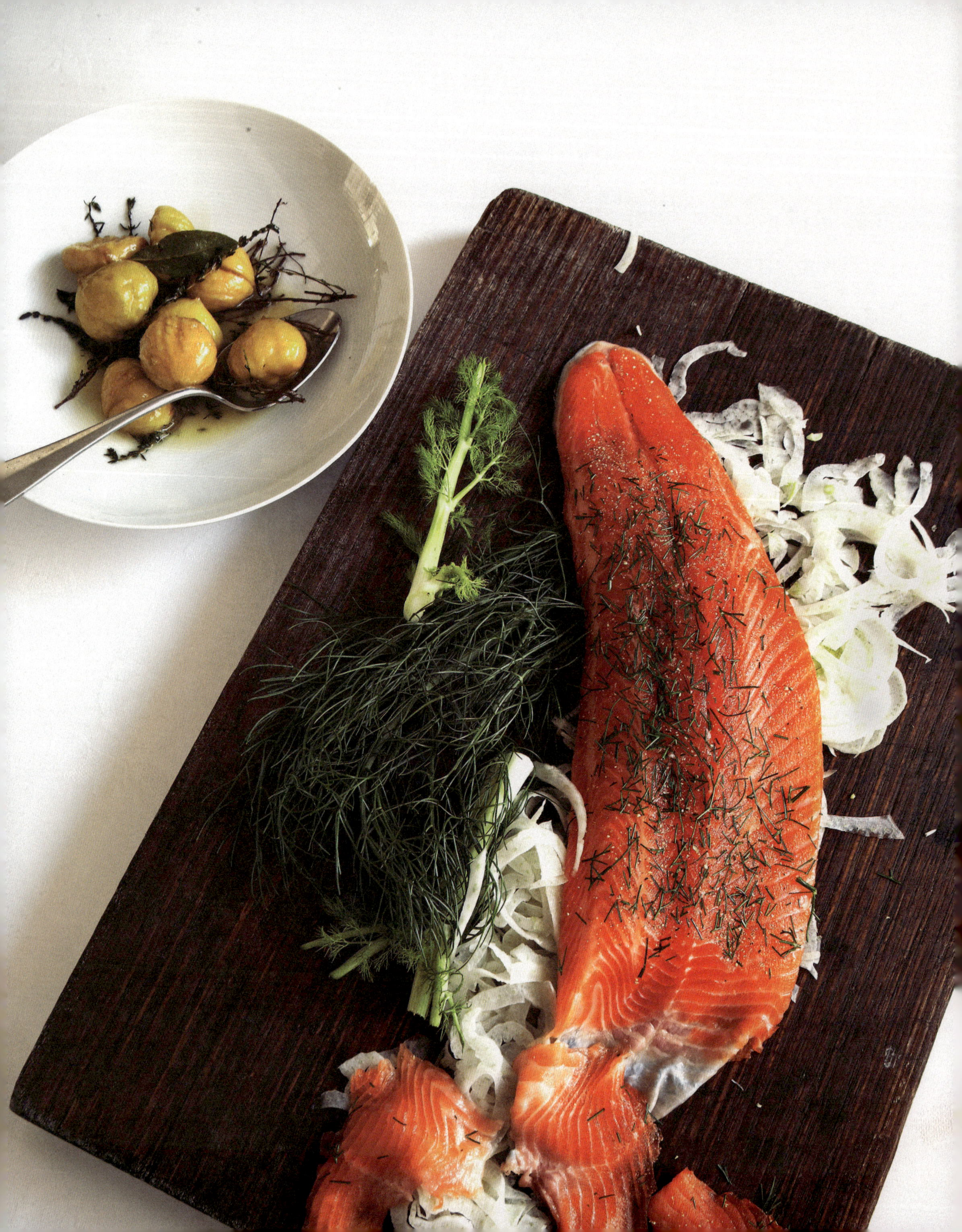

cured ocean trout with fennel & chestnuts

Serves 4-6 | **Prep 20 mins** | **Curing 12 hrs** | **Cooking 45 mins**

1kg side ocean trout (Petuna is our preferred)
1 tsp white peppercorns
1 tsp coriander seeds
100g white sugar
100g sea salt flakes or pink Murray River salt
2 tbsp chopped fennel fronds
Finely grated rind of 1 lemon

FENNEL & CHESTNUT SALAD
50g unsalted butter
250g peeled chestnuts (See Notes, below)
1 clove garlic
1 sprig thyme
Ground white pepper
1 tsp aged sherry vinegar
300ml chicken stock
3 bulbs baby fennel, ends trimmed
Juice of 1 lemon, plus 1 tbsp extra
50ml Pernod, Ricard or pastis (aniseed-flavoured spirits)
2 tbsp extra virgin olive oil
Sea salt flakes or pink Murray River salt

Trim away the fatty belly piece of the trout. The cat will appreciate this morsel. Use a pair of fish tweezers or fine needle-nose pliers to remove the pin bones. Place fish in a shallow dish.

Toast peppercorns and coriander seeds in a small frypan on medium heat for 2-3 mins, until they begin to pop. Transfer to a bowl with sugar, salt, fennel fronds and lemon rind. Mix well and rub over trout, covering both sides evenly. Cover with plastic wrap and refrigerate for a minimum of 12 hrs to cure. Remove trout from marinade and wipe excess off using a clean cloth. Wrap in fresh plastic wrap and refrigerate until using. This can be done up to 3 days in advance.

To prepare salad, melt butter in a large heavy-based frypan on medium heat until foaming. Add chestnuts, garlic and thyme and cook for 4-5 mins, until chestnuts are golden. Season with a little ground white pepper then deglaze pan with sherry vinegar. Add stock and bring to a simmer. Cover nuts with a circular sheet of baking paper (*cartouche*). Tear a little hole in the centre to allow the correct degree of evaporation. Reduce heat to low and simmer gently for 5-10 mins, until chestnuts are tender and juices have reduced to a syrupy glaze. Set aside to cool to room temperature.

Using a mandolin or sharp knife, slice fennel as thinly as possible. Place into a bowl of iced water. Add lemon juice and Pernod, Ricard or pastis and soak for 15 mins, until fennel is crisp. Drain fennel and pat dry with kitchen towel. Place in a large bowl with extra virgin olive oil, extra 1 tbsp lemon juice and season well with salt and ground white pepper.

Remove thyme and garlic from the chestnuts and discard. Add chestnuts and any juice to fennel. Mix to combine, lightly crushing chestnuts into the fennel. Divide between serving plates. Place trout on a heavy board with tail to the right. Starting at the head and using a very sharp, long, thin knife, thinly slice fish across the fillet at a 45-degree angle, into paper-thin slices. Arrange enough trout slices over fennel to cover, and serve.

Notes: We buy an excellent pre-peeled chestnut from Victoria, saving a lot of time and burnt fingers. If you cannot find these, use a method you are familiar with.

– *Marque*

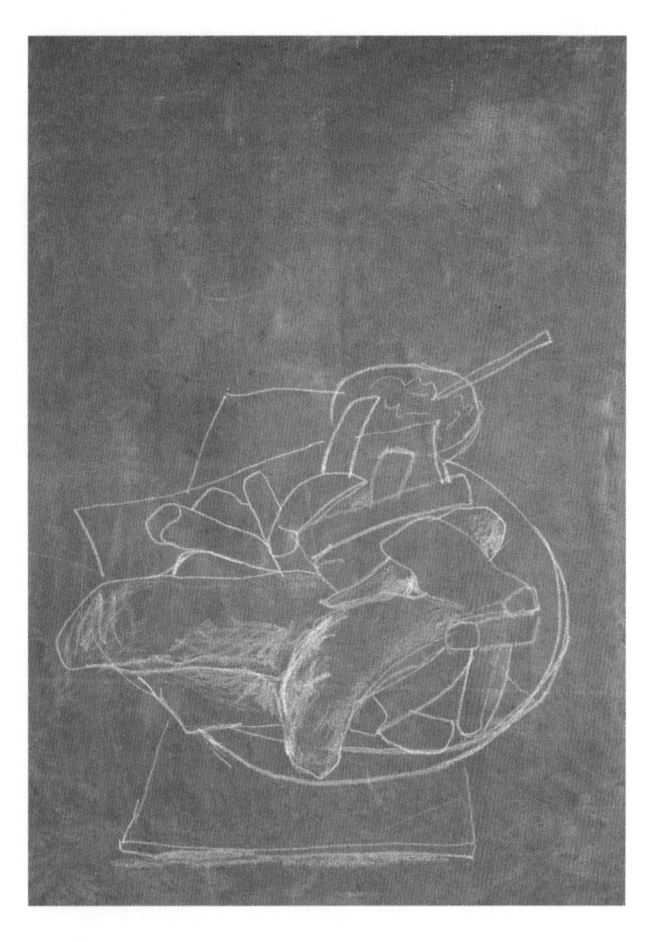

fish & chips

Serves 4 | Prep 5 mins | Cooking 7 mins

4 x 150g pieces of good-quality fresh white-fleshed fish (blue eye, trevalla, snapper, flathead, bream, John dory or silver dory all good options)
4 lemon cheeks, to serve
4 heaped tbsp homemade tartare sauce (see below)
CHIPS
4 large sebago potatoes, peeled
Vegetable oil (for deep-frying)
TARTARE
200ml good-quality whole-egg mayonnaise
1 tbsp chopped capers
1 tbsp chopped cornichons (baby gherkins)
1 tbsp chopped Spanish onion
1 boiled egg, grated through large part of grater
Flat-leaf parsley, chopped
BATTER
300g plain white flour
100g rice flour
20g agave syrup (see Notes)
300ml gin
300ml Coopers Pale Ale (green label)

To make the chips, steam potatoes whole for 5 mins, until just tender. When cool to enough to handle, cut potatoes into thick chips. Heat oil in a large saucepan or deep fryer until a cube of bread sizzles on contact. Cook potatoes for 5 mins, until firm but not golden. Drain on kitchen paper.

Meanwhile, mix tartare ingredients together and season with a little fresh lemon juice to taste.

To make the batter, combine dry ingredients in a large bowl. Add agave syrup, gin and beer and whisk to combine.

Reheat oil. Dip fish into batter, allowing excess to drain off. Cook fish for 2-3 mins, until golden and crisp. Drain on kitchen paper. Reheat oil. Cook chips for final 2-3 mins, until golden and cooked through.

Serve fish & chips with tartare and lemon cheeks.

— The Battery

Notes: Agave syrup gives a hint of sweetness to the batter. Try Spiral brand, available at good delis.

pizza dough

Makes 12 x 220g balls of dough (each ball makes a 30cm pizza)
Prep 10-15 mins | Refrigerate overnight
Proving 1-3 hours | Cooking 20 mins

1L water
5g fresh yeast (from good healthfood stores)
1.8kg unbleached flour (Italian "00" flour is the best)
50g sea salt

Put water in a large mixing bowl, add yeast and mix a little. NB: To stabilise the mixing bowl, place a wet tea towel between it and the benchtop.

Start to add flour quite quickly and mix until amalgamated and dough forms a firm ball shape. Add salt and mix again. If it is too wet, add a little more flour. Turn dough ball onto board or benchtop and rest for 20 mins under a clean, damp tea towel – this stops a crust forming on the dough.

Divide dough into 12 x 220g segments.

Using your hands, roll dough into balls. Place balls on a tray and refrigerate overnight (or freezer if saving for a later date – see Notes, below).

Remove dough from fridge 1-3 hrs before cooking (1 hr on a hot day and up to 3 hrs on a cold day).

Preheat oven to 200°C. Roll dough out on your pizza tray, top with your favourite combination, cook and eat!

Notes: Dough balls can be frozen for later use. Freeze in snaplock bags. Before use, allow several hours for defrosting.

— Pizza Mario

"This is the authentic pizza dough of Naples."

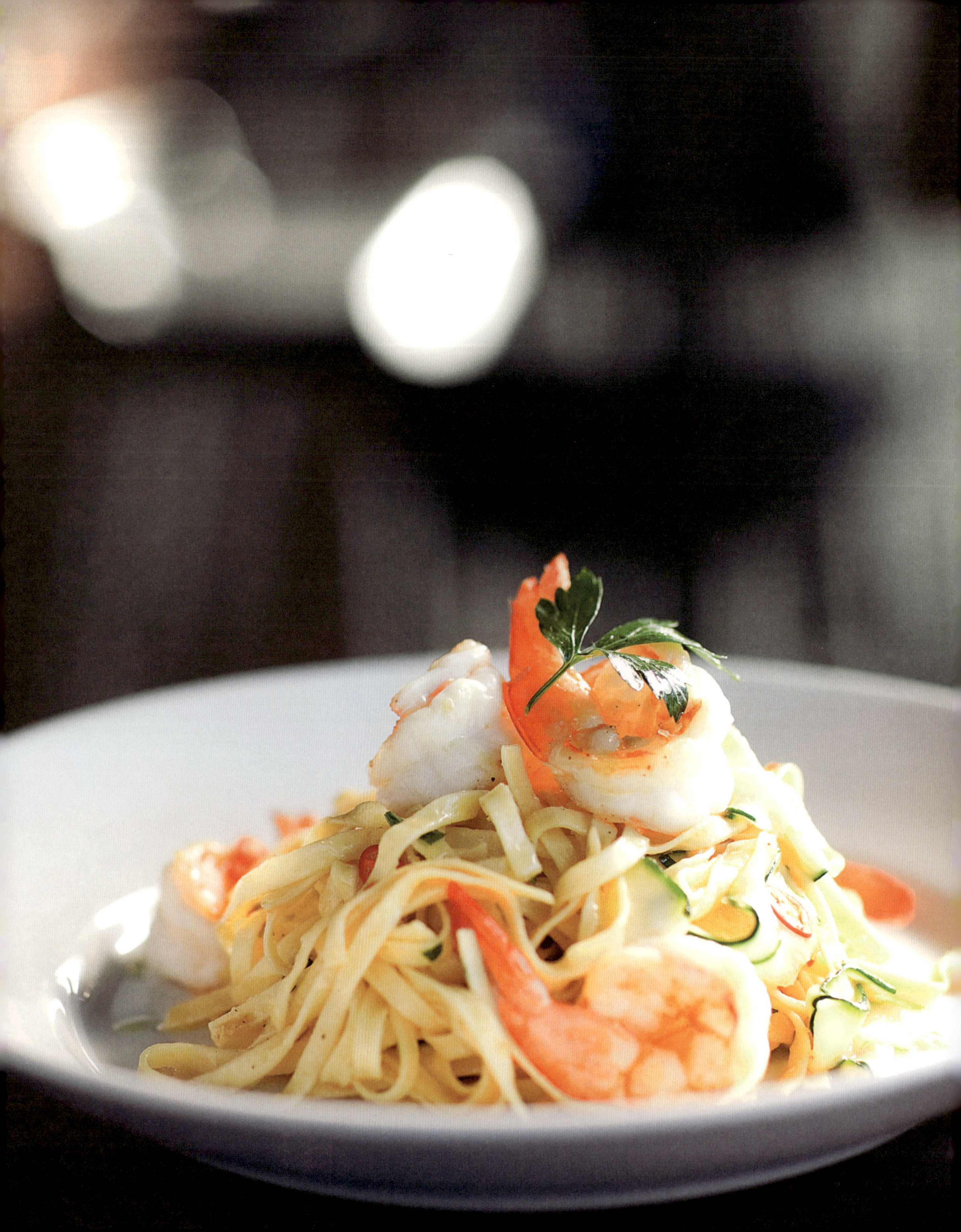

linguine with king prawns, zucchini & lemon

Serves 4 | Prep 20 mins | Cooking 30 mins

PRAWN STOCK
Prawn heads & shells (see below)
½ medium brown onion, roughly chopped
1 stick celery, roughly chopped
½ bulb fennel, sliced
1L water
Salt & pepper
½ bunch coriander

PASTA & SAUCE
400g fresh linguine
Salt
⅓ cup extra virgin olive oil
20 green king prawns, peeled, deveined, tails intact (keep the heads & shells for the stock)
2 tbsp unsalted butter
2 garlic cloves, crushed
2 birdseye chillis, finely chopped
1 cup prawn stock (see below)
¼ cup lemon juice
1 zucchini, ends trimmed, thinly sliced lengthways
⅓ cup grated parmesan
2 tbsp chopped parsley

To make the prawn stock, thoroughly rinse prawn heads and shells under running water. Place in a large saucepan with onion, celery, fennel and water. Season well. Bring to boil on high heat, skimming surface of stock constantly. Reduce heat to low and simmer for 15 mins. Remove from heat, add coriander and sit for 5 mins. Strain stock, discarding solids.

Cook linguine in a large saucepan of boiling salted water according to packet directions. Drain and return to saucepan with half the oil.

Meanwhile, heat a large frypan on high. Add remaining oil and cook prawns for 1 min each side, until opaque. Add butter, garlic and chilli and toss together, until butter has melted. Remove prawns from pan. Add stock, lemon juice, zucchini and parmesan. Simmer for 2 mins, until zucchini is tender and sauce smooth. Return prawns to pan with linguine and parsley. Season to taste and toss to combine.

Notes: You will have prawn stock left over. Pour into a container and freeze for up to 1 month.

— The Clock

olive oil bread

**Makes 2 loaves | Prep 45 mins | Ferment overnight in fridge
Proving 3-4 hrs | Cooking 35 mins**

FERMENT (SEE NOTES)
⅔ cup "00" flour
½ tsp salt
½ tsp olive oil
½ tsp milk
¼ cup water
2g fresh yeast

BREAD DOUGH
580g "00" flour
395ml water
13g fresh yeast
1 tbsp olive oil
1 tbsp milk
3 tsp salt
160g ferment

To make ferment, combine all ferment ingredients in a bowl. Using an electric mixer fitted with a dough hook, beat on low speed for 2 mins. Increase speed to high and beat for 5 mins. Cover and refrigerate overnight.

To prepare the dough preparation by hand, place flour, water and yeast in a bowl. Mix with a spoon and set aside for 20 mins. Add remaining ingredients, except the ferment, and mix until well combined.

Tip dough onto a lightly floured bench and knead for 10 mins. Cover and rest dough for 10 mins. Add the ferment and knead for another 10 mins. Spray a large container with oil and place dough in it. Cover and set aside, in a warm place, for 40-55 mins, until dough has doubled in size. Knock down dough and tip onto a floured bench. Press into a rectangle, about 2cm thick. Fold one-third back onto itself then fold over remaining third. Turn dough 90 degrees, press down and fold into thirds again. Place dough back into container and prove for another 40-55 mins. Repeat this process once more.

Preheat oven to 180°C or 160°C fan-forced. Grease 2 baking trays. Knock down dough and turn onto clean floured surface. Press dough down evenly to a thickness of about 20cm. Cut in half and trim into oblongs about 500g each. Keep dough trimmings as ferment for tomorrow's bread.

Place onto prepared trays and dust with a little flour. Set aside in a warm place for 40 mins-1 hr, until dough has grown two-thirds in size. Touch dough lightly – it should bounce back a little and look airy and spongy. Place trays in oven and spray dough with 2 x 3-second sprays of water. Bake for 20 mins. Turn trays and bake for another 15-20 mins, until the base of the bread sounds hollow when tapped.

Notes:
FERMENT The ferment used in this recipe is day-old dough. It adds texture and flavour. Its role is not primarily as a rising agent, so if your ferment is 2 or 3 days old, it is okay to use. If it's older than this, it is best to make a new one. Always keep your ferment in the fridge. When making your first-ever dough you will need to create some ferment. Once you have done this there is no need to make it again as you will just use day-old dough. The recipe above allows you to make two 500g loaves with enough leftover dough for your ferment for the next mix.

AUTOMATED MIXING Although you will gain a better appreciation of how the dough is changing and developing if you mix a dough by hand, automated mixing is easier and consistently better if you have a good mixer. Follow the directions below and then continue proving as in recipe.

Put everything in bowl; mix on low speed for 2 mins then high speed for 5 mins. Break up ferment and disperse throughout bowl. Then mix again on low speed for 1 min and high speed for 5 mins. The second mix on high speed could take an extra couple of mins. Look for dough to come away from edges of bowl. It should have a silky complexion. When you have this it is ready.

– Bourke Street Bakery

olive oil loaf
- non-organic flour
- salt
- water
- malt
- milk
- xtra virgin olive oil
- yeast

4

olive + rosemary flat bread

4

Pieno
Shop 11, 285a Crown Street, Surry Hills, NSW 2010
| T 02 8354 1303 | 7 days, 7am-5pm

Photo: Michael Wee

crown street eats

Marque
Shop 4,
355 Crown Street
Surry Hills, NSW, 2010
T 02 9332 2225 |
www.marquerestaurant.com.au
Tue to Sat, 6pm-late

Photo: Michael Wee

fouratefive
485 Crown Street,
Surry Hills, NSW 2010
| T 02 9698 6485
E order@fouratefive.com
www.fouratefive.com
Mon to Fri, 7am-4pm;
Sat 7.30am-4pm;
Sun 9.30am-2.30pm

Photo: Tim Robinson

Mahjong Room
312 Crown Street Surry Hills NSW 2010
| T 02 9361 3985 | E info@mahjongroom.com.au
www.mahjongroom.com.au |
Mon to Sat, 6pm-late
Mahjong PlayLunch – last Saturday of each month

Photo: Tim Robinson

crispy duck with chilli & plum sauce

**Serves 4 | Prep 60 mins | Marinating 1-2 hrs
Cooking 1 hr 45 mins | Drying 1-2 hrs**

2¼kg whole duck
2 tbsp light soy sauce
100g cornflour
Oil for frying
MARINADE
8 spring onions, crushed
8 slices ginger, crushed
3 tbsp Chinese rice wine
2 tbsp salt
SAUCE
A little oil
2 spring onions, white part only, finely chopped
1-2 small chillis, seeds removed, chopped
  (leave the seeds in if you like a really hot sauce)
1 tbsp finely chopped ginger
2 cloves garlic, chopped
1 cucumber, thinly sliced
1 small carrot, thinly sliced
1½ tbsp cornflour
2 tbsp plum sauce (found in Asian supermarkets)
¼ cup water

Rinse duck in water and remove the parson's nose and fat from cavity and neck. Mix all marinade ingredients together. Rub inside and outside of entire duck with marinade, setting aside leftover marinade in a large bowl. Put duck, breast facing down, into bowl with rest of marinade and leave to marinate in fridge for 1-2 hrs.

To steam duck, put duck on a heat-resistant plate, breast facing up, and place into a bamboo steamer. If duck is too big you can cut it into halves and use 2 steamers. Place steamer over simmering water in a covered wok and steam lightly for 1½ hrs. You can top up with boiling water as necessary.

When cooked, remove duck and brush off marinade. Let duck cool. Rub duck with soy sauce and then cover in cornflour, which should stick to skin. Place duck in fridge for 1-2 hrs to dry.

To fry duck, heat a wok about ¼ full of oil until very hot. Fry whole duck in oil until skin is crispy and golden. You can ladle oil over top of duck as it cooks. Remove duck from wok and drain off oil. Cut duck into bite-size pieces and place on serving plate.

To make the sauce, clean wok and put back on high heat. Add oil and stir-fry spring onion, chilli, ginger and garlic for less than 20 secs. Add thinly sliced cucumber and carrot and stir-fry for around 1 min. Combine plum sauce and cornflour with water and add to main sauce mixture until it thickens.

Pour sauce over duck pieces and serve.

– Mahjong Room

crown
street
cooks

canard dans la cocotte (duck casserole)

Serves 4-6 | Prep 30 mins | Cooking 1 hr 50 mins

2kg whole duck
Olive oil
CHOUFARCIE – WRAPPED STUFFING BALL
Olive oil
½ brown onion, finely diced
¼ tsp savoury *quatre-épices* (French four-spice mix; available at Herbie's Spices)
½ tsp chopped thyme
100ml white wine
1 tsp brandy
Salt & pepper
150g coarse pork mince
50g duck livers, cleaned, finely chopped
4 pitted dates, finely chopped
1 large outer savoy cabbage leaf, blanched
1 piece caul fat (ask your butcher)
TO FINISH
1L chicken stock
4 turnips, peeled, cut into wedges

Preheat oven to 170°C or 150°C fan-forced.

Remove fat from around cavity and back of duck. Rinse under cold water and pat dry with kitchen paper. Heat some oil in a heavy-based flameproof casserole pan on medium. Cook duck for 5 mins, turning, until golden brown all over. Remove duck from pan.

To make the *choufarcie*, heat a little oil in a small frying pan on low. Cook onion for 5 mins, until transparent. Add *quatre-épices* (four-spice) and thyme. Add white wine and brandy and simmer until reduced by half. Remove from heat. Combine pork mince, livers and dates in a bowl. Pour over wine reduction and season well. Mix well and mould mixture into a ball. Wrap mince in blanched cabbage leaf. Wrap this ball, tightly, in caul fat.

Strain rendered fat from duck pan and set aside. Place *choufarcie* into cavity of duck and return to casserole pan. Pour stock over duck and scatter turnips around. Return to medium heat, cover and bring to a simmer. Transfer to oven and bake for 1½ hrs or until duck legs are very tender.

Remove lid, increase oven temperature to 220°C or 200°C fan-forced and cook for another 5-10 mins, until duck is golden brown. Skim excess fat from surface, chop duck into pieces and serve.

– Tabou

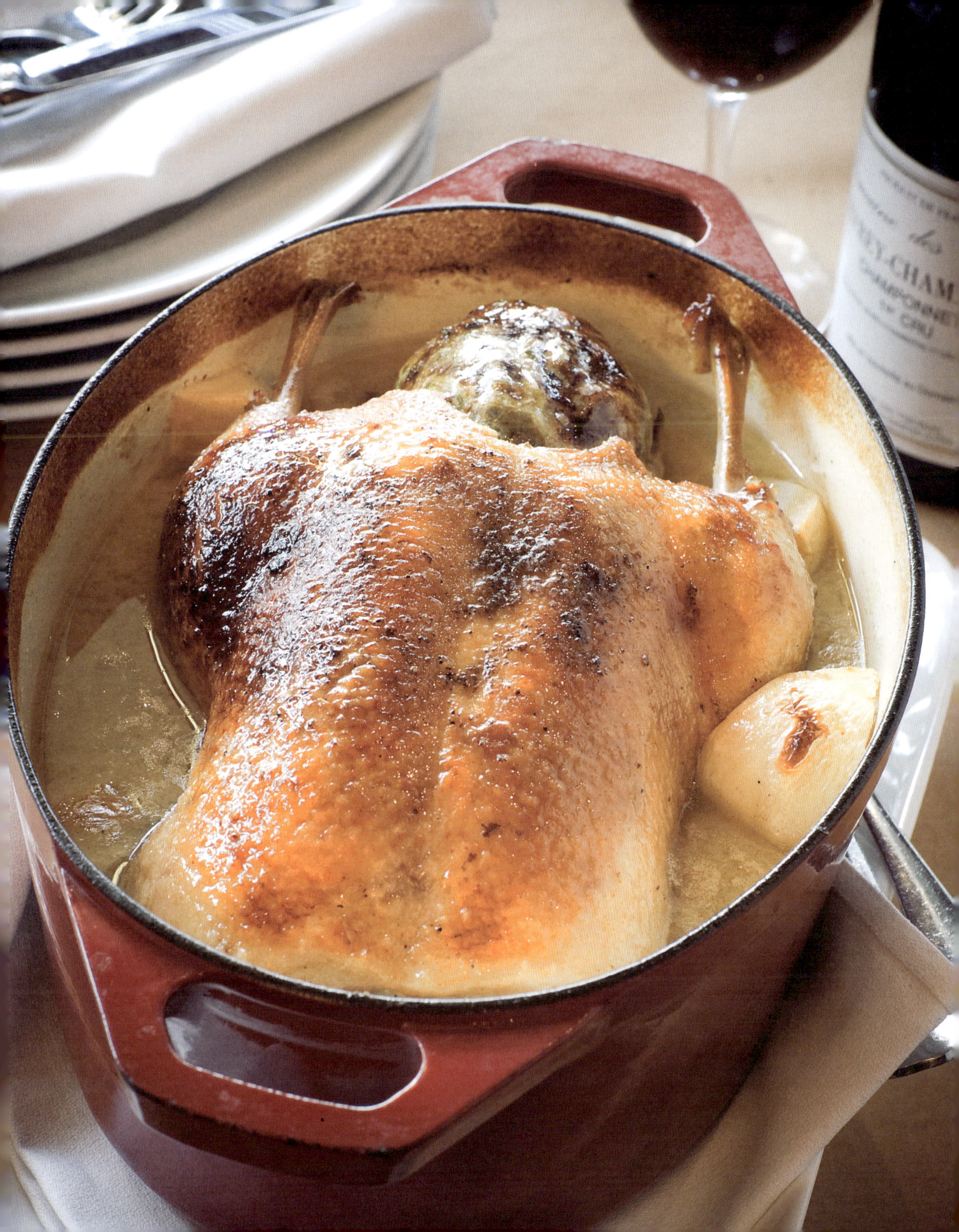

strawberry & pink champagne soup with yoghurt pannacotta

**Serves 6 | Prep 20 mins | Cooking 30 mins
Chilling overnight**

230ml milk
250g caster sugar
2 tsp gelatine powder
230g plain yoghurt
400ml pink Champagne or sparkling wine
300g strawberries, tops removed, washed
6 extra strawberries, tops removed, washed

To make pannacotta, place milk and 50g sugar in a saucepan and bring to just boiling. Stir to dissolve sugar. Remove from heat, add gelatine and stir to dissolve. Allow to cool. Add yoghurt and combine. Pass through a fine strainer to remove any small lumps and pour into 6 lightly greased plastic dariole moulds of approx 120ml capacity. Allow to set in fridge, preferably overnight.

To make the soup, place Champagne in a saucepan, bring to boil and reduce by half. Add 200g sugar and stir to dissolve. Remove from heat and allow to cool. Puree strawberries with a stick blender or regular blender. Pass through a fine strainer. Measure ¾ cup puree and add to Champagne reduction.

Slice extra strawberries lengthways. Turn out pannacotta into soup bowls. Pour soup around and garnish with sliced strawberries. — *Bistrode*

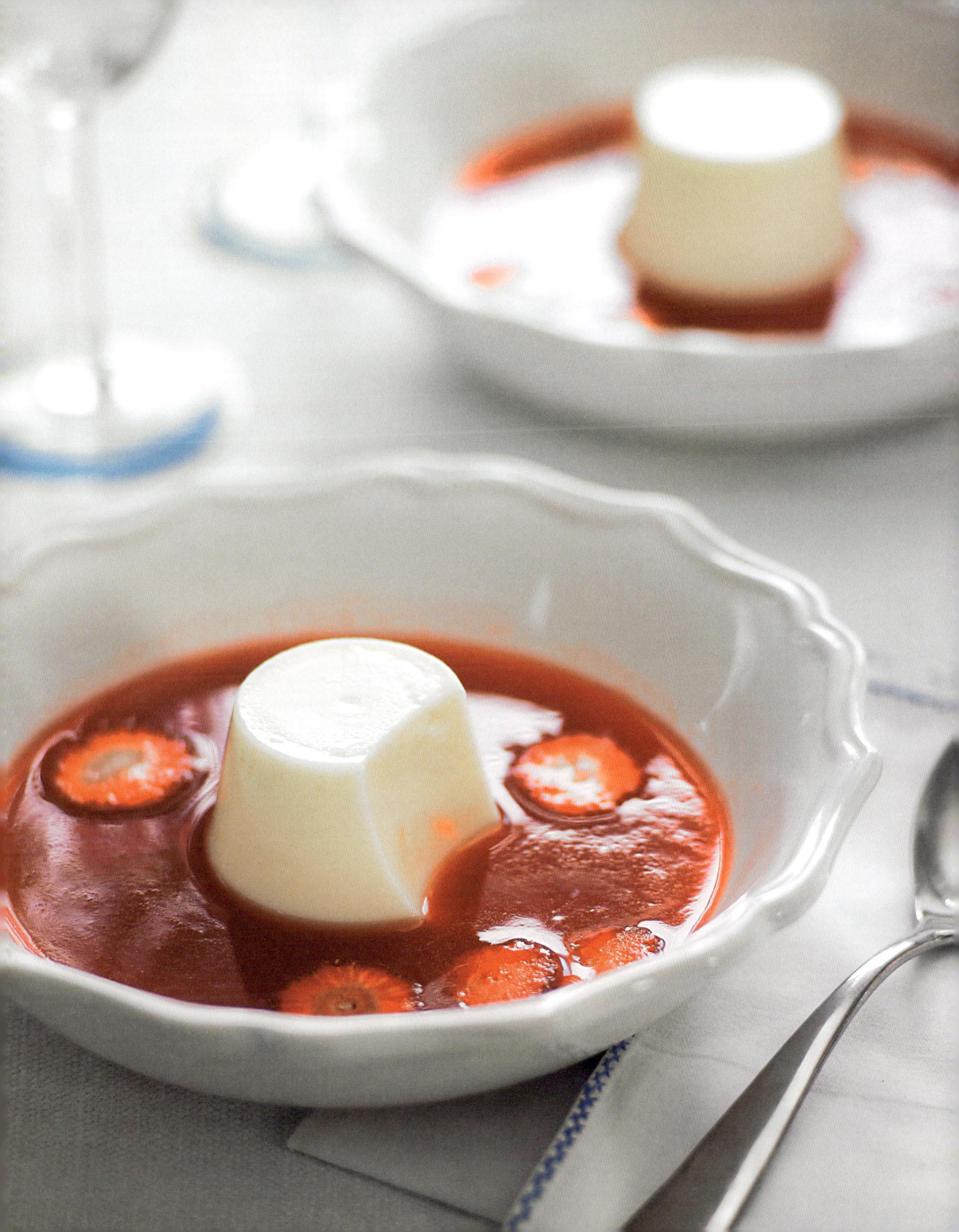

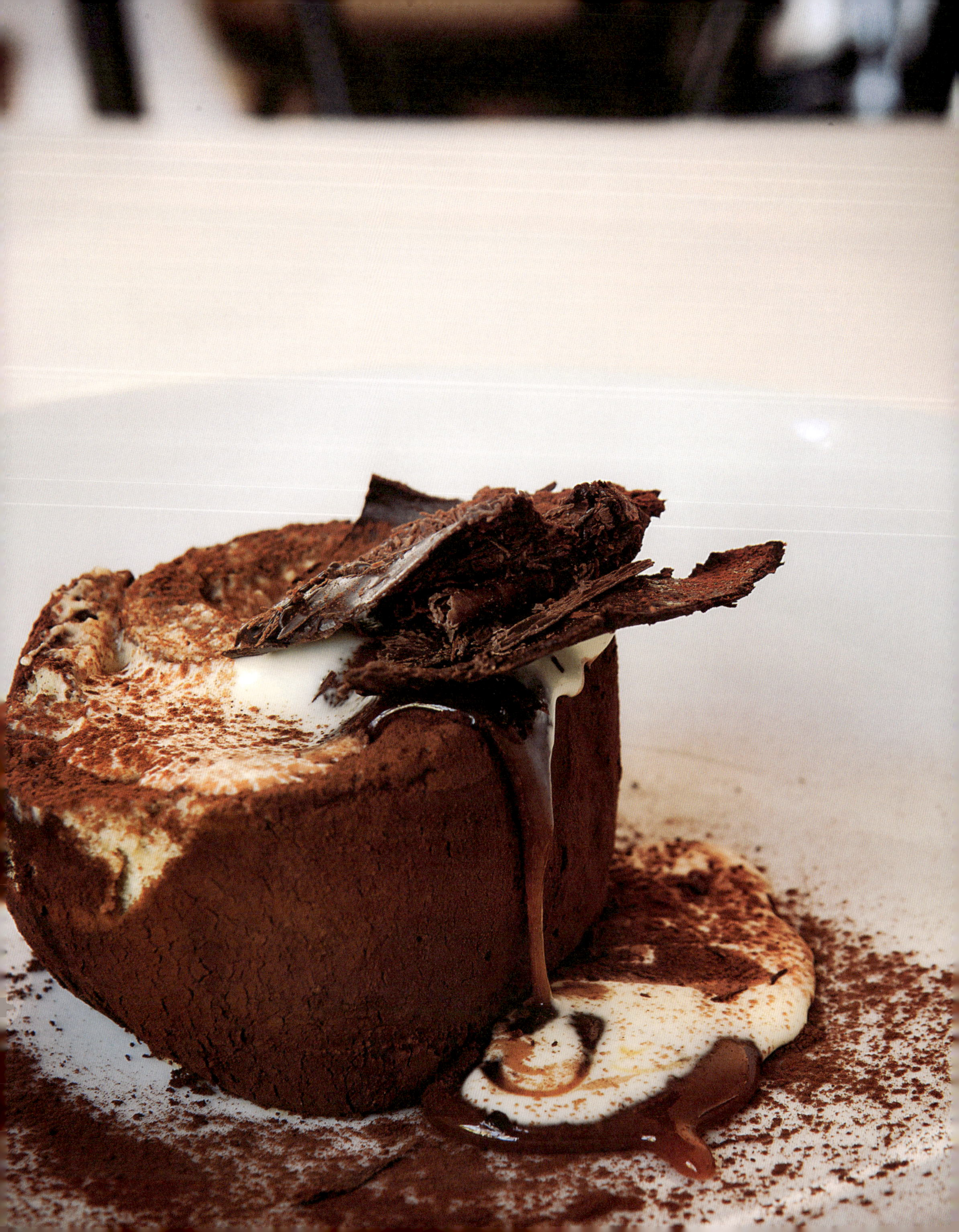

tiramisu roulade

Serves 8 | Prep 45 mins | Chilling 6 hrs | Cooking 20 mins

4 x 60g eggs, separated, + 3 extra egg yolks
85g caster sugar
¼ cup plain flour
40g potato flour
⅓ cup cocoa powder, plus extra to serve
¼ cup espresso coffee, plus extra to serve
Thickened cream & chocolate shavings, to serve

MASCARPONE CUSTARD
6 egg yolks
⅓ cup caster sugar
75ml marsala
1 leaf gelatine
500g mascarpone (Paesanella brand)

Preheat oven to 180ºC or 160ºC fan-forced. Grease a 30cm x 40cm swiss roll pan and line with baking paper.

Using an electric mixer, beat all 7 egg yolks and 60g sugar in a large bowl until thick and pale. Mixture should form a ribbon when beaters are lifted. In a separate, very clean bowl, whisk eggwhites and remaining sugar together with a pinch of salt, until stiff peaks form. Use a large metal spoon to gently fold eggwhites into yolk mixture. Sift both flours together and fold into egg mixture. Fill prepared pan, spreading gently with a metal spatula. Bake for 5-7 mins, until cake is just starting to shrink from the edges. Let cool.

To make the mascarpone custard, in a large heatproof bowl, whisk together egg yolks, sugar and marsala until well combined. Place over a saucepan of barely simmering water and whisk for 4-5 mins, until mixture is thick enough to coat the back of a spoon. Meanwhile, soak gelatine in cold water for 1-2 mins, until soft. Remove custard from heat, add drained gelatine and mix until dissolved. Cover with plastic wrap and refrigerate, stirring every 5 mins to prevent lumps forming, for a total of 30 mins, until completely cold. Place mascarpone in a bowl and mix until smooth. Fold through custard until well combined.

To assemble, on the bench lay a piece of baking paper that is at least 5cm wider than cake on each side. Dust paper with cocoa and invert cake onto paper. Brush coffee all over cake. Spread marsala custard over cake and, using paper as a guide, roll up – just like an old-fashioned sponge roll. Secure both ends with string and roll again in plastic wrap to further support cake. Refrigerate for at least 6 hrs before serving.

To serve, cut into slices and place, cut-side up, onto plates. Drizzle each slice with a little espresso coffee. Dust with extra cocoa powder, top chocolate shavings and a drizzle of thickened cream.

– *Bird Cow Fish*

Notes: Take care not to overcook the custard and curdle it, or you will need to start again!

banana loaf with cinnamon butter

Makes 1 loaf | Prep 20 mins | Cooking 1 hr

125g butter, at room temperature
185g caster sugar
2 eggs
3 small ripe bananas, mashed
1 tbsp milk
1 tsp vanilla
1 tsp bicarb soda
1¼ cups self-raising flour, sifted
CINNAMON BUTTER
125g butter, at room temperature
1 cup honey
1 tbsp ground cinnamon
1 tsp vanilla extract (optional)

Preheat oven to 180°C or 160°C fan-forced. Grease a 14cm x 21cm loaf pan and line with baking paper.

Place butter and sugar in a food processor and process until pale and creamy. Add eggs, process until combined. Add mashed bananas, milk, vanilla and bicarb soda and process until smooth. Add flour and pulse until just combined. Fill pan and bake for 55-60 mins, until inserted skewer comes out clean.

Meanwhile, to make cinnamon butter, use an electric mixer to beat butter until pale and creamy. Add honey, cinnamon and vanilla and beat until combined. Place butter on a piece of plastic wrap and roll into a sausage shape, using plastic as a guide. Twist ends and place in fridge 1 hr for flavours to infuse and butter to firm up.

To serve, cut butter into discs and serve with a slice of the warm banana loaf. — *fouratefive*

pumpkin ravioli with brown butter & sage

Serves 4 | Prep 70 mins | Cooking 1 hour

DOUGH
1kg plain flour
8 eggs
¼ cup olive oil
FILLING
1kg butternut pumpkin, chopped
4 garlic cloves, unpeeled
1 small red chilli
1 tbsp olive oil
Salt & pepper
1½ cups grated parmesan & extra shaved parmesan, to serve
1 cup finely chopped flat-leaf parsley
TO FINISH
250g unsalted butter
1 cup sage leaves
Salt

Sift flour into a large bowl, make a well in centre and add eggs and oil. Mix until combined and mixture comes together and forms a dough. Turn onto a lightly floured surface and knead for 10 mins until smooth. Cover with plastic wrap and rest at room temp for 1 hr.

To make filling, preheat oven to 200°C or 180°C fan-forced. Place pumpkin, garlic and chilli in a baking pan. Drizzle with oil and bake for 45 mins, until soft. Squeeze garlic from skin. Place in bowl with pumpkin and chilli. Mash until very smooth. Season to taste. Add parmesan and parsley and mix to combine.

Divide dough into 4 pieces. Wrap 3 pieces in plastic wrap to prevent drying out. Press 1 piece of dough into a rectangle about 10cm wide. Set pasta machine at setting No. 1 and dust rollers with flour. Feed dough through twice. Narrow the settings, 1 notch at a time, rolling dough through once, until you reach setting No. 5. Lay the long piece of dough on a lightly floured bench. Drop 1 tsp pumpkin filling onto the dough every 5-6cm, leaving a border around each mound. Brush edges with water. Repeat rolling with another piece of dough. Lay over pumpkin filling, pressing firmly around each edge to seal. Use a ravioli cutter to cut each square of ravioli. Repeat with remaining 2 pieces of dough and pumpkin filling.

To finish, melt butter in a small saucepan on low heat. Increase heat to medium and cook for 10-15 mins, until nut brown. Strain and return to saucepan with sage leaves. Cook for 1-2 mins, until sage is crisp.

Meanwhile, cook ravioli in large saucepan of boiling salted water for 5 mins or until ravioli float to surface.

To serve, remove ravioli with a slotted spoon and divide between serving plates. Top with nut-brown butter, sage and shaved parmesan. — *Pazzo*

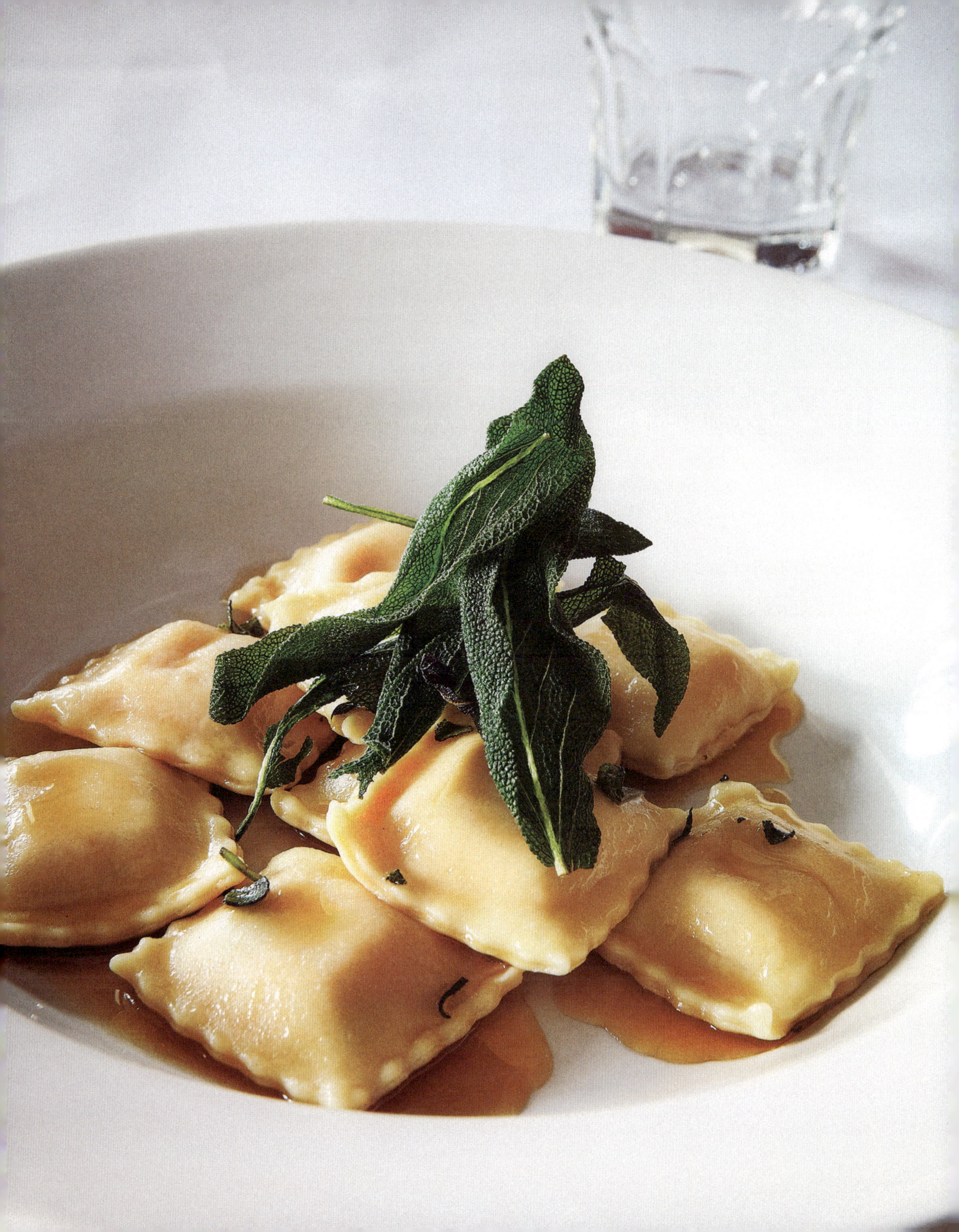

twice-cooked pork belly with braised cabbage & pancetta

Serves 4 | Prep 30 mins | Cooking 3 hrs 45 mins

MASTER STOCK
2L water
150ml light soy sauce
150ml Chinese *shaoxing* cooking wine
1 garlic clove
2cm piece ginger, peeled, chopped
1 cinnamon stick
3 star anise
1½ tbsp brown sugar
800g piece pork belly

BRAISED CABBAGE
4 slices pancetta
50g butter
1 garlic clove, finely chopped
1 small leek, white part only, chopped
1 brown onion, diced
1 small green cabbage, finely shredded
100ml white wine
2 cups chicken stock
100ml veal jus
¼ bunch parsley
Salt & pepper

For master stock, place water, soy, wine, garlic, ginger, cinnamon, star anise and sugar in large saucepan. Bring to boil, reduce heat and simmer for 30 mins.

Preheat oven to 160ºC or 140ºC fan-forced. Line a deep baking pan with baking paper. Score rind of pork belly and place in prepared pan. Pour master stock over pork and cover with foil. Bake for 2½ hrs, on centre shelf until pork is very soft. Remove pork from stock and refrigerate until cool (easier to cut).

Meanwhile, to make the braised cabbage, increase oven to 180ºC or 160ºC fan-forced. Lay pancetta on a baking tray and bake for 5-8 mins, until crisp. Set aside. Melt butter in a large frypan on medium heat. Cook garlic, onion and leek for 5 mins, until soft. Add cabbage and cook for 4-5 mins, until soft. Deglaze pan with wine and simmer for 5 mins, until reduced. Add stock and jus and simmer for 10 mins to reduce by half again. Stir through parsley and season to taste.

Increase oven to 210ºC or 190ºC fan-forced. Cut pork belly into 4 pieces. Line a heavy-based pan with baking paper and add pork, skin-side down. Bake for 15 mins or until skin is brown and crisp.

To serve, divide cabbage between 4 deep plates and crumble over the pancetta. Top with pork, skin-side up, and drizzle with juices.
— *The Dolphin Hotel*

chicken liver pâté

Serves 6 | Prep 30 mins | Soaking overnight | Cooking 10 mins
Setting 2 hrs

1kg chicken livers
350ml milk
125g butter
2 tbsp vegetable oil
Salt & pepper
¼ cup brandy
4 eschalots (French shallots), finely chopped
2 garlic cloves, chopped
½ cup chopped thyme leaves
½ cup pouring cream
100ml port
1½ gelatine leaves
36 green peppercorns

Trim and clean livers. Place in a bowl with milk and soak overnight. Drain livers very well in colander.

Dice butter and allow to soften. Heat a non-stick pan on high. Season livers and sauté in oil for 2-3 mins each side, until cooked to medium. Transfer to a food processor. Deglaze pan with brandy. Pour brandy over the livers.

Reduce heat to medium and, in same pan, melt 1 tsp of the butter. Sauté eschalots, garlic and thyme for 3-5 mins, until soft but not coloured. Add to livers with rest of softened butter and process until smooth. Add cream, season to taste and pulse until combined.

Fill 6 x ½ cup ramekins with pâté and place in fridge to cool rapidly.

Meanwhile, heat port in a small saucepan on low, until just simmering. Soak gelatine in cold water until soft. Drain and add to port, stirring until gelatine dissolves. Allow to cool to room temperature then spoon on top of pâté. Sprinkle with peppercorns and refrigerate for 2 hrs, until set. — *The Winery By Gazebo*

Notes: Do not overcook or undercook the livers.

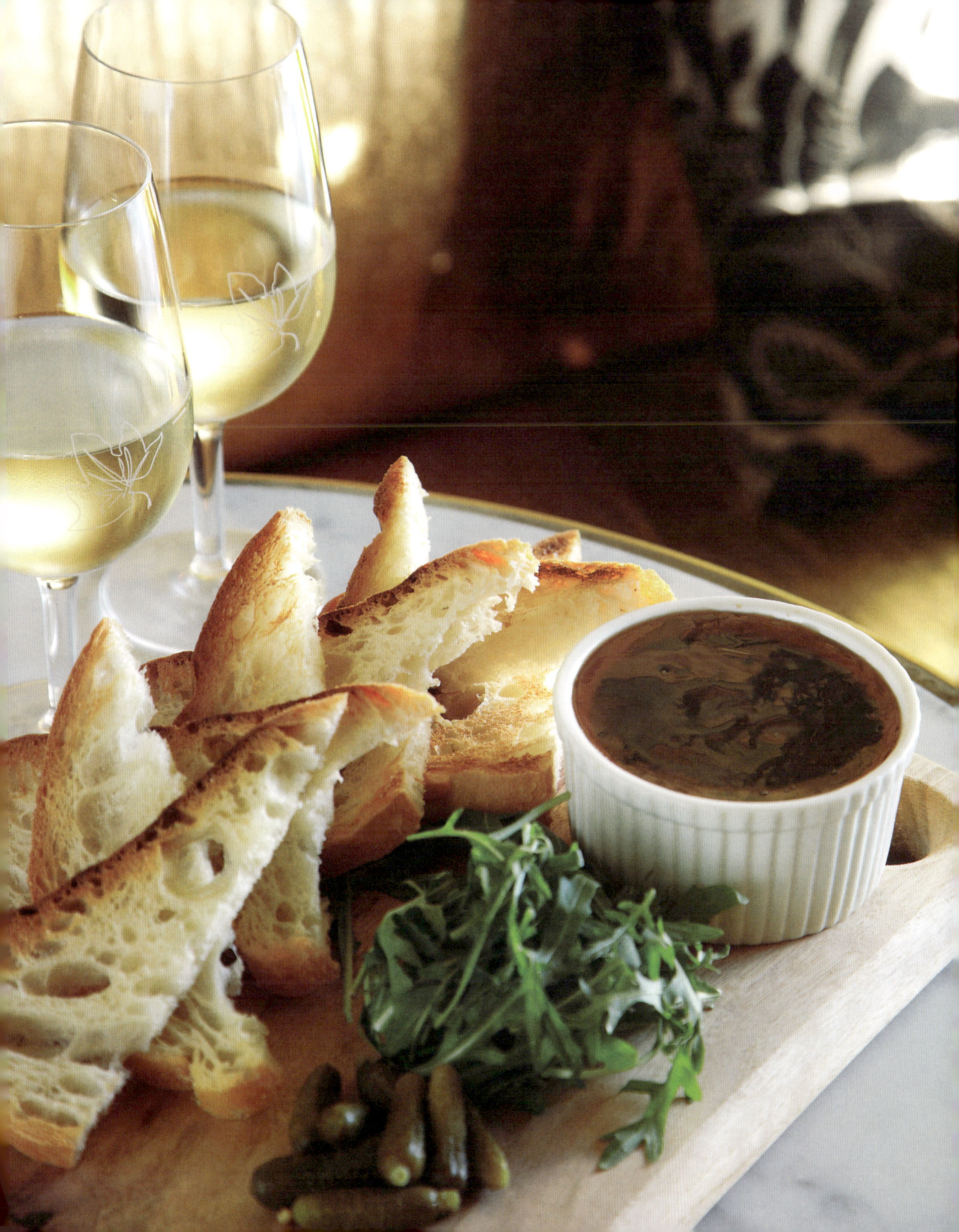

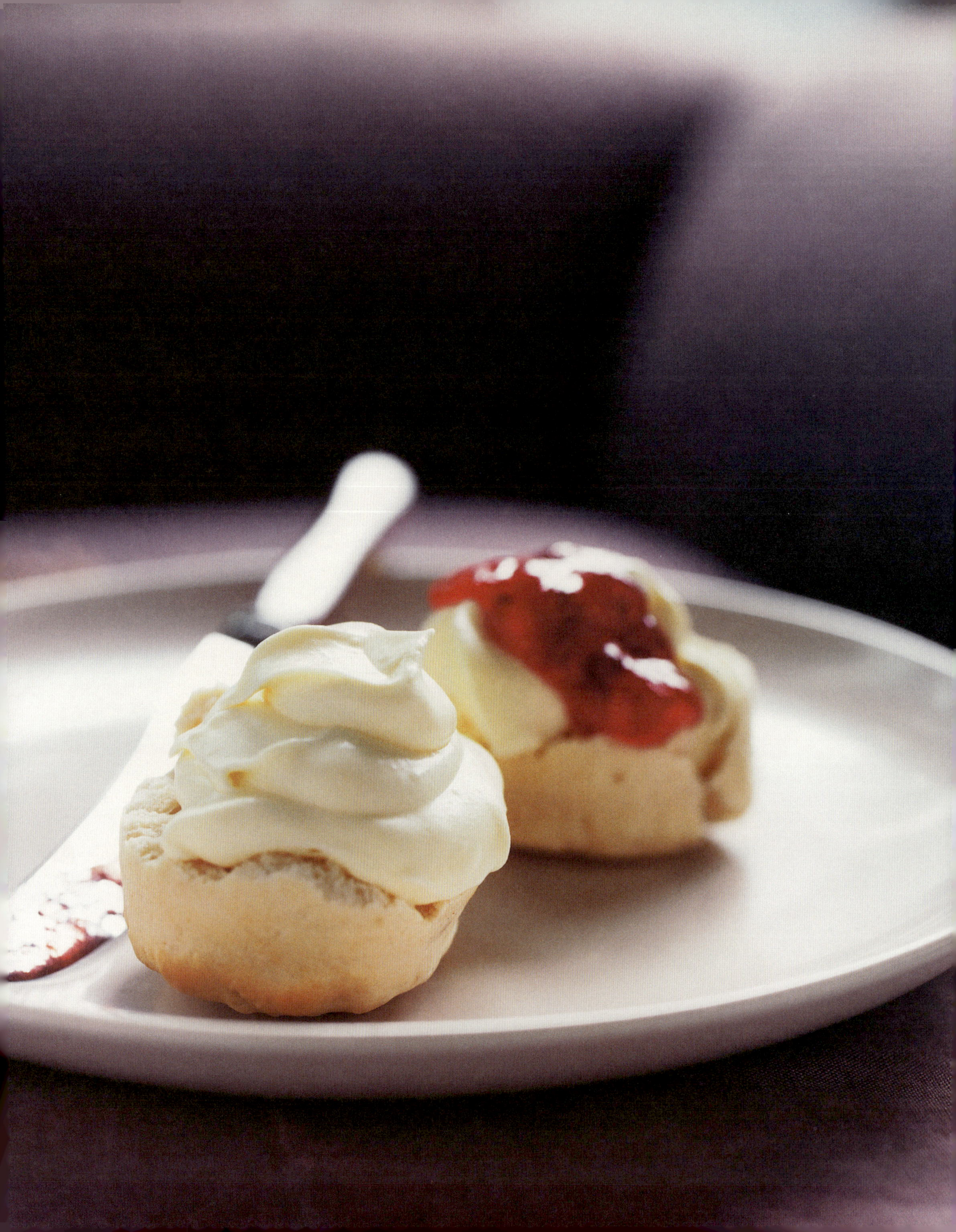

bill granger's simple scones

Makes 8 | Prep 20 mins | Cooking 8-10 mins

1 tbsp icing sugar
2½ cups plain flour
1½ tsp baking powder
Pinch salt
1 cup milk
30g butter, melted
Jam, to serve
Whipped cream, to serve

Preheat oven to 200ºC and grease a baking tray. Sift icing sugar, flour, baking powder and salt into a large bowl. Add milk and butter and stir with a knife to combine. Knead quickly and lightly until smooth and then press out onto a floured surface.

Use a glass to cut out rounds roughly 5cm diameter and 3cm deep and place close together on greased baking tray. Gather scraps together, lightly knead again, then cut out more rounds. Bake for 8-10 mins, until puffed and golden.

To serve, top with jam and lightly whipped cream.

– bills

vietnamese char-grilled beef skewers

Serves 4-6 | Prep 20 mins | Chill 2 hrs | Cooking 10 mins

600g sirloin steak, cut into 2cm cubes
10-12 okra, cut in half
1 red onion, peeled, cut into 2cm squares
1 can pineapple slices (save juice), cut into pieces
Watercress or green coral lettuce
Fresh Asian herbs (Vietnamese mint, Thai basil, perilla)
Fresh rice vermicelli noodles (optional)

MARINADE
1 stalk lemongrass, finely chopped
3 cloves garlic, crushed
1 birdseye chilli (optional), finely chopped
3 tbsp raw sugar
2 tbsp honey
2 tbsp sesame oil or olive oil
2 tbsp oyster sauce
¼ cup fish sauce
¼ cup mushroom soy sauce (from Asian grocers)
¼ cup pineapple juice (saved from tin of pineapple slices)
1 tbsp cracked black pepper

DIPPING SAUCE
¼ cup lime juice, or to taste
1 tsp raw sugar
1 tbsp salt
1 tsp cracked black pepper

GARNISH
Grated lime zest
Toasted sesame seeds

For the marinade, in a large bowl mix lemongrass, garlic, chilli, sugar, honey, oil, sauces, pineapple juice and pepper. Add steak and mix well. Cover and refrigerate for 2 hrs. Soak skewers in water for 15 mins.

To prepare the dipping sauce, in a small bowl mix juice, sugar, salt and pepper. Stir. Garnish with zest.

Thread steak cubes, okra, onion and pineapple onto skewers. Grill on high, direct heat for 2 mins or until medium-rare.

To serve, layer plates with a bed of watercress or coral lettuce. Place skewers on top and sprinkle with sesame seeds to garnish. Serve with dipping sauce and fresh Asian herbs and cooked vermicelli noodles, if desired.
— Xage

goi cuon (soft rice paper rolls with prawns & pork)

Makes 12 rolls | Prep 10 mins | Cooking 20 mins

80g dried rice vermicelli noodles (Golden Swallow brand)
18 x 22cm sheets rice paper
18 cooked small prawns, peeled, halved lengthways
120g cooked pork neck, finely sliced
1 cup shredded iceberg lettuce
1 bunch perilla leaf (available from Asian grocers)
1 bunch mint
1 bunch garlic chives
3 tsp roasted peanuts, crushed
1 birdseye chilli, thinly sliced

NUOC TUONG NGOC – HOISIN DIPPING SAUCE
½ cup hoisin sauce
1½ tbsp white vinegar
½ cup milk

Cook vermicelli in a saucepan of boiling water for 5 mins. Turn off heat and allow noodles to stand in water for a further 5 mins. Drain and rinse under cold water. Drain again and set aside for 30 mins to dry. NB: Try to have vermicelli cooked and strained for at least 30 mins prior to rolling. This allows the noodles to dry off a little and cling together.

To assemble rolls, cut 6 rounds of rice paper in half. Fill a large bowl with warm water and dip 1 whole sheet of rice paper in water then lay it on a flat surface. Dip a half-sheet of rice paper in water and lay it vertically in middle of round sheet. This will strengthen the roll. Place 3 pieces of prawn, horizontally, in middle of rice paper, 4cm from top. Below prawns, place a little pork, lettuce, perilla leaves, mint and vermicelli.

Fold sides into centre over filling, then roll up from bottom to enclose filling tightly, placing 2 garlic chives in towards the end, so they stick out at one end. Repeat with remaining rice paper and filling.

To make the *nuoc tuong ngoc* (hoisin dipping sauce), combine hoisin and vinegar in a saucepan and heat on medium. Stir in milk and heat until just at boiling point. Set aside to cool.

To serve, top rolls with peanuts and chilli and serve with dipping sauce on side.
— Red Lantern

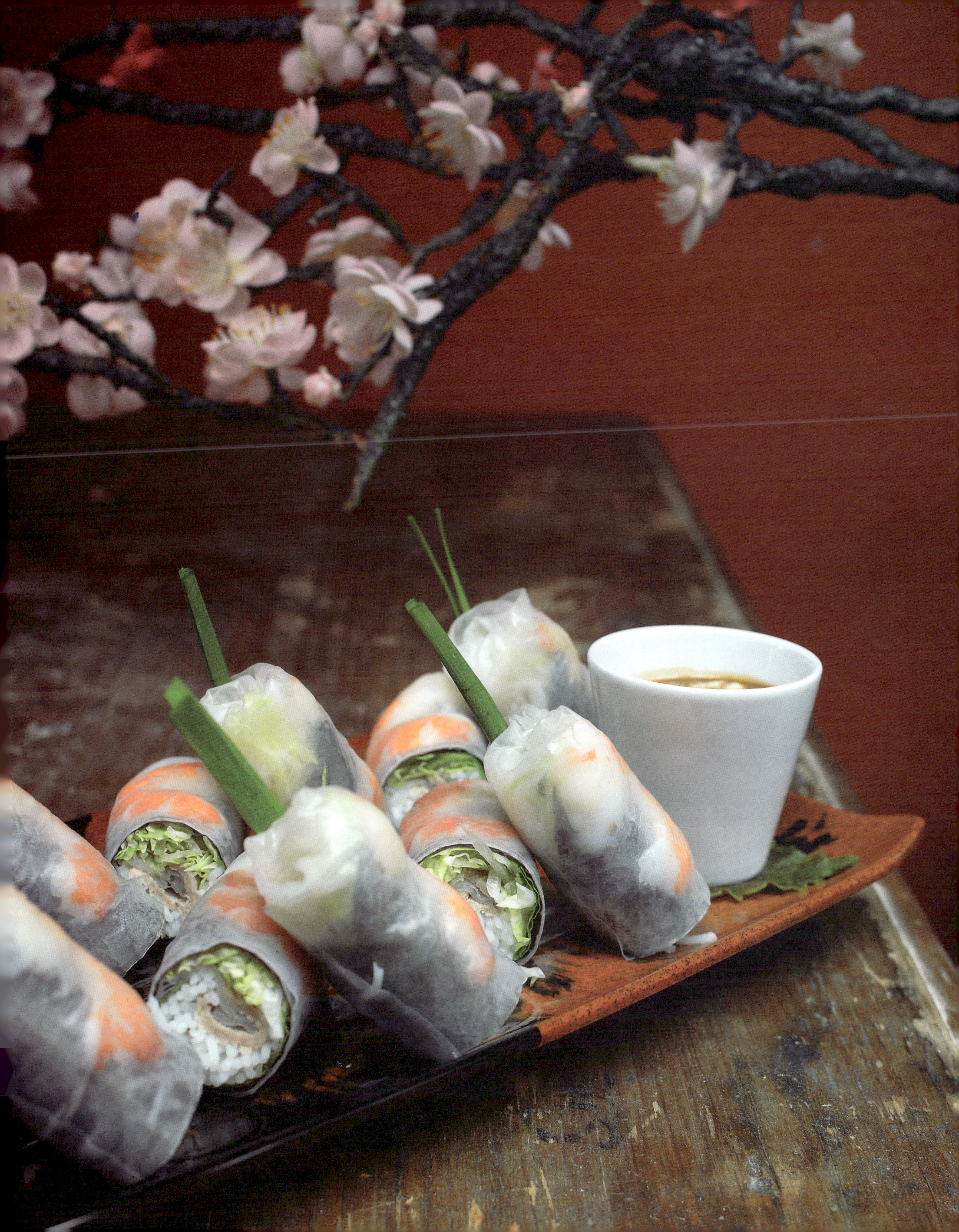

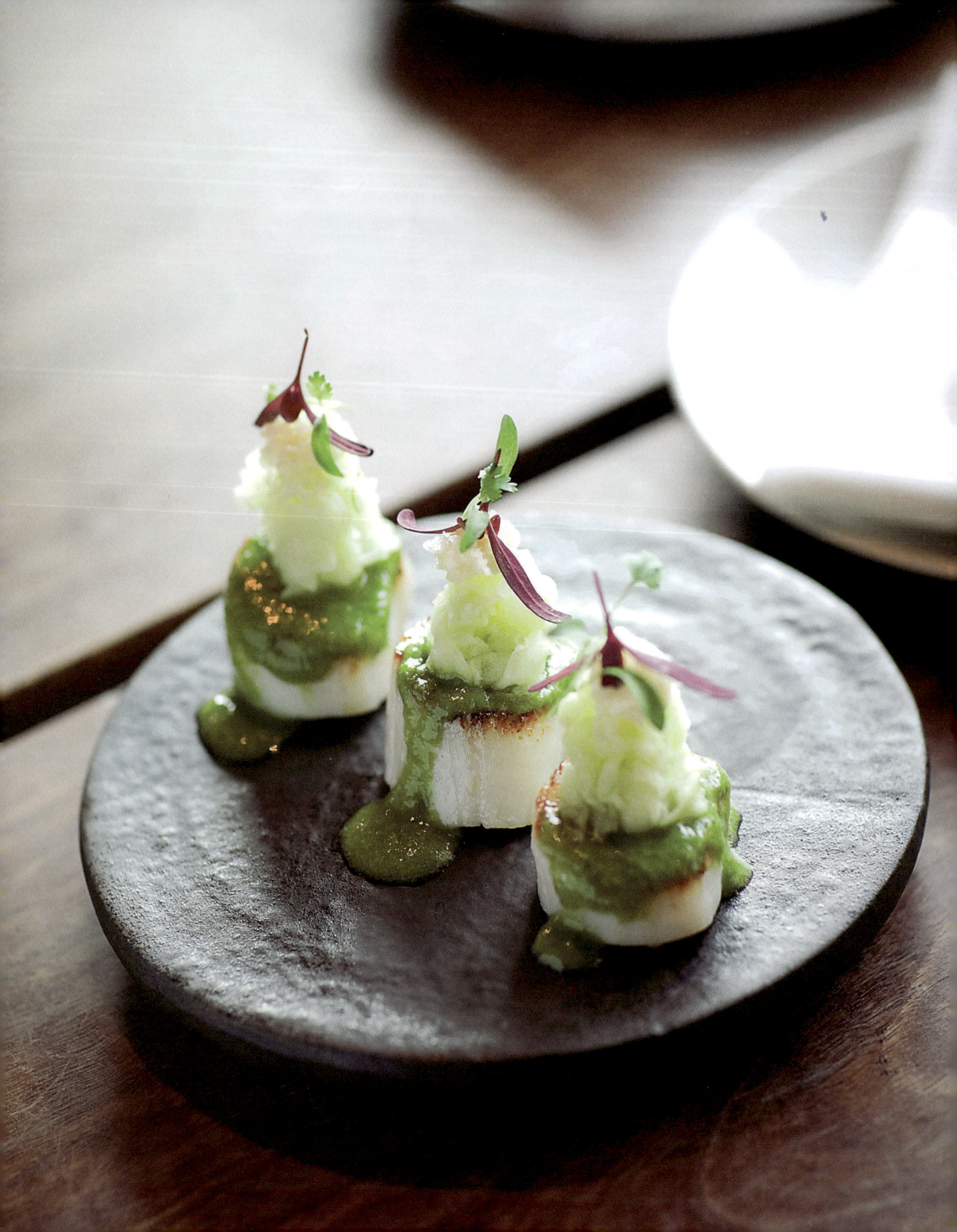

scallops with jalapeño sauce

Serves 4 | Prep 30 mins | Soaking 30 mins | Cooking 5 mins

12 scallops, roe removed
1 tbsp olive oil
Garlic mayonnaise, micro herbs,
   panko (Japanese breadcrumbs) to serve
APPLE AMAZU
5 Granny Smith apples
Salt
1 cup apple juice
1 cup sushi vinegar
JALAPEÑO SAUCE
60g jalapeño chillies
1 tsp chopped ginger
1 tsp chopped garlic
100ml rice vinegar
100ml mirin
100ml pomace olive oil or vegetable oil
1½ tbsp chopped spring onion
1 tbsp coriander leaves

First make the apple *amazu*. Peel, core and quarter apples. Finely slice, lengthways, and place in a bowl of salted water. Set aside for 30 mins, until apples have softened slightly. Drain and rinse off salt under running water. Drain again. Combine apple juice and sushi vinegar in a large bowl. Add apple and toss to combine. Refrigerate until ready to serve.

To make the jalapeño sauce, place jalapeño, ginger, garlic, vinegar and mirin in a food processor or small spice blender. Blend until smooth and paste-like. Add oil, onion and coriander and pulse until finely chopped and well combined. Season to taste and set aside.

Lightly oil and season scallops. Preheat a chargrill, barbecue or large frypan on high. Cook scallops for 1-2 mins, each side, until seared.

To serve, place scallops on plates and drizzle with jalapeño sauce. Top with 1 tbsp pickled apple (squeezing excess liquid out first), a little garlic mayonnaise, micro herbs and a sprinkle of *panko*.

Notes: *Panko*, or Japanese breadcrumbs, are available from Asian sections of supermarkets.   – *Toko*

osso bucco

Serves 6 | Prep 1 hr | Cooking 2 hrs 20 mins

100g brown onion, diced
150g carrots, diced
50g celery, diced
40g butter
1 garlic clove, chopped
Rind of ½ a lemon (no pith)
100ml vegetable oil
2kg veal osso bucco
50g plain flour, for dusting
200ml white wine
200ml chicken stock
450g can peeled tomatoes, chopped, with juice
1 tsp fresh thyme leaves
1 bay leaf
A few parsley stalks
2 tsp sea salt
1 tsp freshly ground black pepper
100g orzo pasta
GREMOLATA
1 tbsp parsley, chopped
1 tsp garlic, finely chopped
1 tsp lemon zest, grated

In a heavy-based casserole, over medium heat, cook onion, carrot, celery and butter for 6-7 mins. Add garlic and lemon peel and cook for another 2-3 mins until vegetables soften, then remove from heat.

Add vegetable oil to a large frypan and turn heat to medium-high. Turn shanks in flour and shake to remove excess. Place shanks in frypan and brown all over in hot oil. Remove and place on top of sweated vegetables in saucepan. Drain oil from frypan and add wine to deglaze pan. Reduce wine over medium heat. Pour pan juices over shanks.

Preheat oven to 180°C. Add stock to frypan, bring to boil and pour over shanks. Add tomatoes, thyme, bay leaves, parsley, salt and pepper. The liquid should come ⅔ of the way up the shanks.

Bring liquid to a simmer, cover tightly and place in oven. Cook for about 2 hrs (turn and baste shanks every 20 mins) until meat is tender and falls off bone.

Remove shanks. Sauce should be dense and creamy. Remove meat from bones and return it to sauce. Add orzo pasta and return dish to oven for 10 mins or until pasta is cooked.

To serve, divide among bowls and top with gremolata.

Notes: Meat can be left on the shanks if desired, and served accordingly.

— The Beresford Hotel

Sparkle Cupcakery
132 Foveaux Street, Surry Hills,
NSW 2010 | T 02 9361 0690
celebrate@sparklecupcakery.com.au
www.sparklecupcakery.com.au

Photo: Toby Burrows

crown street eats

Longrain
85 Commonwealth Street,
Surry Hills, NSW 2010
T 02 9280 2888 | www.longrain.com
Lunch, dinner, cocktails
& bar food 7 days

Photo: Tim Robinson

Photo: Tim Robinson

Bourke Street Bakery
633 Bourke Street, Surry Hills,
NSW 2010 | T 9699 1011
| E info@bourkestreetbakery.com.au
Mon to Fri 7am-6pm; Sat & Sun 8am-5pm

Photo: Tim Robinson

crown street eats

Gaslight Inn
278 Crown Street, Darlinghurst, NSW 2010 | T 02 9360 6746
gaslightinnhotel@aol.com | Fine lager, friendly service

Photo: Michael Wee

directory

The cafes, restaurants, pubs & food suppliers of CROWN STREET, SURRY HILLS, NSW 2010

a **Agave Restaurante Mexicano**
Shop 2, 410 Crown Street
(02) 9326 9072

Alchemy Cafe Restaurant
572 Crown Street
(02) 9699 2455

Aree's
413 Crown Street
(02) 9698 5522

Azafran Tapas
555 Crown Street
(02) 9319 2976

b **Bay Hong Vietnamese Restaurant**
294 Crown Street
(02) 9360 8688
www.bayhong.com.au

Bills Surry Hills
359 Crown Street,
(02) 9360 4762
www.bills.com.au

Billy's Convenience Store
Level 1, 418 Crown Street
(02) 9331 5504

Billy Kwong
Shop 3, 355 Crown Street
(02) 9332 3300
www.kyliekwong.org

Bismillah Food Indian Cuisine
581 Crown Street
(02) 9698 6895

Bird Cow Fish
Shops 4 & 5,
500 Crown Street
(02) 9380 4090
www.birdcowfish.com.au

Blue Wok
666 Crown Street
(02) 9699 2829

c **Cafe Mint**
579 Crown Street
(02) 9319 0848
www.cafemint.com.au

Cortile Pizza
265 Crown Street
(02) 9356 2888
www.cortilepizza.com.au

Cossie's Cafe Restaurant
638a Crown Street
(02) 9699 8482

Crown Street Grocer
Shop 1, 365 Crown Street
(02) 8668 5326

Crust Gourmet Pizza Bar
610 Crown Street
(02) 9698 9668
www.crust.com.au

d **Dimitris Pizza**
324 Crown Street
(02) 9361 6068

Essenza Italian
560 Crown Street
(02) 9698 8907
www.essenzaitalian.com.au

e **Fifi Foveaux's**
428 Crown Street
(02) 9380 6881

f **Four Ate Five**
485 Crown Street
(02) 9698 6485
www.fouratefive.com

Gaslight Hotel
278 Crown Street
(02) 9360 6746

g **Gnome Espresso**
536 Crown Street
(02) 9332 3191

Grill'd Healthy Burgers
241 Crown Street,
Darlinghurst.
www.grilld.com.au

h **Hudson Meats**
410 Crown Street
(02) 9332 4454
www.hudsonmeats.com.au

i **Icafe & Restaurant**
Shop 2, 265 Crown Street
(02) 9356 2200

In the Mood for Thai, Surry Hills
379 Crown Street
(02) 9380 8097
www.thairiffic.com.au

k **Kawa**
348a Crown Street
(02) 9331 6811

Koko's Pizza Pasta Ribs
415 Crown Street
(02) 9318 0044
www.kokospizza.com

l **Lemon Cafe**
393 Crown Street
(02) 9380 5242

Low 302
302 Crown Street
(02) 9368 1548
www.low302.com.au

m **Mad Mex – Fresh Mexican Grill**
2/241 Crown Street
(02) 9331 7788
www.madmex.com.au

Maddy's Café Patisserie
612 Crown Street
(02) 9690 2940
www.maddys.com.au

Mahjong Room
312 Crown Street
(02) 9361 3985
www.mahjongroom.com.au

Maloneys Grocer
Shop 4, 490 Crown Street
(02) 9331 3811; www.
maloneysgrocer.com.au

Marque
Shop 4, 355 Crown Street
(02) 9332 2225; www.
marquerestaurant.com.au

Mashallah Indian Cuisine
624 Crown Street
(02) 9699 6366

Matsuri Japanese Restaurant & Takeaway
614-618 Crown Street
(02) 9690 1366

MFC Supermarket
435 Crown Street
(02) 9319 5211

Mille Vini
397 Crown Street
(02) 9357 3366

Monkey Magic
Shop 3, 410 Crown Street
(02) 9358 4444
www.monkeymagic.com.au

n **Nandos**
535 Crown Street
(02) 9698 0138
www.nandos.com.au

Nua Exotic Thai
Shop 3, 265 Crown Street
(02) 8354 0123
www.nuathai.com.au

o **O Organic Cafe**
487 Crown Street
(02) 9319 4009
www.organicproduce.com.au

p **Pazzo**
583 Crown Street
(02) 9319 4387; www.
pazzorestaurant.com.au

Pieno
Shop 11, 285a Crown Street
(02) 8354 1303

Pizza e Birra
Shop 1, 500 Crown Street
(02) 9332 2510

Players, Crown Hotel
589 Crown Street
(02) 9699 3460
www.crownhotel.com.au

r **Red Lantern**
545 Crown Street
(02) 9698 4355
www.redlantern.com.au

Room 9
289 Crown Street
(02) 9331 2433
www.citycrownmotel.com.au

s **St Mina's Fruit & Vegetable Wholesale**
563 Crown Street
(02) 9699 3098

Style Dish Thai
395 Crown Street
(02) 9331 0859

Surry Hills Fine Wines
557 Crown Street
(02) 8399 2199

Tabou
527 Crown Street
(02) 9319 5682
www.tabourestaurant.com.au

Tandoori 567
567 Crown Street
(02) 9699 4535

Terrace Thai on Crown
577 Crown Street
(02) 9318 1263

Thanh Long
622 Crown Street
(02) 9319 3206
www.thanhlongoncrown.com

The Bentley Restaurant and Bar
320 Crown Street
(02) 9332 2344
www.thebentley.com.au

The Clock Hotel
470 Crown Street
(02) 9331 5333
www.clockhotel.com.au

The Clove Indian Eatery
249 Crown Street
(02) 9361 0980
www.theclove.com.au

The Dolphin Hotel
412 Crown Street
(02) 9331 4800
www.dolphinhotel.com.au

The Goods Organic
253 Crown Street
(02) 9357 6690

The Nepalese Kitchen
481 Crown Street
(02) 9319 4264

The Original Maltese Cafe
310 Crown Street
(02) 9361 6942

The White Horse
381-385 Crown Street
(02) 8333 9999
www.thewhitehorse.com.au

The Winery by Gazebo
285a Crown Street
(02) 9331 0833
www.thegazebos.com.au

Thomas Dux Grocer
285a Crown Street
(02) 8354 0388
www.thomasdux.com.au

Thyme on Crown
479 Crown Street
(02) 9690 2244

Toko Restaurant & Bar
490 Crown Street
(02) 9357 6100
www.toko.com.au

Tokonoma Shochu Bar & Lounge
490 Crown Street
(02) 9357 6100

Trinity Bar & Bistro
505 Crown Street
(02) 9319 6802
www.trinitybar.com.au

Triple Shot Café
533 Crown Street
(02) 9319 6605

Turkish Delight Pide & Kebab
662 Crown Street

Wood & Stone
559 Crown Street
(02) 9319 0757

Xage Vietnamese
333 Crown Street
(02) 9332 3344
www.xage.com.au

Yai
628 Crown Street
(02) 9698 2097
www.yai.com.au

Yok Yor
Shop 3, 241 Crown Street
(02) 9380 8860

Yulli's
417 Crown Street
(02) 9319 6609
www.yullis.com.au

Zeno Restaurant & Pizza
389 Crown Street
(02) 9331 5040

and...

IN THE NEIGHBOURHOOD

Assiette
48 Albion Street, Surry Hills
(02) 9212 7979; www.restaurantassiette.com.au

Berta
17-19 Alberta Street,
Sydney. (02) 9264 6133

Bistrode
478 Bourke Street, Surry Hills. (02) 9380 7333
www.bistrode.com

Bodega
216 Commonwealth Street,
Surry Hills. (02) 9212 7766
www.bodegatapas.com

Boteco
421 Cleveland Street,
Surry Hills. (02) 9318 2993
www.boteco.com.au

Bourke Street Bakery
633 Bourke Street,
Surry Hills. (02) 9699 1011

Cafe Zoe
688 Bourke Street,
Surry Hills. (02) 8399 0940

Chu Bay
312a Bourke Street,
Darlinghurst. (02) 9331 3386

Erciyes Turkish Restaurant
409 Cleveland Street,
Redfern. (02) 9319 1309

Green Chillies Thai
13 Oxford Street,
Darlinghurst. (02) 9361 3717

Il Baretto
496 Bourke Street,
Surry Hills. (02) 9361 6163

La Sala
23 Foster Street, Surry Hills.
(02) 9281 3352

Longrain
85 Commonwealth Street,
Surry Hills. (02) 9280 2888
www.longrain.com.au

Pizza Mario
9/417-421 Bourke Street,
Surry Hills. (02) 9332 3633
www.pizzamario.com.au

Spice I Am
88 Wentworth Avenue,
Surry Hills. (02) 9280 0928
www.spiceiam.com

Strangers With Candy
96 Kepos Street,
Redfern. (02) 9698 6000

Sushi Suma
421 Cleveland Street,
Surry Hills. (02) 9698 8873
www.sushisuma.com

The Battery
St Margarets, Shop 15,
425 Bourke Street,
Surry Hills. (02) 9357 3000
www.thebattery.com.au

The Beresford
354 Bourke Street,
Surry Hills. (02) 9280 2888
www.theberesford.com.au

The Book Kitchen
255 Devonshire Street,
Surry Hills. (02) 9310 1003
www.thebookkitchen.com.au

Tumnak Thai
101 Oxford Street,
Darlinghurst. (02) 9331 3364
www.tumnakthai.com.au

Uchi Lounge
15 Brisbane Street,
Surry Hills. (02) 9261 3524
www.uchilounge.com.au

Vini
Shop 3, 118 Devonshire Street, Surry Hills.
(02) 9698 5131
www.vini.com.au

Wafu
460 Cleveland Street,
Surry Hills. (02) 9319 1880

Woolworths St Margarets
413-417 Bourke Street,
Surry Hills. (02) 9326 0100

Zensation Tea House
656 Bourke Street,
Redfern. (02) 9319 2788
www.zensation.com.au

Three cheers for the testers!

BACK ROW: Margaret Cox, Heather Laurie & Rowan, Rebecca Ritchie, Georgia Hawkins, Fiona Macneall, Amanda Lintott, Amy Burrows, Briony Schofield.
MIDDLE ROW: Lucy, Georgia & Matthew Mather, Nia McAneney, Terina Stibbard, Leeanne Lightfoot, Helen Bouropoulos, Sally Chesher, Emma Rees-Raaijmakers with Izaak, baby Adela & Freja.
DOWN THE FRONT: Ella Eizenberg, Lara Schofield, Olivia Burrows, Sarah MacMaster with Tika, Hugh & Jessica, Helen Biggs & baby Noah, Tracy Hausler with Liam & Anna.
MISSING IN ACTION: Louise Bickle, Mrs Bickle, Trent Chapman, Katrina Cook, Michael Eizenberg, Michelle Findlay, Kate Hannaford, Lesley Holden, Analisa Kirby, Maria Leonardis, Mrs Macneall, Gregan McMahon, Bronwyn Shelsher, Henrie Stride.

PHOTO: MICHAEL WEE

thank you

thank you to the mums and dads, grandparents, children, teachers, cafes, restaurants, grocers, pubs, businesses and other generous folk for your belief in and support of this project. We are ever grateful to you, and to the long list of people below for your advice and assistance:

Photography: Michael Wee (Brunch, Lunch, Dinner and Soups, Salads, Sides, ads, streetlife); Toby Burrows (Cake Stall, Eats, ads); Michael Fotoulis (Eats, ads and streetlife); Andre Martin (Dessert, Celebration); Paul McMahon (Cake Stall); Tim Robinson (Eats, ads and street life); John Colette (Celebration); Petrina Tinslay (Bill's scones image). Shao Tren (school, students, teachers, streetlife); Mr Robb (students); David Iacono (students, school); Frankie Te Rangatahi Taniora (students, streetlife); Katrina Kritikaksis (streetlife); Lesley Holden (streetlife, ads); Fiona Macneall (streetlife)

Photography assistant: Mitch Hay for Tim Robinson

Production: Louise Bickle; Amy Burrows for Toby Burrows
Shoot chefs/home economists: Sharon Kennedy (Lunch and Dinner); Kim Meredith (Celebration); Elizabeth Sharaq (Soups, Salads, Sides); Jane Strode (Brunch and Dessert)
Ably supported by: Margaret Bickle (Celebration); Alexa Clayton-Jones (Celebration); Nia McAneney (Soups, Salads, Sides and Celebration); Fiona Macneall (Brunch, Dessert and Soups, Salads, Sides); Briony Schofield (Brunch); Sandra Toi (Soups, Salads, Sides).
Food prep assistants: Margaret Cox (Cake Stall); Annie Paris (Cake Stall); Nia McAneney (Soups, Salads, Sides and Celebration)

Styling assistant: Annie Paris (Cakestall and Eats)
Hand model: Eloise Gibson (Soups, Salads, Sides)

Props: Chee Soon & Fitzgerald; Ici et Là; Major & Tom; Mrs Red and Sons; Mud Australia; No Chintz Textiles & Soft Furnishings; Jean-Claude Wane

Art & production:
Digital prepress & production: Jorgen Jansson
Illustrations: Lucas S. Noble – Year 4/5P
Calligraphy: Raymond Leung

Financial support:
City of Sydney Council;
Westpac Bank, Surry Hills

IT: John Couani, Acme Computer

Website:
Andy Maynard
www.yeahdesign.com.au

Sage advice: Pamela Clark, Susan Tomnay, Victoria Jefferys, Elizabeth Hooper – ACP Books; Rob Bosschieter and Simon Kenny – Northern Beaches Cooks; Lesley O'Brien; Henrie Stride; Lynn Lewis – Murdoch Books; Julie Robb – Banki Haddock Fiora Lawyers; Bilkay Kitapli – Turkish translation; Victoria Moxey – Urban Walkabout; Peter – Christopher's Cake Shop

Locations:
Lesley and Jack Holden (Lunch and Dinner)
Stephen Prodes and Louise Bickle (Brunch and Dessert)
Jason Downing and Amanda Lintott (Celebration)
Original Finish (Soups, Salads, Sides)

Recipe wrangling: Fiona Macneall, Briony Schofield
Recipe editing: Mandy Sinclair **Indexing:** Jo Rudd
Guest testers: Betty Baboujon, Amy Lees, Tamarah Pienaar, Vanessa Walker

Proofreaders: Gail Darcy, Louise and Richard Kirwan, Helen Biggs, Trent Chapman

Copyright:
We thank the following people and publishers for permission to reprint recipes: Denise Smart's Apple Crumble Sundae: *Cookbook For Girls*, Penguin Books/Dorling Kindersley; Sally Wise's Rhubarb Sparkling: *A Year In A Bottle*, ABC Books – with permission from HarperCollins Publishers Australia; *Australian Women's Weekly* cookbook recipes: Salt & Pepper Tofu with Chilli Lime Dressing, and Lemon-Crusted Teacake, reproduced with permission from ACP Books. Sue Fairley-Cunningham for permission to print an adaptation of her late mum Joan Campbell's baked ham recipe; Petrina Tinslay for Bill Granger's scones pic.

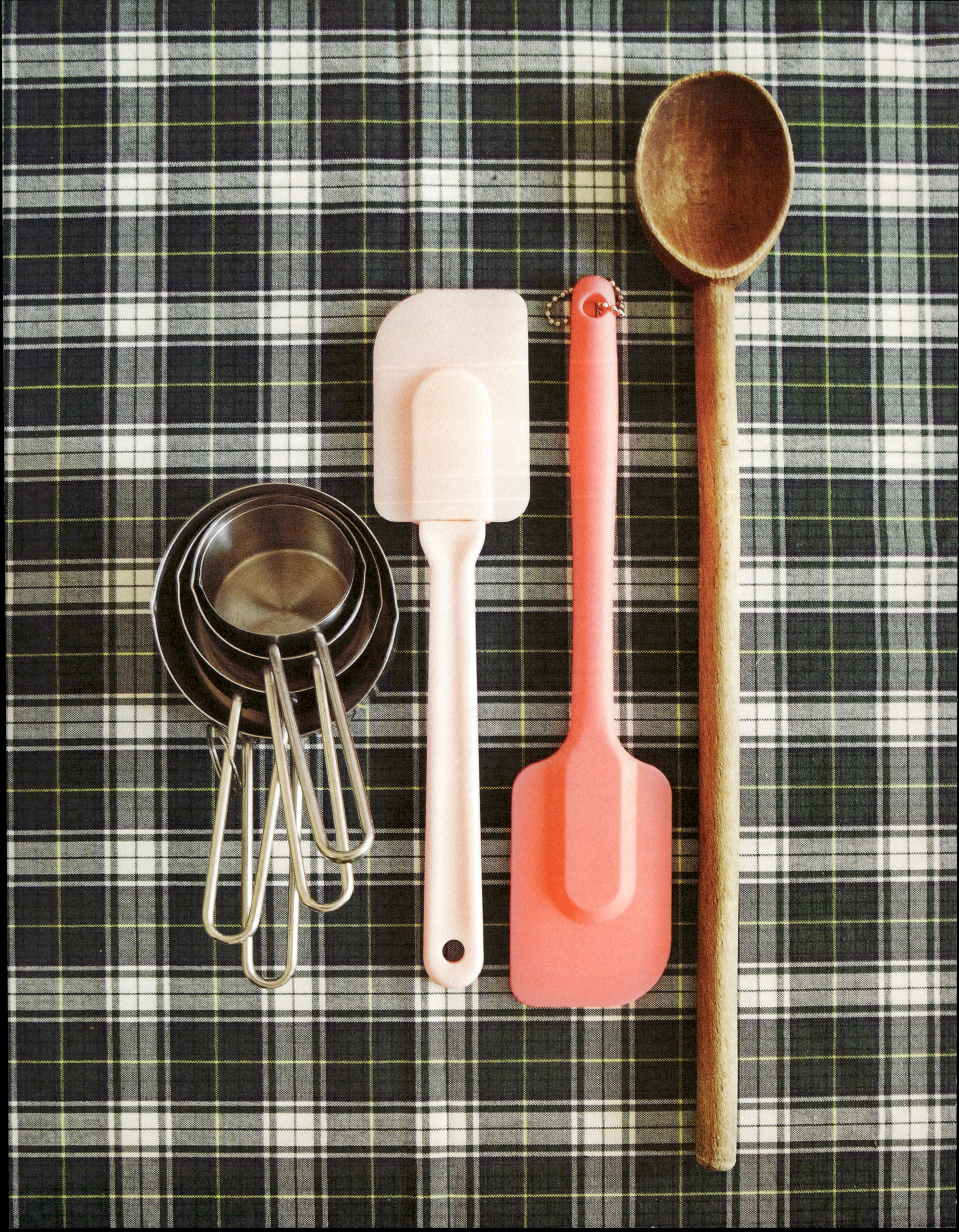

1 x 🍵 =

1 tsp = 5ml
1 tbsp = 20ml
1 cup = 250ml

Liquid Measures

30ml	1/8 cup
60ml	1/4 cup
80ml	1/3 cup
125ml	1/2 cup
180ml	3/4 cup
250ml	1 cup

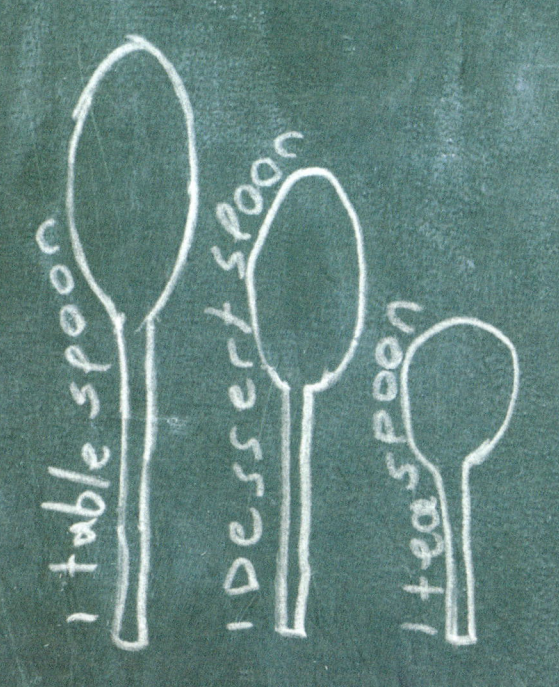

1 tablespoon · 1 dessert spoon · 1 teaspoon

Oven Temperatures

Celsius	Farenheit	Gas Mark	Description
105°	225F	1/4	Very Cool
120°	250F	1/2	
130°	275F	1	Cool
150°	300F	2	
165°	325F	3	Very Moderate
180°	350F	4	Moderate
190°	375F	5	
200°	400F	6	Moderately Hot
220°	425F	7	Hot
230°	450F	8	
245°	475F	9	Very Hot

index

A
aloo gobi 82
appeltaart 100
apple crumble sundae 93
Argentinian marinating sauce 53
Asian lamb salad 83
Aunt Rosie's no-cook coconut ice 118
Aunty Marina's *faki* 74

B
bacon & egg pies, winner 13
baked beans with chorizo & eggs 14
bananas
    banana loaf with cinnamon butter 168
    best banana bread ever 17
    chocolate & banana muffins 13
    Indonesian ladyfinger bananas in coconut sauce 97
Bangladeshi chicken curry 55
bánh xèo 33
beef
    beef, Stilton & Guinness pie with tomato chutney 31
    bulgogi grill 68
    Indian curry 67
    Korean BBQ 68
    Marie's Greek-style bolognese 65
    Mongolian 43
    ragù 51
    Vietnamese chargrilled skewers 173
beetroot & fetta salad 79
Beijing pie (Olympics fare) 48
berry dessert, simple 94
bill granger's simple scones 173
bircher muesli 20
biscuits *see* **cookies**
black chicken 50
blueberry griddle cakes 14
bolognese, Marie's Greek-style 65
bougatsa 95
Brazil's national cocktail 129
breads
    banana loaf with cinnamon butter 168
    best banana bread ever 17
    New Zealand Maori fried bread 74
    olive oil bread 158
    pizza dough 154
    Swiss bread 19
breakfast couscous 10
bruschetta, Crown Street Public School's garden club 36
bulgogi grill 68
butter chicken 62

C
caipirinha 129
cakes
    best-ever chocolate 122
    blueberry griddle 14
    carrot 123
    coconut 117
    Dutch ginger 124
    fig & pecan 106
    Grandma Melville's kiss 117
    hazelnut 120
    lemon-crusted teacake 119
    Lena's rum roll 138
    Marcia's apple chocolate 105
    moist orange 124
    Molly's Christmas 129
    pineapple fruit 118
    Sparkle's vanilla cupcakes 114
canard dans la cocotte 162
carrot cake 123
chefs' recipes
    baked lemon tart 88
    baked pineapple ham 133
    banana loaf with cinnamon butter 168
    bánh xèo (Vietnamese pancakes) 33
    bill granger's simple scones 173
    blueberry griddle cakes 14
    breakfast couscous 10
    canard dans la cocotte (duck casserole) 162
    chicken liver pâté 170
    crispy duck with chilli & plum sauce 161
    cured ocean trout with fennel & chestnuts 153
    fish & chips 154
    goi cuon (soft rice paper rolls with prawns & pork) 174
    Indian beef curry 67
    linguine with king prawns, zucchini & lemon 157
    Meg's organic minestrone 77
    Mongolian beef 43
    olive oil bread 158
    organic mushroom salad 150
    organic Thai-spiced chicken salad 84
    osso bucco 177
    pizza dough 154
    pesto & cherry tomato prawn pasta 34
    pork chop with fennel-seed crust, fennel & pear purée 133
    pumpkin ravioli with brown butter & sage 168
    scallops with jalapeno sauce 177
    scallops with jalapeño sauce 177
    Sparkle's vanilla cupcakes 114
    strawberry & pink Champagne soup with yoghurt pannacotta 164
    sweet & sticky chicken wings 48
    tiramisu roulade 167
    twice-cooked pork belly with braised cabbage & pancetta 170
    vanilla bavarois with toffee shards 138
    Vietnamese chargrilled beef skewers 174
Cherry Smith's pikelets 106
chicken
    Bangladeshi curry 55
    black 50
    butter 62
    flat roasted 58
    Malaysian-inspired curry 53
    nasi goreng 29
    organic Thai-spiced salad 84
    paella 46
    prosciutto-wrapped with polenta 57
    spicy Indonesian fried 56
    sweet & sticky wings 48
    liver pâté 170
chimichurri 53
Chinese apple pear drink 114
choc chip cookies, Pat Stride's 105
chocolate
    best-ever cake 122
    & banana muffins 13
    mousse 142
    Ma Stibbard's chocolate coconut slice 120
    Marcia's apple chocolate cake 105
    piping hot chocolate 10
    tiramisu roulade 167
Christmas cake, Molly's 129
Christmas pudding, Scottish 137
coconut
    Aunt Rosie's no-cook coconut ice 118
    coconut cake 117
    Ma Stibbard's chocolate coconut slice 120
    oaty coconut slice 123
cookies
    double gingernut biscuits 122
    Grandma Melville's kiss cakes 117
    Pat Stride's choc chip cookies 105
corn fritters 21
cracked wheat salad, Turkish 82
Crown Street Public School's garden club bruschetta 36
crunchy granola 16
curry
    Bangladeshi chicken 55
    dry potato & cauliflower 82
    Indian beef 67
    Malaysian-inspired chicken 53

D
desserts
    apple crumble sundae 93
    baked lemon tart 89
    black sticky rice 98
    chocolate mousse 142
    Dutch apple pie 100
    foolproof pav 90
    French rice pudding 132
    Greek custard & filo treat 95
    hokey pokey 98
    Indonesian ladyfinger bananas in coconut sauce 97
    Indonesian sweets 97
    lemon delicious 93
    rich vanilla ice-cream 94
    simple berry dessert 94
    strawberry & pink Champagne soup with yoghurt pannacotta 164
    tiramisu roulade 167
    vanilla bavarois with toffee shards 138
double gingernut biscuits 122
doughnuts, East African 17
drinks
    Brazil's national cocktail 129
    caipirinha 129
    Chinese apple pear drink 114
    fresh lemon cordial 114
    Middle Eastern lemonade 114
    mint tea 11
    piping hot chocolate 10
    rhubarb sparkling 129
dry potato & cauliflower curry 82
duck
    crispy duck with chilli & plum sauce 161
    duck casserole 162
Dutch apple pie 100
Dutch ginger cake 124

E
East African doughnuts 17
East African onion salad 84
East African pilaf 57
eggplant parmigiana 49
eggs
    baked beans with chorizo & eggs 14
    Mediterranean eggs 20
    traditional Greek red eggs for Easter 141
    winner bacon & egg pies 13

F
faki 74
fig & pecan cake 106
fig and prosciutto salad 78
fish
    cured ocean trout with fennel & chestnuts 153
    fish & chips 154
    gravlax crostini 134
    Greek baked fish 46
    Greek marinated fish 49
    salmon with soba noodles 31
    steamed fish with ginger & spring onion 26
flapjacks, Molly's 21
flat roasted chicken 58
foolproof pav 90
French rice pudding 132
fresh lemon cordial 114

crown street cooks

G
German cheesy noodles 62
goi cuon 174
Grandma Melville's kiss cakes 117
granola, crunchy 16
gravlax crostini 134
Greek baked fish 46
Greek baked lamb & pasta 132
Greek custard & filo treat 95
Greek lentil soup 74
Greek marinated fish 49
gruyère soufflés, twice-baked 142
guacamole from the Texas Hills 80

H
ham, baked pineapple 133
hazelnut cake 120
hokey pokey 98
homemade yoghurt 16

I
ice-cream, rich vanilla 94
Indian dry potato & cauliflower curry 82
Indian beef curry 67
Indonesian fried rice 29
Indonesian ladyfinger bananas in coconut sauce 97
Indonesian sweets 97
Italian meat sauce 51

J
Japanese clear soup 83
Japanese grill sauce 58

K
kachumbari 84
kaese spaetzle 62
kisir 82
kokkina avga 141
Korean BBQ 68
kue lapis sagu 97

L
lamb
    Asian salad 83
    Greek baked pasta 132
    tandoori cutlets with dahl 68
    winter casserole 55
lemon
    baked lemon tart 88
    fresh lemon cordial 114
    lemon delicious 93
    lemon-crusted tea cake 119
Lena's rum roll 138
linguine with king prawns, zucchini & lemon 157

M
Ma Stibbard's chocolate coconut slice 120
Malaysian-inspired chicken curry 53
mandazi 17
mango & prawn salad 79
Marcia's apple chocolate cake 105
Marie's Greek-style bolognese 65
marinating sauce, Argentinian 53
meat sauce, Italian 51
Mediterranean eggs 20
Meg's organic minestrone 77
Middle Eastern lemonade 114
minestrone, Meg's organic 77
mint tea 11
miso grill sauce, Japanese (for BBQ beef/chicken/pork) 58
Moist orange cake 124
Molly's Christmas cake 129
Molly's flapjacks 21
Mongolian beef 43
Moroccan orange salad 80
muesli, bircher 20
mui choy kau yuk 61

N
Nanna Patz's savoury tart 33
nasi goreng 29
New Zealand Maori fried bread 74
North African carrot salad 84

O
oaty coconut slice 123
olive oil bread 158
Oma's *gemberkoek* 124
organic mushroom salad 150
organic Thai-spiced chicken salad 84
osso bucco 178
oyster shooters 130

P
paella 46
pancakes, Vietnamese 33
pasta
    baked pasta & lamb 132
    linguine with king prawns, zucchini & lemon 157
    pesto & cherry tomato prawn pasta 34
    pumpkin ravioli with brown butter & sage 168
    spaghetti & meatballs 44
    spring pasta 26
Pat Stride's choc chip cookies 105
pear, goat's cheese & walnut salad 78
pesto & cherry tomato prawn pasta 34
pies
    beef, Stilton & Guinness pie with tomato chutney 31
    Beijing pie (Olympics fare) 48
    Greek custard & filo treat 95
    winner bacon & egg pies 13
pikau ya nyama 57
pikelets, Cherry Smith's 106
pineapple fruitcake 118
piping hot chocolate 10
pizza dough 154
pork
    chop with fennel-seed crust, fennel & pear purée 133
    slow-cooked Cantonese belly 61
    soft rice paper rolls with prawns & pork 174
    spaghetti & meatballs 44
    twice-cooked pork with braised cabbage & pancetta 170
potato scones, Scottish 18
prosciutto-wrapped chicken with polenta 57
psari marinato 49
psari plaki 46
pumpkin
    pumpkin ravioli with brown butter & sage 168
    roast pumpkin & pea risotto 56

R
ragù 51
red velvet sauce 65
rhubarb sparkling 129
rice
    black sticky rice 98
    East African pilaf 57
    French rice pudding 132
    paella 46
    roast pumpkin & pea risotto 56
    tofu & snow pea fried rice 34
roast tomato, red lentil & cumin soup 74

S
salads
    Asian lamb 83
    beetroot & fetta 79
    cracked wheat 82
    East African onion 84
    fig & prosciutto 78
    mango & prawn 79
    Moroccan orange 80
    North African carrot 84
    organic mushroom 150
    organic Thai-spiced chicken 84
    pear, goat's cheese & walnut 78
salmon with soba noodles 31
salt & pepper tofu with chilli lime dressing 29
sauces
    Italian meat 51
    Japanese miso grill 58
    red velvet 65
    spicy seafood dipping 79
savoury tart, Nanna Patz's 33
scallops with jalapeño sauce 177
Scottish Christmas pudding 137
Scottish potato scones 18
Scottish shortbread, traditional 119
seafood
    linguine with king prawns, zucchini & lemon 157
    mango & prawn salad 79
    Nanna Patz's savoury tart 33
    oyster shooters 130
    paella 46
    pesto & cherry tomato prawn pasta 34
    scallops with jalapeño sauce 177
    soft rice paper rolls with prawns & pork 174
    spicy dipping sauce 79
    see also fish
shortbread, traditional Scottish 119
soft rice paper rolls with prawns & pork 174
soufflés, twice-baked gruyère 142
soup
    Greek *faki* (lentil) 74
    Japanese clear 83
    Meg's organic minestrone 77
    roast tomato, red lentil & cumin 74
    strawberry & pink Champagne with yoghurt pannacotta 164
spaghetti & meatballs 44
Sparkle's vanilla cupcakes 114
sparkling rhubarb 129
spicy Indonesian fried chicken 56
spicy seafood dipping sauce 79
spring pasta 26
steamed fish with ginger & spring onion 26
stoff pisang 97
strawberry & pink Champagne soup with yoghurt pannacotta 164
sumashi-jiru 83
sweet & sticky chicken wings 48
Swiss bread 19

T
tandoori lamb cutlets with dahl 68
tattie scones 18
tea cake, lemon-crusted 119
teurgoule 132
Thai-spiced chicken salad, organic 84
tiramisu roulade 167
tofu
    salt & pepper tofu with chilli lime dressing 29
    tofu & snow pea fried rice 34
Turkish cracked wheat salad 82

V
vanilla bavarois with toffee shards 138
veal
    osso bucco 178
    spaghetti & meatballs 44
Vietnamese chargrilled beef skewers 173
Vietnamese pancakes 33

W
winner bacon & egg pie 13
winter lamb casserole 55

Y
Yiouvetsi 132
yoghurt
    homemade 16
    strawberry & pink Champagne soup with yoghurt pannacotta 164

Z
zopf 19

Published by Crown Street Cooks Pty Ltd
in 2010 as a fundraising project on behalf of
Crown Street Public School P&C

Publisher: Crown Street Cooks
356 Crown Street, Surry Hills, NSW 2010
Contact: Helen Bouropoulos
+ 61 2 9360 4187
E: crownstreetpublicschool@pandcaffiliate.org.au

Project director: Lesley Holden
Editor: Lisa Green
Art director: Andrea Healy
Production & styling: Louise Bickle
Recipe producer: Fiona Macneall
Sub-editor: John McDonald
Business manager: Helen Bouropoulos

Contributing photographers: Toby Burrows,
John Colette, Michael Fotoulis, Andre Martin,
Paul McMahon, Tim Robinson,
Petrina Tinslay, Shao Tren, Michael Wee

Illustrations © Lucas S. Noble
Calligraphy © Raymond Leung

Publication: Crown Street Cooks –
Food From the Heart of Surry Hills
Copyright © 2010
All rights reserved

ISBN 978-0-646-53692-7

All recipes included in this book are family favourites and have been edited for accuracy and clarity by the recipe editor. The use of these recipes is beyond the control of the authors and publisher who cannot take any responsibility for the results you may achieve or any consequences that may arise from your cooking. When preparing these recipes please take care when using sharp implements and hot cooking equipment. Be aware of all potential hazards. As a parent or carer, please be responsible in choosing the appropriateness of any recipe you cook with your children. Do not leave children unsupervised. The recipes contained in this publication have been contributed by members of the Crown Street Public School community and invited local chefs. **Crown Street Cooks** has made every effort to trace copyright holders and the publishers would like to hear from anyone who believes they have not been acknowledged correctly. All material has been included in good faith. Trademarks used are acknowledged as the property of their owners.

Printed by Toppan Printing Co, China

First printed in 2010

www.crownstreetcooks.com.au